THE
HARVEST
DIARIES

THE
HARVEST
DIARIES

DAVID G. CÔTÉ

ISBN: 978-0-578-06445-1

Printed in the United States of America

CONTENTS

This book is dedicated to my first love, my wonderful, beautiful, loving wife, Denise. She is the one with whom I share my second love—wine. It is also dedicated to my children, Nicole and Adam, who have begun their own love affairs with wine.

I also owe a huge debt of gratitude to Dane Stark, the winemaker at Page Mill Winery. We have been friends for nearly 20 years. He gave me the gift of a lifetime by sharing his world with me during the Harvest of 2008. His knowledge of winemaking is extraordinary and his joy in making wine is infectious. And the results are among the most outstanding, yet underrated wines I have ever enjoyed, particularly the Merlot!

And finally, my thanks to Dane's A-Team, Gary Brink, assistant winemaker, retail sales manager, carpooler and overseer of the Côté Merlot Harvest, Michael Curran, part-time winemaker and mechanic extraordinaire, and Lynn Hearn of Buster's Lab at the Stable who helped me remember how much fun chemistry can be. I have never worked or laughed so hard in my entire life. Thank you all!!

PROLOGUE

We have a vineyard, and I was given a gift. For nearly thirty years, I was on the fast track in Silicon Valley. I had the great pleasure of working at Apple Computer during most of the eighties, when "One Person, One Computer" was really about changing the world. It was also the "First Golden Age of Apple," when the Macintosh really did change the world. I spent much of the nineties in the world of networking, connecting all those computers together to create a new system, one that would enable the Internet and the way we interact today. I spent some time at a semiconductor company. Silicon and software are the building blocks of computers and networks, so this was a tremendous learning experience in one of the seminal technologies that enable the high-tech industry. Here I helped found and lead a division and got my first real general-management experience. In 2002, I got the best job I have ever had: CEO and president of Packeteer, Inc., a $50 million public company employing two hundred people. In five and a half years, we built it up to 450 people and $145 million in revenue. The gift I was given is that we sold the company to another player in the industry, and they had no need of my services.

I took a break. I pulled weeds, pruned and picked berries, and made jam. I exercised regularly, and I was outdoors most days. My son was home from college, and we spent lots of time together. My daughter worked nearby, and we saw her all the time. My wife, Denise, and I got to spend time together— a real treat for both of us!

The real gift was that I went to work for my winemaker throughout the 2008 harvest, something I had thought about for years. But before I tell you about that, I have to provide some background as to why this really matters. Did I tell you we have a vineyard?

PART 1
MY SECOND LOVE

Do You Believe in Magic?

There is just something about wine and grapes that is spiritual. It starts with being Catholic, and the importance of wine to the central ideas of Catholicism. Wine, along with bread, is transmuted into the blood of Christ in the most important sacrament of the Catholic faith, the Eucharist. Wine and vineyards are used metaphorically throughout the Bible, likening God to a vineyard owner in one parable, his church to the branches, and Christ himself to the vine.

His first public miracle was the changing of water into wine at the wedding feast at Cana. As a child I remember hearing the line from the chief steward, who says to the bridegroom, "Everyone serves the good wine first and then the inferior wine after the guests have become drunk. But you have kept the good wine until now."

After many years of drinking wine, I can fully understand that statement. Of course, that notion has been superseded by a Côté family rule, which is, "Life is too short to drink bad wine."

Another of the spiritual elements of wine for me is the connection to my mother's family of farmers. I spent several summers in Minnesota as a young boy, most of the time on the farms of my uncles and cousins in southern Minnesota around Fairmont and Blue Earth. Most of the days were filled with wandering around the farm with my three brothers, and for suburban LA kids who loved the outdoors, this was heaven. My cousin once noted that we found more animals in the week or two we spent with them than they did in a year. We were constantly on the lookout for animals, from garter snakes to raccoons.

One summer I found a two- or three-foot diameter snapping turtle buried in the "crick." All I could see were some eyes buried in the silt. I kept poking farther and farther back and watching the eyes twitch. When I reached a couple feet back and it was still twitching, I got up and ran up to the farmhouse and asked my cousin Steve what the heck I could have found. He jumped up excitedly and said, "It's probably a big ol' snapper". We ran down together, and he reached into the mud and, sure enough, pulled out the biggest turtle I had ever seen. It was mad, too. Steve wore steel-toed boots, and when he poked at the turtle to get its attention, it bit down hard on his boot. He grabbed it and put it into a cistern so everyone in the family could get a look at it. It was huge. I think he eventually put it back into the pasture.

But the highlight of our time on the farm was when we went to work for our cousins, or their neighbors. We would be sent off to "walk beans." This meant we went through the soybean fields and pulled all the big weeds. I'm sure that today they have some equipment or spray that takes care of the weeds, but back then, it was a manual job. While this was our least favorite job, the point was that we got paid for it. As a kid growing up, we were always looking for ways to make money: washing cars, mowing lawns, collecting bottles. But this work paid more than we could have imagined. After a day of walking beans, we might get ten dollars each. This amount, in the days when babysitting netted you fifty cents an hour, meant we were living.

The ultimate job, though, was baling hay. We either stood on the hay wagon and loaded the bales coming off the baler, or we worked in the hay barn, stacking bales coming off a large conveyor belt. Again we made good money. Another aspect of this work we always enjoyed was that my aunt, or the neighbor's wife, would bring out dinner in the middle of the afternoon, and then we would always have a spectacular supper at the end of a long day.

Once when I was working the hay wagon, we had finished loading the conveyer that moved the bales into the hay barn. We were leaving the yard as the tractor went right over a very fresh cow pie. Unfortunately, I was sitting on the front edge of the hay wagon and took a full frontal hit of the muck all over. The two guys with me (one of my brothers and the neighbor's son) couldn't stop laughing. I wiped it off my face, but the rest would stay with me throughout the day. The adults chuckled when they saw me, but no one batted an eye at the end of the day when I came in and sat down at the supper table. My face and arms were clean, but my clothes smelled like cow shit. But then everything smelled like that outside, so nobody really cared.

All of these experiences created a view of farming as a connection with the outdoors and a community of people working together. The outcome was incredible—soybeans, corn, alfalfa, and other crops grew right before your eyes. It was magic.

My brothers and I didn't really grow up around wine, though. As was typical of my parents' generation, they tended to drink cocktails, and the summer specialty of the house was grapefruit juice and vodka. We had a number of mature grapefruit trees in our yard, as did most of the houses in our subdivision in Woodland Hills, which was out in the San Fernando Valley, northwest of Los Angeles. The homes had all been built amidst mature grapefruit and orange groves. Sunkist would come through every year and pick the fruit, paying us a small amount. My parents held back on picking one tree every year. This produced a summer's worth of grapefruit juice for their favorite cocktail, and my brothers and I would take wheelbarrows full of grapefruit to sell on the other side of town. It was a great way to make a little money when we were kids.

My only remembrance of wine in my family was that my mom and dad went out to Brookside Winery. I didn't realize it at the time, but these were essentially tasting rooms and outlets for their wines located throughout Southern California. My parents came home with a few gallons of Brookside Sauterne every once in awhile, and I remember the gallon jugs in a cupboard in the kitchen. In fact, Brookside was one of the oldest wineries in the San Bernardino area, a grape-growing region that prospered from the late 1800s until after World War II, when grapes gave way to houses in the postwar Southern California land boom. Who knows, maybe they only went there once, but it is my only remembrance of wine during my childhood.

A related side story involves the Italian Vineyard Company, a winery founded in the late 1800s by Secondo Guasti. This winery at the base of the San Gabriel Mountains in Southern California was the largest winery in the world in the early 1900s, boasting five thousand acres of vineyards. The town of Guasti was built by Secondo for his workers, and today it is a modern development preserving the Guasti estate and winery buildings in downtown Ontario.

These experiences, and the rest of my childhood enjoying the outdoors (camping, hiking, working summer camps), all added to the joy I found in living things, both plants and animals. It is the foundation that led me to go to college at the University of California at Davis to study zoology—and to learn about the wonders of wine in the valleys nearby.

Bringing all of this together, I remember that I was in my first wedding party the summer before I left Southern California for Davis. The couple was two good friends of mine from high school who dated throughout high school and the first few years of college and decided to get married. I will never forget that the groom made a special request of the priest at the wedding mass. Rather than using the typical sacramental wine used at most masses, would the priest use a Charles Krug Cabernet Sauvignon? I wasn't familiar with this or any other wine. Quite frankly, it didn't taste that good to me at the time. But that too would change.

Higher Learning, Napa Style

Now, you may remember me saying earlier that I was taking a break from a thirty-year career in high-tech marketing and management, so where does the zoology degree fit in? I believe that there was a brief period in the twentieth century when people went to college to study what they were interested in, not just what would get them a job. That period was very brief. It lasted from the late sixties to the late seventies. Prior to that, people went to college to study the field in which they would eventually work, or at least with the intent of applying what they were doing to their life's work. These days, particularly as I have seen my own children and their friends grow up, there is again the focus on studying what will get you the best job.

Or maybe this is just the rationale I created for studying zoology, which was a great experience for me.

Davis, California, is situated about twenty miles west of Sacramento in the middle of California's agricultural heartland. In fact, UC Davis was originally the University Farm back when Berkeley was *the* University of California. While Davis had become a full-fledged university in the 1950s, it still had a strong heritage in agriculture. In the seventies, Davis was a typical college town that revolved around the university. An interesting quirk of the old university laws around alcohol and college campuses was that UC Davis still had a law in the seventies prohibiting the sale of any alcohol except 3.2 beer within two miles of the campus. As a consequence, there were two liquor stores, Jake's and

L&M, where you could buy wine and other alcohol, and they were exactly two miles from campus.

When I arrived at UC Davis as a junior transfer, I was still only twenty years old, and as it was a college town, all of the merchants were very tight about selling alcohol to minors. Needless to say, there were students who were of age, and they bought alcohol for everyone else. At the time, the universal beverage of choice was beer. In fact, I remember two girls moving into the dorms on my floor, and they rolled in a hand truck stacked with five or six cases of beer, "just to get started." These two were in fact the first girls I met who actually had beer bellies to rival a guy's. The difference was that guys with beer bellies were generally overweight. These two were fairly petite girls with little bellies that almost made them look four months pregnant—not a pretty sight.

Wine was not something many of us drank. Occasionally someone would buy a large bottle of jug wine. One of our favorites was Gallo Hearty Burgundy. It was actually a pretty good wine, and very inexpensive. Most people associated Gallo with cheap bulk wine, though the third generation is making some great wines in the Sonoma area. But it is not well known that the brothers Ernest and Julio Gallo did as much as anyone in the California wine industry to raise the standard for fine wine.

In the fifties and sixties, the word burgundy in the United States, as associated with wine, took on an interesting characteristic as a semi-generic term. Legally it could be used to designate nearly any red wine. This obviously caused disagreements with Europe, particularly France. While it may still be legal, the practice has generally fallen out of favor in recent years. Hearty Burgundy is still produced by Gallo and is actually made from Zinfandel, among other varieties. It's a rather funny twist on its namesakes, the much lighter, subtle wines we know as French burgundy and Pinot Noir.

Today French burgundy (made from Pinot Noir grapes) and Pinot Noirs from around the world are extremely popular, due in no small part to a movie about wine tasting on the Central Coast of California called *Sideways*. In the movie, the lead character extols the virtues of Pinots and makes one small reference to disliking Merlot. The movie was so influential that most California wineries and others now produce a Pinot Noir, and Merlot has fallen a bit out of favor.

Back to Davis in the mid-seventies, I remember thinking we had truly arrived as connoisseurs when we took a step up to a 1.5-liter Almaden

Mountain Red Wine or the penultimate Lancer's Rosé in the crockery bottle. But this was all before I learned about the wonders of Napa.

In the spring of 1975, I made my first trip to Napa Valley. At the time, the valley was nothing compared to what it is today, in both the number and kinds of wines, and the number of people. Also, at that time, Napa winery tasting rooms were all free, and they tended to serve a large variety of wines.

By the time I came to the valley for the first time, it seemed to begin just north of Yountville with the large, mission-style winery that was Robert Mondavi Winery. I didn't have much of a palate at that time, so my tastes tended toward lighter, fruitier wines—not sweet, but definitely fruitier. The white wines of the time were Chenin Blanc, which is difficult to find anymore, and Johannisberg Riesling. Robert Mondavi had just introduced a Fumé Blanc, which I learned much later was simply the beginning of the Mondavi marketing machine, which had renamed Sauvignon Blanc as Fumé Blanc. Next up the valley were two of the oldest wineries in California, Beaulieu and Inglenook, located in Rutherford, the heart of the valley. Both had tremendous history in Napa Valley.

The Inglenook winery still had much of the old winery in operation and a grand tasting room complete with winery history over all the walls. Inglenook was founded in 1879 by Gustav Niebaum. At this point, Inglenook had lost a lot of its cachet, and the winery, purchased by the beverage giant Heublein in the late sixties, was selling jug wines. In 1975, the year I first visited Napa, the movie director Francis Ford Coppola purchased a portion of the Inglenook estate, later purchasing the winery itself and renaming it Rubicon Winery.

Beaulieu Vineyards was across Highway 29 from Inglenook, and it had modernized its facilities, including a brand-new tasting room. Founded in 1900 by Georges Latour, BV was also one of the granddaddies of Napa Valley wineries and a frequent stop for many of us coming from Davis. The back way from Davis through Winters and Lake Berryessa that came out through the eastern mountains into Napa Valley cut across the valley, ending up at Highway 29, right at the Beaulieu tasting room, so that was usually our first stop.

In those days, there weren't very many wineries, with reports of as few as twenty wineries in Napa Valley in 1975. In contrast, there were two hundred wineries by 1990, and today there are approximately 250 wineries operating in Napa Valley. The ones I can remember visiting during my college days were the three I mentioned (Mondavi, Inglenook, and Beaulieu) and Louis Martini, Franciscan, Beringer Brothers, Christian Brothers, Charles Krug, and the brand-new Sterling Vineyards with the tram ride to the winery on top of a hill.

Louis Martini and Franciscan were not big favorites in those days, so we didn't go there too often. They were both a mile or so south of the town of St. Helena, which was the main town in Napa Valley proper. Just north of St. Helena is what I now call the "Disneyland of Napa Valley," the Beringer Brothers Winery, now simply called Beringer Vineyards. As the name implies, it was started by two brothers from Germany. It is the oldest operating winery in Napa, founded in 1876. As with most of the wineries at the time, they liked guests to take a tour of their winery to learn about winemaking. At Beringer, the tour was quite interesting, particularly because the brothers had carved out tunnels in the hillside to age and store wine. But the main event was tasting, and at Beringer, tasting was done in the beautiful Rhine House, as it is today.

Right up the road from Beringer was the Christian Brothers Winery. It was housed in a fantastic stone building called Greystone, named for the original winery built in 1880, later purchased by the Christian Brothers in 1950. In the 1990s, they sold it, and later in the 1990s it was converted to a Culinary Institute of America school.

In 1975, it was going strong as the Christian Brothers Winery, and their claim to fame for us college students was that they served all of the wines made by the Christian Brothers, and they stayed open later for tasting than anyone else (except for maybe Louis Martini, but more on that later).

On that first trip, and on a number of subsequent trips, my favorite winery was Charles Krug. Founded in 1861 by Charles Krug, it is probably more famous as the Mondavi winery. Purchased by Cesare and Rosa Mondavi in 1943, they ran the winery with their children, primarily Robert and Peter. In late 1965, there was a famous falling-out between Robert and the rest of the family that prompted Robert to start the Robert Mondavi Winery in 1966. That is a fascinating story.

Maybe because my friend Steve had talked the priest into using Krug Cabernet for communion, or maybe because the winery had a great reputation for reds, or maybe just that the tasting area was very casual and down to earth, Charles Krug was my favorite winery at that time.

Wine tasting was a great weekend activity for many of the students at UC Davis. While most of us probably went for the free wine, the reality was that we were being introduced to flavors and variety in wine that never would have been possible without the diversity of grapes and wineries even in those early days in Napa. My own palate began to change as I was introduced to bigger, tannic red wines. I still couldn't afford to buy many of these wines, so beer was still the staple for my undergrad drinking.

One highlight of my college days was the weekend my mom came to visit. I had decided not to go through the graduation process at Davis. This was for one simple reason: Davis in June is hot and humid. In those days, graduation took place on the football field in the middle of the day, and the temperatures were routinely in the nineties and sometimes in the hundreds. As much as I was proud to have graduated, I had no intention of sitting through the heat of the ceremony.

As a side note, in the two years between my graduation in 1976 and Denise's (my wife) graduation in 1978, the university built a beautiful new field house that, among other things, housed a wonderful, air-conditioned graduation ceremony that we attended to celebrate Denise's graduation in 1978.

Back to the story. My mom came to visit the weekend before graduation, and as part of our celebration, we took a trip to Napa Valley. It was a beautiful summer day, and the vines were freshly leafed out, and the grapes were just beginning to form throughout the valley. The trip got off to a rocky start as I missed the turn-off to cross the valley and end up in Rutherford. Instead, we headed south for a few miles, with my mom suggesting that I stop and ask for directions. Being a typical male, and since I was the tour guide, I couldn't possibly ask for directions. So I just headed west at the next road and ended up on Highway 29, somewhere south of Yountville. We'd only lost a little time—about an hour!

We went to the usual places, Inglenook and Beaulieu, Beringer and Christian Brothers, and Charles Krug. We wandered around Inglenook, which always felt like you had just stepped back in time to the turn of the last century. The imposing stone-and-wood winery building had that great earthy smell of wine. The tasting room was also filled with photos, old wine bottles, and memorabilia of the early days of Inglenook.

At the time, I had no idea that this beautiful winery had been purchased by a large East Coast beverage company, Heublein. In fact, in the years afterward, many of the large, well-known wineries were bought out by large consumer conglomerates in the United States and even Japan. At one point, Coca-Cola owned the Sterling Vineyard. And there is the well-known story of the Mondavi Winery going public in the early nineties and ultimately being sold to Constellation Brands in 2004.

But in the mid-seventies, it still felt like an old-style family agricultural business. The people who worked the tasting rooms and gave tours were eager to share their love of grapes and winemaking. The weekends at the wineries were busy, but by no means were they the crowded tourist attractions they became through the nineties and today.

We had fun taking tours and trying wines at all my favorite wineries, but I remember Christian Brothers making a particular impression on my mother. Maybe it was the connection to our Catholic roots, or maybe just the imposing Greystone building, but we spent a good amount of time there—until they closed at 4:30. Now, maybe it was just the end of a great day and we were feeling the effects of a day of wine tasting, but my mother was in a great mood. I had never seen her even tipsy, so it was very funny when she said to me as we were leaving Christian Brothers, "Is there another winery we could go to?" I thought this was hilarious. I remembered that Louis Martini stayed open until 6:00 PM, so off we went to get our last taste of Chenin Blanc.

That night, my mom treated several of my friends and me to a wonderful dinner in Old Sac, which was an area of Sacramento down near the river that had been revitalized with restaurants, bars, and shops but had maintained the character of the buildings, most of which were built in the late 1800s. Needless to say, we didn't drink any wine that night. I probably had a beer.

As an aside, that phenomenon would be a recurring theme in all of our future wine tasting. After a day of tasting a number of wonderful wines, beer was often the beverage of choice for dinner. In fact, on a recent trip with our daughter and her boyfriend, we kept a steady flow of water going the entire meal, as we all needed to rehydrate after the day's tasting.

After I graduated in 1976, I moved back to Southern California for the summer. I wasn't sure what I was going to do, but it had finally dawned on me that the zoology degree I had obtained wasn't opening any doors for me. The one exception was that I was offered a job at Orange County's Lion Country

Safari (long since defunct). For the sum of $3.75 an hour, I could have the pleasure of caring for the large African antelope called kudu—among other things, picking up the kudu doodoo. (My apologies to many friends for that old and tired attempt at a joke.) As fun as all of that sounded, I headed back up to Davis to sort out my next step and hang out with my friends, most of whom were still in school.

MY ONE AND ONLY

Moving back to Davis turned out to be the single most important decision I have made in my life. I came back because that was where my friends were, and since I didn't have any idea what I was going to do, it seemed like the perfect escape—a place where everyone went to class as an excuse to live and play around a large number of young people. The difference for me was that I wasn't going to classes, so I needed to find a job. I had waited tables in Southern California for the summer, so that seemed like a logical step. I found a unique opportunity at Cassidy's, a new restaurant that would be opening in a month or so.

Since I needed a job right away, I was hired on as a laborer to complete the construction of the restaurant. It was a beautiful place, with all of the interiors done in heart redwood. It was billed as a restaurant, bar, and club. They would serve lunch and dinner, but at 9:00 PM Thursday through Sunday, they booked musical acts and it became a club. The place had a great stage and a great bar. For me, it went one step further. When they finally opened, I worked lunches and dinners, but the real treat was that on Tuesdays, they paid me fifteen dollars an hour to play music from 9:00 to 11:00 PM. The staff was a great group of people, and it was a fun place to work.

I had moved in with an old friend from the dorms, Kent Littlehale, who was still a student, and a number of our friends that were still in school lived in apartments in the north end of Davis, so it was a great life. Lacking any real furniture for my room, I found a box spring in another apartment complex, steam cleaned it, and bought a refurbished mattress and frame, at a total cost of twenty dollars. I bought an unfinished dresser, built a desk from a file cabinet and a piece of knotty pine I found, and added the staple of college rooms, a cinderblock and pine bookcase. I was now set, as Kent had all the other furniture in the house.

On October 15, 1976, a Friday, I went to a party in a nearby apartment. Debbie Claridge and I had been resident advisers in the dorms during my last year in school. She and her roommate were having a party to kick off the new school year. It seemed like a great excuse for a party. I was still working construction at the restaurant, so my evenings were free.

Being the gentleman I was, I quickly gravitated to the keg, where I was happily serving anyone who needed a beer—and, of course, making sure I was never dry myself. Somewhere in this happy time, I got to talking to a beautiful girl. She looked very familiar. She had lived in the dorm complex next to my own the previous year, but somehow I couldn't place her. As we kept talking, it dawned on me that I did know her, and that she had cut her hair short, changing her appearance somewhat from what I remembered from school. And believe me, I did remember her. A friend of mine knew a girl in the same complex who looked similar to this girl, but I thought there was no real comparison—this girl was stunning. She is the most beautiful woman I have ever met, and this was just the beginning of a lifetime together.

I was telling stories of one of my roommates, a real ladies' man. One story was one of my favorites. I had come back to our room from studying, and he was asleep on the floor. I came in quietly and turned on the light at my desk to finish up a few things. The next thing I felt was a hand gently caressing my inner thigh. I froze and looked at Steve, who looked back at me with eyes that were just opening. His eyes snapped wide open when he saw it was me. He immediately said, "Oh, man, I thought you were Brooke. I am so sorry." We had a great laugh.

But the best part of the story was my telling it the next day to a group of our friends, with Brooke in the group. She was a wonderful girl, and I don't think they were dating at the time, just friends. So when I got to the part about the inner thigh, which I probably embellished, and then described Steve exclaiming, "I thought you were Brooke," she began to protest. And that was actually the best part of the story, particularly when the two of them started dating.

But back to the keg. I remember talking to this girl and her friend for a while, and then we went our separate ways. I ran into Debbie, the girl hosting the party, and said, "Who's that girl?"

She said, "Oh, that's Denise Anderson, but forget it. She has a boyfriend for three years now." I was devastated, and I went off to find my friends. I ended up dancing with Debbie's roommate. Both of us were pretty far gone and were merely holding each other up rather than dancing. The next thing I remember is standing on an outside balcony at the front of the apartment. I remember thinking that I had probably had enough to drink and needed to think about heading home. Just then, up the stairs came Denise, returning from somewhere. I saw her and asked where she had been. She came over and told me that she had taken a friend home and really should have stayed home herself, but that Debbie had begged her to come back.

Over the next hour or so, we stood on that balcony and talked about all kinds of things. At one point, I remember thinking that I wanted to know if I had a chance. I broached the subject of her boyfriend, and she told me that the summer had been difficult for them and she wasn't sure where the relationship was going. By this point she was standing very close to me, and we were touching. It was electric. I looked at her and said that I thought something important was happening and that I needed coffee to make sure I was in the best shape to talk with her. She agreed, and we walked off to find coffee. Somewhere along the way, I kissed her. After coffee, we went back to my apartment and spent the entire night talking. In later days, we would describe something about our lives to each other and find ourselves saying, "You told me that, the night we met." I think I even took out photo albums and showed her my family and friends. In the early morning, we went to the old Milk Farm coffee shop and had breakfast. Denise had to go home to Hayward, California, to get her hair cut, and I had to go to work at the restaurant. It was difficult to say goodbye—a problem that persisted for a long time.

At work that day, I was so tired that my boss sent me home at noon. I went home on cloud nine. I told Kent that I had met the most amazing girl, and I spent the next day and a half waiting for her to come back to Davis. When she did, we immediately went back to Debbie's house to tell her we were together—and that it was her fault. She was very excited for us.

The next few weeks were a blur. When Denise wasn't in school or I wasn't working, we were together. She left me notes on my car in town, and I would surprise her by finding her in the quad in between classes. We were truly in love.

Our first real date the next weekend was a drive up into the foothills of the Sierra to a town called Grass Valley. We stopped to get food and wine for a picnic. I wanted to impress her, and I bought a bottle of wine with a cork in it. At the time, that was impressive, or at least I thought so. We got to a park and set about to have our picnic when I realized that I didn't have a corkscrew. No problem—I just pushed the cork into the bottle, and we enjoyed the wine with our lunch.

I think we both knew that first night that we were right for each other. There always has been a magic that surrounds our relationship and our love for each other. So it was fitting that we got engaged three weeks after we met. I asked Denise to marry me, and she said yes.

We didn't speak about it again for about a month. We had returned from Thanksgiving with her family at the ranch owned by her grandmother in Mendocino, a truly special place. We were talking about where I would go to graduate school the next year. I had been accepted at Colorado State, Fort Collins, and Oregon University, for their master's program in student personnel, which is the degree for working in student housing. These programs required that I take the GMAT, which is essentially the test for graduate business school programs. Someone had said to me, why get a degree in student personnel when you can get an MBA and still work in housing, if that's what you want to do? This led me to also apply to Cal State Sacramento's business school as a backup (at the time, Davis didn't have a business school). This was another decision that would have a profound influence on my life.

As we discussed the upcoming year, I really had no desire to leave Denise. In the conversation, she asked when I thought the two of us should get married. This was the first mention of the subject since I had first asked her. I told her I had been thinking about the summer. She still had a year to finish her degree, and she wanted to finish at Davis. In that conversation, we decided that I would go to Cal State part time the next year, working full time as she finished her degree, and then she would work while I finished my MBA. We didn't even think about what we would do after that. For now, we were getting married a short nine months later.

This was a truly wondrous time. We were in love and spending every moment together we could. We often made dinner together with Kent. Dinner was typically a huge salad with dressing Kent had invented, followed by something from the barbecue, as we had a large gas barbecue near the pool in our apartment complex. Many times we'd end the evening alone or with friends in the jacuzzi. Often we'd bring a bottle of wine to share.

At this point we were still fairly limited white-wine drinkers, not really able to afford finer red wines, and not really mature enough wine drinkers. Cost was a big factor. A popular white wine at the time was Blue Nun, a Liebfraumilch, which was a somewhat sweet white wine from Germany. Even though it was probably reasonably priced, it was too expensive for us. While we could have bought jug wine as a better value, and we often did when we had parties, we were beginning to see ourselves as "wine people," and thus we wanted to share a "nice" bottle of wine at the jacuzzi. We found the perfect fit for us. It was a Liebfraumilch that I recall as Sohne Perle Liebfraumilch. I cannot find any reference to it, but I have found Schmitt Sohne Liebfraumilch, which is sold today. At the time, this wine was less than two dollars a bottle at Jake's, so it fit our view of ourselves and our wallet perfectly. We enjoyed many a well-chilled bottle of that wine during the winter and spring of 1976–77.

At the time, Denise was only twenty, so when we went to Jake's, I was in charge of buying the wine. Ironically, one time as she waited for me outside near the car, a young guy walked up to her and asked her what time it was. She happily told him the time, and then he asked, "Could you buy me some beer?" All she said was no. He walked away, obviously disappointed. By the time I got back to the car, she was still trying to figure out why he had asked her the time and then asked her to buy him beer. I think she was confused because she was underage and had never bought beer before herself, but we had a good laugh about it anyway.

A side note on our evenings in the jacuzzi: Kent was more sophisticated than either Denise or me. His drink of choice in the jacuzzi was Courvoisier. This was long before Tim Meadows made it famous in his "Ladies' Man" sketches and movie from *Saturday Night Live*. But Kent had it all over Tim Meadows. Kent would arrive at the jacuzzi with his snifter of Courvoisier, wearing a robe that was made up of squares of bright colors. Sometimes he would sit outside the jacuzzi, sipping his Courvoisier, looking every bit the bon vivant, or so we all thought. At the time it was too strong a drink for me, and for Denise. I am still not a big cognac drinker. When I go for harder stuff, I tend to bourbons, with Pappy van Winkle topping the list. (Thanks and appreciation for this to our friends Alain and Penina Sotto of Toronto for introducing me to Pappy at a great dinner at Bouchon in Yountville in 2008 – now I am way ahead of myself.)

As the spring of 1977 unfolded and our wedding plans were being made, we enjoyed many trips to Napa Valley. At this point, due to proximity and our own knowledge, we tended to visit Napa Valley.

We did venture into Sonoma one time that spring to visit Buena Vista, which may be the oldest winery in California, having been founded in 1857 by Agostin Harazsthy, considered the founder of the California wine industry. He was the first to bring cuttings from some of Europe's greatest vineyards to California. He introduced hundreds of grape varieties to California. Buena Vista also boasted caves for storing and aging wines.

The other famous Sonoma winery we visited in those days was Sebastiani. This winery was located just outside of the city of Sonoma and had a very casual family feel to it. At the time, it was actively being managed by the second generation, August Sebastiani, son of Samuele, the founder. Besides serving some very nice wines, one of the highlights of the winery was the cask carvings of waterfowl. As I heard the story, August had hired someone to carve waterfowl into the oak doors of the winery. He liked them so much that he hired the gentleman full time to carve all over the winery. By the time we visited in the mid-seventies, there were examples of the beautiful carvings throughout the winery and tasting room.

Spring in Napa Valley seemed to epitomize our lives. The vines were coming alive with the promise of magic, turning grapes into wine. Our lives were full during this time, living in the country atmosphere of Davis and the peaceful surrounding countryside.

Spring became summer, and we attended nine weddings the summer before we got married on August 13, 1977. It was a spectacular day, among the very best of our lives. We were married by Father John Boll at St. Joseph's Church, which was filled with family and friends. The reception was held at the Rec Pool Lodge in Davis, which cost us a mere $150, as Denise was a student. (My guess is that nothing will cost $150 when either of our children gets married.) It was a great day!

Our honeymoon was quite modest by today's standards. We spent our first night at Harvey's, the casino in South Shore Lake Tahoe. One of the highlights of the evening was that while we were waiting in line for the buffet—yes, our honeymoon night dinner was a buffet—we played a roll of nickels in the slots. As we were getting close to going in, we decided to play five nickels at a time the last few times. Amazingly, we hit a fifty-dollar jackpot! This money made it possible for us to eat out two nights of our four-day honeymoon. After that first night at Harvey's, we had booked rooms with kitchenettes so we could cook and save money. At this point Denise was a student with a year to go, and I was working at Wells Fargo Bank as a teller. (Cassidy's had closed due to mismanagement, but that's a whole different story.) So the jackpot was a major upgrade for us.

Our second day and night were spent at Fallen Leaf Lodge, a group of rustic cabins on the shores of Fallen Leaf Lake near Lake Tahoe. That night we watched a movie outdoors, and Denise cooked stuffed flank steak for the first time, which has become a family favorite.

One of the wedding gifts that we took on our honeymoon was a picnic basket with two wineglasses and a bottle of Charles Krug Cabernet. By now we had ventured into red wine territory, and while I cannot say we were in any way experts, this was deemed a treasure. We bought some lunch supplies at the lodge and took off on a hike up the small river that fed the lake. It was a beautiful day in the Sierras. I thought we were in for it at one point, though. I was leading us up what seemed like a path that abruptly ended. It ended right at a beaver dam. So there we were, in the middle of nowhere, "up a creek." Rather than turning around, I forged ahead, a trait that has generally held me in good stead. But this time, it served to force Denise and me through a thicket of wild berry bushes before we came back out on the original trail. On my second day of married bliss, I had succeeded in severely scratching my beautiful new wife's legs, as we both were wearing shorts in the beautiful Sierra summer weather.

The day was saved by our picnic. We were both famished, and the food and wine in the summer air served to replace our earlier trauma with a wonderful experience. I have never quite lived this story down, though, as thirty-two years later, when we are out for a hike, I will still get the occasional "Do you know where we're going?"—said with great love and affection.

As most newlyweds do, we discussed our plans for the future: children, jobs, houses, dogs, you name it. But one of the things we both shared serendipitously, from the beginning, was the idea that someday we wanted to have a vineyard. It was not a well-formed idea. It wasn't about making wine or anything else at the time. It was really about having land and being surrounded by the vines, which was one of those things we just shared from our earliest conversations.

MARRIED LIFE
AND FINE RED WINE

In the late seventies, as Denise was finishing her undergraduate degree and I was starting my graduate program, we lived a very simple life. We had little money; in fact, our combined income in 1977, the year we were married, was a little over seven thousand dollars. Even for that time, we didn't make much.

But we were in love with each other, we had many friends, and we were blessed to live in a beautiful part of the state. The Sacramento area had all kinds of outdoor activities, from boating to camping to hiking to river rafting, all of which could be done very cheaply. Also, we had the Gold Country, with its rich history, particularly at places like Sutter's Mill (where the Gold Rush in California got started) and Columbia, a town that had been preserved from the era and was now a state park. We also had Tahoe and Yosemite close by. Since we were both students, we could ski for five dollars a day midweek at Heavenly Valley on the South Shore of Lake Tahoe.

We also had the Napa and Sonoma valleys and the growing number of wineries to visit. In the fall of 1977, we spent Denise's twenty-first birthday wine tasting with her parents. They enjoyed visiting the Wine Country with us, and in those days, it was an easy trip for all of us: Denise and me from Davis, and her parents from Hayward, near Oakland, California, where Denise grew up. This trip, we had agreed that after wine tasting, we would all go back to our apartment in Davis to have dinner and celebrate Denise's birthday. We lived in married student housing near the UC Davis campus. It was a large one-bedroom apartment with all utilities paid at $135 a month. As we got to the door, I unlocked it and stepped back for Denise to enter. As she stepped in, she heard a big "Surprise!" I had arranged to have our friends join us for the celebration. Denise was shocked and jumped back into me. After she recovered, we had a great party, and so began the back and forth of the two of us surprising each other on major birthdays, which you would think might become obvious, but we became more and more devious, as you will hear later.

An interesting note on the wine business in those days is that there were very few Chardonnay wines being made in California. Chardonnay is the primary grape in the white wines from the Burgundy region of France, but the California wine industry had not embraced it until an interesting change began to occur in the drinking habits of Americans. Cocktails at lunch or to begin a meal began to give way to a glass of Chardonnay. Because of this move from hard alcohol to wine by many Americans in the early eighties, big, oaky Chardonnays began to dominate the white-wine scene, and wines like Chenin Blanc and Riesling seemed to disappear from Napa. These Chardonnays were much fuller-bodied wines than the white burgundies of France; but then, they were being made to replace the martini. Since then, Chardonnay has become the staple white wine for wineries throughout the world, and the variety of Chardonnays, from big oak to buttery malolactic, to leaner, crisper styles, has contributed to the continued dominance of Chardonnay for white wines.

One of the real treats for us in the early years of our marriage was visiting Denise's grandmother, who lived on two hundred acres of ranchland that hugged the rugged Northern California coast near Elk in Mendocino County.

By the time I met Gram in the late seventies, she was already in her eighties. She was Denise's dad's mom. They had lived in the Bay Area up until the late sixties and had owned the Anderson Sanitarium, a convalescent hospital in Hayward. When they sold the sanitarium, they bought this property in Elk and moved there permanently. Sometime in the early seventies, Denise's grandfather died, and Gram lived on the ranch alone, taking care of about twenty-five head of cattle. She was a tiny Belgian lady who still had a thick accent.

She was very eccentric. She did yoga every day in the old barn on the property, which was a huge structure built at the turn of the century from beautiful heart redwood. She hauled bales of hay into the pasture to feed her cattle, all of which she had named and treated like her pets.

But for Denise and me, this was a vacation. We loved the land and the ocean. The property had forested hills of Douglas fir and coastal redwoods that swept down to the pastureland that overlooked the ocean. It was a picture postcard of the California coast, and we enjoyed weekends there at least once a month until Gram's death in the mid-eighties.

On these visits to Gram's in Mendocino, we drove through Anderson Valley. There were a couple of small wineries that we visited during these trips. One of them was Edmeades Winery. Edmeades was started in 1963 by cardiologist Dr. Donald Edmeades and was the first to grow grapes in Anderson Valley. In 1972, after selling his grapes for nearly ten years, they began to make their own wine. Sadly, that year, both Dr. Edmeades and his wife died of cancer, but their son Deron finished the vintage and, along with his sister and partners, ran the winery until they sold it to Jess Jackson in 1988. By the time we visited in the late seventies, they were mostly known for their big Zinfandels. The other winery we visited was a new winery at the time, Navarro Vineyards, founded in 1974. Both of these wineries helped put Anderson Valley on the map as a wine-producing area, still largely undiscovered. Oddly enough, someone gave us a bottle of Navarro Vineyards Pinot Noir about two years ago. It was very good.

By the early eighties, we were living in the Bay Area. Our first house was in the town of Milpitas. Both of us worked across the bay; Denise drove up the peninsula to San Carlos, and I went directly across the bay to Cupertino, where I worked for Apple Computer through most of the eighties. We put all of our money into buying our first house, so even though we were both making decent money, we were "house poor," but we were very happy.

Our real estate agent, who was a wonderful motherly type named Bea, had told us that we should stretch to get into as much house as we could afford. We took her advice then and continued to take her advice, ending up today in what we call Chateau Côté, which is our dream come true—but again, I am ahead of myself.

While at Apple, in the spring and summer, a group of us would sometimes go up into the mountains above Stevens Creek Reservoir for lunch at

Ridge Winery. The winery, dating from the late 1800s, was on the top of a ridge on Monte Bello Road. It afforded a spectacular view of Santa Clara Valley. They didn't serve any food, but in those days they didn't mind if we came up the hill with our sandwiches and enjoyed the view for a while. It wasn't until a few years later that I actually went up on a weekend to taste their wines.

It is little known that Ridge Winery played an interesting role in the famous 1976 Judgment of Paris, the wine tasting that put Napa on the map. In this famous blind tasting done in Paris with French judges, the Stags Leap Wine Cellars 1973 Cabernet Sauvignon beat the best of the French Bordeaux. This gave Robert Mondavi and others the fuel they needed to begin the now-famous marketing of Napa Valley as the premier wine-producing region in the United States and a contender for premier region of the world.

The fifth-place wine in that competition and the second-place finisher for California Cabernets was the Ridge Monte Bello 1971 Cabernet Sauvignon. Because Ridge was in the Santa Cruz Mountains, which was a little-known wine-producing region in the mid-seventies, there was little attention paid to this wine.

Interestingly, Steven Spurrier, the English wine merchant that had organized the 1976 tastings, held a thirtieth-anniversary blind tasting of the very same wines in France and California in 2006. This time, top honors went to the Ridge Monte Bello 1971, with the Stags Leap placing second. California Cabs ranked as the top five wines by the judges. This prompted some of the original judges from 1976, ones who also participated thirty years later, to admit that the California wines held up extremely well over time. Many of them had predicted that the California wines wouldn't age anywhere near as well as the French Bordeaux.

The Ridge Monte Bello, along with their single-vineyard Zinfandels, have been excellent wines, finally gaining notoriety in the nineties when the Santa Cruz Mountains became better known. And because it was so close by, we enjoyed Ridge wines and their spectacular view on a regular basis. In fact, I would credit Ridge with introducing us to Zinfandels, with their Lytton Springs Zinfandel leading the way. Lytton Springs Zinfandel comes from two tracts of vineyard land in Sonoma County where Dry Creek Valley and Alexander Valley meet, a prime area for "old vine" and newer Zinfandels.

In 1982 we made a move up the peninsula to the town of Belmont. It was a crazy time in the California real estate market. (Some say it's always crazy, but this was extreme.) We were in the middle of a recession, but inflation was roaring, and interest rates were at all-time highs. In fact, in the latter part of 1981 and through most of 1982, the National Average Contract Mortgage Rate, based on a survey conducted at that time by the former Federal Home Loan Bank Board, was above 15 percent! I don't think it has ever been higher.

Not knowing any better, we had decided to move nearer to where Denise was working so that one of us didn't have to commute. Fortunately for us, we found a very aggressive real estate agent, and a man who had built a beautiful new house "on spec" and needed to get out from under it. We arranged a very creative deal, in which the builder carried back a note at a very aggressive interest rate, allowing us to make the payment. He got himself a seller, and we upgraded to a great new house, in a beautiful wooded canyon called San Juan Canyon. We lived in Belmont for seven years. Both of our children were born when we lived at that house. We have wonderful memories of that house.

It was the first house where we put in a wine cellar of sorts. We had a space under our stairs that was accessed through a door at the back of the bathroom off the living room. It was a very cool spot, as the house, like many in Belmont, was built partially into a hill. One of the walls was solid cement and acted as part of the foundation. It was a fairly constant temperature in the low sixties. As a result, we didn't refrigerate or add additional insulation. I'm not sure we would have noticed a difference anyway because at the time, while we had certainly expanded our tastes in wine, we couldn't afford to "put down" fine wines, and we consumed most of them in the year or two after we got them. But we had redwood racks and a real wine cellar!

Mike and Cindy, friends of ours who lived in Los Altos, down the peninsula near Stanford University, had already begun to join several high-end wine clubs, including Williams Selyem, one of the finest Pinot Noir wineries in the world. The winery was located in the Russian River area of Sonoma County. It was founded in 1981 by Burt Williams and Ed Selyem (later sold in 1998 to John and Kathe Dyson). It wasn't open to the public, but they made some wine available to restaurants. They sold most of their wines through what has come to be called "the list." Two other choices of theirs were noted for their California Cabernet Sauvignons, Dunn Winery and Caymus Vineyards.

Since they had started collecting these and other fine wines, they made the decision that as part of a major home remodeling project, they would dig a basement and build a true wine cellar. Within a year or so, it was finished. It was very exciting to go down into the cellar, where Mike had catalogued all of his wines. Denise and I thought that someday we would like to do something like this.

We held the first of many large parties at the Belmont house. We decided to have a pasta feed in the fall. We set up long tables with red-checked tablecloths in our garage. We worked for two days preparing fresh tomato sauce and pesto sauce, and we accompanied the pasta with garlic bread and Caesar salad. About fifty of our friends and family joined us for this party. Denise's father, who was a very gifted artist, created a huge banner depicting all things Italian that was posted at the back of the garage. This party also featured a great Merlot that we had found earlier that summer.

We had visited a small, fairly new winery in the Stag's Leap District called Pine Ridge. It was founded in 1978, and today it boasts a winemaker from Davis (Go, Aggies!), Stacy Clark, who joined them in 1983. She then became their winemaker in 1988. We had fallen in love with their Merlot and joined their wine club. We also bought a case of their Merlot and served it at our party. It was a hit! At the time, this was one of the hidden gems that we felt represented great wine and yet fit the budget of a young family. As is the case for many of these wineries, they have gone on to become more successful and have grown beyond the small tasting room, to include a beautiful tasting room and caves for both storage and events.

On July 9, 1984, I turned thirty, so it was Denise's turn to create her first big surprise. We woke up on my birthday, and she told me to stay in bed while she went down to fix breakfast. I could watch Wimbledon on TV, she said. I thought that sounded good and promptly went right back to sleep. Unknown to me, a number of our friends were gathering across the street at the home of our neighbors Glen and Connie Morgan. So my surprise was waking up to thirty of our best friends shouting, "Happy birthday," with a few even jumping on the bed. Fortunately, they let me get up and take a shower, but we had a wonderful party featuring a Ramos Fizz recipe Denise had gotten, a wonderful brunch, followed by an afternoon of Chardonnay and some very nice gifts, including many bottles of wonderful wine.

In the fall of 1985, my college roommate (now our veterinarian) was getting married. Kent had asked me to be his best man, which was a real honor for me. A month or so before the wedding, I asked him what he'd like to do for his bachelor party. He had a great idea. At the time, there were two other couples besides Kent and Kim and Denise and me that had been friends from our time at UC Davis. Kent had the idea to spend the day together, starting with brunch at Domaine Chandon, the sparkling winery in Yountville in Napa Valley. After brunch we would do some wine tasting as a group. For an old married guy like me, that sounded great.

The day dawned gloriously, as so many do in California. We all drove to Domaine Chandon and began our celebration with a glass of sparkling wine. We had a wonderful meal and many bottles of Chandon sparkling wines. The meal lasted at least four hours. By the time we were ready to leave, we had all had plenty to drink, and the thought of wine tasting was not high on our lists. But here we were in Napa Valley, and that was the plan for the day. We agreed to go to Clos du Val, which was directly across the valley on the Silverado Trail. We arrived, tasted a few wines, and agreed we were all done for the day. Interestingly, the 1985 Clos du Val Cabernet Sauvignon was a favorite of ours a few years later, along with a number of the great 1985 reds from Napa.

The wedding also produced a great story, though not a wine story. As the best man, it was my job to drive the bride and groom from the church to the reception. In our days in the dorms at UC Davis in the early seventies, I had introduced my floor to Bruce Springsteen. In the fall of 1975, he was on the cover of both *Time* and *Newsweek* the week of October 27, 1975. Fortunately for me, he also played a concert at the Sacramento Civic Auditorium that year. I introduced a number of friends, including Kent, to the joys of "the Boss" and Clarence Clemmons. My anthem was a song called "Rosalita" from the album *The Wild, the Innocent, and the E Street Shuffle*. It is still my favorite. I played it all the time and would get ready for intramural basketball games by listening to "Rosalita." Okay, what does that have to do with Kent's wedding? This is a true story. We got in the car in front of the church, and as I pulled out, I turned on the radio to the opening strains of "Rosalita." Kent was blown away (so was I)! He kept asking if I'd had it planned. I said no, but we thoroughly enjoyed the ride, with the sunroof open and all of us belting out the lyrics to "Rosalita." Amazingly, just as we pulled up to the reception, the last notes of the song faded away. It remains a highlight of Kent's wedding, and he's been my friend for over thirty-five years.

A year later, in the fall, was Denise's big birthday. She turned thirty in October 1986. I knew she would be expecting something, so I put together a layered approach to surprising her. The overall concept was to pick her up from work and stay at the Fairmont Hotel in San Francisco by ourselves, which really meant going to dinner and then coming back to all of our friends in the suite for a party. Then, because I had just come off a major product launch at Apple that had kept me busy pretty much 24/7 for six months, I added a vacation to Hawaii. It would begin with a few days by ourselves, and then Grandma and Grandpa would bring our beautiful six-month-old daughter, Nicole, over to meet us for another week.

I let her assistant know the entire plan, so whenever Denise made an appointment for the time we'd be gone, her assistant just canceled it. The other thing that made it work was that her birthday was midweek, so the surprise would be a few days before. I arrived in a limo at her office on a Friday afternoon. (I had completely over-packed for her, to be sure I had everything). She was quite surprised and asked what we were doing. I told her we were staying the weekend in San Francisco at the Fairmont. When we arrived in the beautiful suite, she asked why we had gotten such a big room. I told her that a small perk from the crazy hours was that the event group at Apple had worked with the Fairmont to comp us the suite. Denise told me later that she had no idea what was happening, figuring that this would be a weekend for us, with a bigger party on her actual birthday.

We went to dinner across the street at the Stanford Court Hotel, at their restaurant, Fournou's Oven, which at the time was an excellent restaurant. We had a great meal and a great bottle of wine. As we headed back to our hotel, I asked Denise if she wanted a nightcap sent to our room. Thankfully, she said yes, giving me the excuse to call the room and warn everyone that we were on our way up. When she arrived, she was greeted at the door by everyone shouting, "Happy birthday." She was blown away. She was even more surprised to find that we were leaving the next morning for Hawaii by ourselves, and that Nicole and her parents would join us in a few days. But she was most surprised that I had also packed for her and that her parents had brought the bags with them. As the party in our suite began to wind down, a number of us decided to continue the party, ending up in the famed Tonga room of the Fairmont Hotel, a nice segue to the tropical experience we were headed toward.

By the late eighties, we were getting restless in Belmont. We loved the house, but it was essentially built into the hillside, and we had no land. This was also a big problem for our kids, with no real yard to play in. We had been looking to get farther down the peninsula for a number of reasons. Denise had left her position as vice president of human resources with the birth of our son, Adam, and I was working at Apple, which was thirty minutes down Highway 280. We wanted warmer weather and a yard for the kids to play in. And we hoped to get enough land to put in a vineyard, though as yet, we had no idea what that meant. Throughout the late eighties, our weekend routine became breakfast at the Stagecoach restaurant in Woodside (now Buck's Restaurant and a venture capital hangout), review the open house listings in Woodside, Atherton, Menlo Park, and Portola Valley, and go visit them, looking for that affordable house with land. For two or three years, we had little luck.

In 1989, we began to look a little farther south, into Los Altos Hills. This was a small community that was formed as a city in 1954, the year I was born. It had one-acre-minimum parcels and was noted for being rural. We found a house on two hilly acres that had been built in the 1950s and hadn't been remodeled. The structure and "bones" of the house were excellent. And to top it off, there seemed to be a hillside that might be perfect for a vineyard. We had to look beyond the house itself and envision what it could become.

In fact, the day we moved, I stayed at the Belmont house to do the final cleanup, and Denise went on ahead to the Fernhill house (because it was on Fernhill Lane) with the kids. By the time I got there two hours later, all of the draperies had been torn down and thrown into the backyard and Denise was scrubbing the family room floor. The only owner of the house had been a smoker, and the house reeked of smoke. Why we didn't notice it when we were touring and buying the home, I'll never know. As Denise scrubbed the floor, a thick layer of smoke and dirt began to melt away. Underneath was rust-colored linoleum that actually wasn't too bad.

Over the next few weeks, we tore up all the carpets and found beautiful oak hardwood flooring. We repainted the inside of the house. We redid one of the bathrooms that had been done in red and black velveteen wallpaper. In a short while, the house was more than livable. We had a beautiful piece of property and views of the south bay from Palo Alto to San Jose.

We were starting to get a vision of remodeling this home and putting in the vineyard. It was essentially a classic ranch-style home, except that the garage was below the rest of the house with a glassed-in sunroom off the kitchen and above the garage. The kitchen was in desperate need of remodeling, so that end of the house was first. The kitchen was a triangular room, and there was no dining room. We decided to turn the existing family room into a large dining room, add a few square feet to increase the size of the kitchen, and redo the sunroom as a structurally sound family room off the kitchen. This room had huge pieces of flagstone that we refinished as one of the most beautiful floors I have ever seen.

The garage was below the house, and it turned out that the staircase from the kitchen into the garage was not up to code, and we couldn't make it so, as the distance below the kitchen was not high enough to accommodate the number of stairs. As we discussed what to do, one of the options was to build a new garage structure up on the level of the main house. The old garage could then be used for storage. I began to see an extensive wine cellar down below the house, built into the bedrock. But as we explored the cost, the garage alone would cost $25–35,000, and that was without doing anything to the storage area. Then our contractor made a great suggestion that would forestall the wine cellar for a time. He suggested we put in a residential elevator to go from the laundry room into the garage. It would cost about $10,000, so it was quite economical. We did it, and the remodeling turned out great. We had a brand-new kitchen, a huge dining room, a stunning family room with 270-degree views, and an elevator. Our kids were ecstatic.

I purposely left out the nine months of living in a few rooms as the remodeling occurred. It was an adventure, and one that would figure in our next move, which was the most serendipitous but important of our lives; more on that later.

Back to wine. Sometime in the early nineties, we decided to go "bike wine tasting" in Napa Valley. We stayed at a small B&B on Zinfandel Lane, just south of St. Helena in Napa Valley. We got up on Saturday and rode our bikes to a number of wineries in the valley. We bought wine at several of the wineries and asked the staff to hold it, as we would be back to pick it up the next day.

One of the funny experiences of the day was our "visit" to Opus One. Opus One at the time was a very famous joint venture between Robert Mondavi and the Baron Phillipe de Rothschild. Opus One wine became the first ultra-premium California wine, selling for more than fifty dollars a bottle when it was first available in the mid-eighties. By 1991, a beautiful winery had been built near the Robert Mondavi Winery, but it was not open for tasting. As we rode by on our bikes, the gate was open, so we decided to ride in, on the chance that we could get a look around. We rode down the long driveway and ended up at the entrance to the winery. We were met immediately by two people who kindly but firmly asked us to leave the premises.

We went on our way and stopped just up the road at V. Sattui Winery. We had had enough of wine tasting and needed a break and some food. V. Sattui, in addition to offering its wines to the public, had an extensive deli and picnic grounds. It was a great place to stop. By the time we were back on our bikes, the wine and food had all set in, and it was quite a trek to go the short distance back to our B&B, especially as we were riding along the busiest stretch of Highway 29, the main artery through Napa Valley.

The next day we picked up our wine, and we agreed that while it was an adventure, we would separate bike riding and wine tasting from now on.

This period, in the late eighties and early nineties, was about looking for great wines that hadn't been "discovered" yet. It was also when we really discovered the Sonoma area for the first time. Unlike Napa Valley, which is just that, a valley, Sonoma County ranges from the Russian River with its coastal influences, to Dry Creek Valley and Alexander Valley, with much warmer climates and home to much bigger reds, notably "old vine" Zinfandels and big Cabernets. But our first exposure was to Sonoma's Valley of the Moon, the stretch of Highway 12 that starts just south of the town of Sonoma and extends up to Santa Rosa. The Valley of the Moon is not unlike Napa Valley, though at the time it was much less traveled, and it seemed to us like Napa in the late seventies.

The north end of the valley is home to our absolute favorite winery in the Sonoma area, St. Francis Winery. We discovered St. Francis Merlot first. (Seeing a pattern here yet?) It is still one of the finest Merlots on the planet.

But they have grown to make wonderful Cabernets, Zinfandels, Petite Sirah, Syrah, and even a Mourvèdre, which is one of the lesser-known Rhone grapes, and Cabernet Franc, a Bordeaux blending grape. We joined their wine club years ago and get the benefit of a number of these wines that are only available at the winery or through the club.

Another beautiful winery is Château St. Jean. The centerpiece of the winery is the chateau itself. Built in 1920, it was fully restored when the winery was established in 1973. It helps create an elegant atmosphere, both for the grounds and for the wonderful tasting areas. In particular we love their reserve wines, among them the Merlot, Chardonnay, and Cabernet Sauvignon

On one of these trips, we also ventured out on Bennett Valley Road to Matanzas Creek Winery, which has wonderful reds and a beautiful setting, with huge lavender plantings. They sell a variety of lavender-based products, from soaps to oils. It is also a beautiful drive to this winery.

Another find almost went undiscovered. As we were leaving Sonoma Valley one Sunday, we saw a sign for Schug Winery. I had heard stories that Walter Schug, who was the original winemaker at Joseph Phelps (more about Phelps later), had left in the eighties to found his own winery. We decided to stop by. What a treat! The winery is situated southwest of the town of Sonoma in the cool Carneros appellation, which spans both Napa and Sonoma counties. Here we discovered their wonderful Pinot Noirs and Chardonnays. They also made what they called Heritage Reserve wines, a Merlot and a Cabernet Sauvignon among them. They were excellent, but at the time, we couldn't really afford them. Meanwhile, the Schug Pinot was excellent and reasonably priced. I remember that we bought a case on that first visit. We have been Schug Pinot fans ever since and often close out a trip to Sonoma saving time for a visit to Schug Winery.

As we began to branch out in these years, we visited the Russian River Valley, home to the best Pinot Noirs in the world—just my opinion. Wines from Gary Farrell Winery, Rochioli Winery, and the aforementioned Williams Selyem are among the very best, and they can be quite expensive. On one of these trips we happened upon Robert Stemmler Winery, which was actually in the Dry Creek Valley. Robert Stemmler was a legendary figure in the wine business in California. He worked at Charles Krug with the Mondavi Brothers in the sixties and was the winemaker at Simi Winery in

Healdsburg in Sonoma County. He also consulted for a number of wineries before founding his winery in the early eighties. He began to make a wonderful Pinot Noir from Russian River fruit, and it became one of our great finds. Sadly for us, he retired in 1989 and sold his label to the owners of Buena Vista Winery. It was revived in 2001 or 2002, with a tasting room on the historic Sonoma town square.

During this time we also rediscovered Dry Creek Valley. We had visited Dry Creek Vineyards in the very early eighties along with Rodney Strong and Simi in Healdsburg and Chateau Souverain in Geyserville, all on trips returning from Denise's grandmother's ranch in Mendocino.

One of our favorites was A. Rafanelli Winery. This was an example of having tried a wine in a restaurant and needing to find it. I am not sure why, but we had tried an A. Rafanelli Zinfandel at a local Italian restaurant in Los Altos. It was wonderful. I remember reading the label and seeing that the winery was in the Dry Creek area. The first time we tried, we found out that they weren't open for tasting and that you could only get wines at the winery. On one of our next trips, we set up a tasting and visited the winery. It is completely family run, with Dave Rafanelli in charge of the winery and the vineyards; his daughter is the winemaker, and his wife runs marketing and sales. They have a small percentage of their wine in restaurants, but the rest is sold through their club or at the winery. They also make a wonderful Merlot and Cabernet and, when the grapes are just right, their Terrace Select Cabernet Sauvignon.

During these years, we also visited Napa many times. Napa was becoming so famous and so crowded that we had to find off-peak times to visit. We were very fortunate because Napa was only two hours away, so we could afford to be flexible. On these trips, we visited some of our old friends, like Beringer, buying a bottle or two of their private reserve Cabernet Sauvignon or Beaulieu, and their Latour Reserve Cab. But we also were trying a number of the newer wineries that had become popular, wineries like Trefethen and ZD, Duckhorn (for Merlot of course) and Cakebread.

One of those amazing finds happened completely by accident. In the early to mid-nineties, I worked for a networking pioneer called SynOptics. It later merged to become Bay Networks and was later acquired by Nortel, the telecommunications giant in Canada. But in the SynOptics years, we were a fast-growing, exciting Silicon Valley start-up. One of the things we did was to celebrate our successes. My team had created a promotion that was very successful, and I got agreement from the company to take them on a wine tasting trip to Napa Valley to celebrate. Oh, yeah, this was all for them!

There were about fifteen of us, and we rented the equivalent of a rock band's touring bus. It had captain's chairs everywhere, TV, and a staff to serve breakfast on the way up to Napa. I had chosen the wineries for the group, but I can't remember a single one, given what happened. One of the people in my group, Betty, asked if we could stop at Whitehall Lane Winery, as she enjoyed their white wines. By now, I was pretty firmly a red wine fan. I enjoyed white wine, but red was the typical choice. I didn't think anything more about it, as I had seen Whitehall Lane, which sat in a fairly modern-looking building right on Highway 29 just south of St. Helena.

Unknown to any of us, the winery had been purchased by Tom Leonardini in 1993. When we got there, we were treated to a great tour of what was becoming a brand-new modern winery. Tom had brought in a new wine-maker and was outfitting the winery with the latest equipment. He had also secured grapes from the famous Morisoli vineyard, which is right in the middle of the Rutherford area, prime for red wines, primarily Cabernet. We barrel-sampled the upcoming releases of the Morisoli Cabernet Sauvignon and their reserve Cabernet Sauvignon that also had Morisoli fruit. We also tasted some of the first vintage from the new Leonardini Vineyard Merlot. Along the way, Betty did get to try their whites, and she liked them. I was so taken with their Cabs and the Merlot that I remember buying futures on these new wines and signing up for their wine club.

About nine months later, in the fall, we went up to the winery with friends to pick up our futures and enjoy a celebration of new releases at the winery. It was one of those warm fall days you only see in Wine Country. The air was warm but crisp, and the leaves had begun to turn, so the surrounding vineyards were stunning. We enjoyed great food and wine, and we got the opportunity to meet Tom Leonardini, who was a very down-to-earth guy. As we talked with him, thoughts turned to football. In the mid-1990s, the San Francisco 49ers were a major power, and Tom had grown up in San Francisco and loved the 49ers. The game was on TV in his guesthouse. He invited us over to watch it. That afternoon was one of those experiences I will never forget: a beautiful setting, tremendous wines, good food, and a great host. Since then, Whitehall Lane has had great success.

THE DREAM IS REALIZED

In the late summer of 1990, we were invited to a party at the home of Karen and Gary Campi. The Campi's were a very active family at St. Nicholas School, where our daughter, Nicole, was entering the second grade. Denise had met Karen Campi the year before, partly because our daughters (Nicole and Jaclyn) were in the same grade. This particular beautiful afternoon, we were invited to a party at their house in Los Altos Hills. The backyard was full of people, but the first thing I noticed was the vineyard stretching up the hill beyond their yard. By this time, the grapes were well along. I could tell they were white wine grapes, as they were still green. If they had been red grapes, they already would have been red in color by this late in the season.

I didn't know Gary and Karen Campi, but as we spent the day at their party, I found that they were two of the most welcoming people I had ever met. As I said, Denise knew Karen, but I didn't know Gary at all. Nonetheless, he was a very gracious and friendly host. He was, and is, larger than life, and no one likes a party more than Gary Campi. When we got a chance to talk for a few minutes, I asked him what kind of grapes he was growing. He seemed excited that I was interested, and he told me that they grew Chardonnay and sold their grapes to Page Mill Winery, taking finished wine in return. This was the dream Denise and I had, so I was anxious to learn more. But that would have to wait.

On that day, little did Denise or I know that Karen and Gary would become great friends of ours in the years to come—and that they would be instrumental in helping us to achieve our dream.

It was probably six months later, in the spring of 1991, after we had finished our remodel of the Fernhill House, that we invited Karen and Gary over for dinner. This was one of the first dinner parties since the completion of our new kitchen, and we were happy to share it with our new friends, the Campi's. They brought along a couple bottles of their 1989 Chardonnay, the first Chardonnay bottling since they had planted their vineyard. (Actually, it was the second harvest, but they had made sparkling wine out of those first grapes. Chardonnay is a key ingredient in many of the finest French champagnes and sparkling wines from all over the world. I don't know what happened to that original bottling of sparkling wine—and I probably never will.)

This was their first vintage from the winery that would become such an important part of our lives, Page Mill Winery. We admired the bottles, which were simply labeled "Page Mill Winery, Chardonnay, Campi Vineyard." "Campi Vineyard"—that said it all; that was what Denise and I wanted to do with our land. Just as important, the wine was wonderful. We drank both of the bottles they brought. One had been for dinner and the other for us to keep. But as Karen and Gary soon learned, they had met kindred spirits when it came to wine. In fact, they said they hadn't even been sure that they should bring wine to the house, as they didn't know us well enough to know if we really enjoyed wine. I think that evening helped them understand our love of wine. It was the first of many, many evenings spent with great wine, a great meal, and the best of friends.

But for this story, the most important discussion of the evening was talking about the Campis' vineyard. How did it happen? What did they do? Who did they use? We had so many questions, and they excitedly shared it all with us.

When they moved into their house, they had a large hillside above the house and yard that was undeveloped. As they thought about landscaping options for this piece of their yard, they discovered that a neighbor behind them had a vineyard. They saw how beautiful it looked and how it filled the entire hillside, and they thought it might be the right option for them. They found a company called Devine Consultants, which was a husband-and-wife team, Nancy and Eddy Szyjewicz, who installed home vineyards. In the nearly fifteen years I have known them, I have never been able to pronounce their last name. For us, they are simply Eddy and Nancy, and we were lucky enough to work with them ... but I'm ahead of myself.

For Karen and Gary, this was an option that made sense, not only for the vineyard, but given that Campi Properties was their business, the idea of vineyard property didn't hurt the resale prospects either. (Of course, twenty years later, they're still in their wonderful home.) As they were having the vineyard installed, they were also fortunate to meet their neighbor up the street, Dick Stark.

Dick and Ome Stark founded Page Mill Winery in 1976, when Dick excavated a cellar below the family's home on Page Mill Road in Los Altos Hills. Dick made wonderful, approachable wines, and he had a particular love for producing small lots of vineyard-designated wines from local growers. That vineyard behind the Campis' that helped inspire them was the Garbett vineyard, named for Elizabeth Garbett. Dick made a wonderful Chardonnay from the Garbett vineyard. Because of the high quality of the Garbett fruit and the fact that Eddy and Nancy were caring for the Campi vineyard, Dick agreed to produce Gary and Karen's Chardonnay. The plan was that either Dick would pay the Campis per ton of grapes, or they could take back wine in trade. Obviously they chose wine!

In the fall of 1992, I experienced my first "up close and personal" wine harvest. Karen and Gary invited friends over to harvest their grapes and then go up to Page Mill for the crush. I thought I had died and gone to heaven. The vines were everywhere, and the grapes were beautiful. They were so sweet, with the juice as thick as syrup. I couldn't get enough of picking the grapes. Their vineyard was on a very steep hillside, and some people found it hard to climb, but I had such an adrenaline rush from being among the vines, filling bins with beautiful, ripe fruit that the climb didn't matter. I just couldn't get enough of it, and I think everyone noticed. Gary made the comment that he thought I looked sad when we were finished. He was probably right. All of the fruit was collected in small plastic bins, holding twenty-five to thirty-five pounds of fruit each. These were stacked on a flatbed truck to be transported the short distance up the road to Page Mill Winery.

A number of us drove up the road to Page Mill with the fruit, as Dick was going to crush it right away. We pulled into a nondescript driveway with a half cask holding up the mailbox—no sign, nothing to let anyone know this was actually a winery. We pulled up in front of a shingled ranch-style house. Now you could tell it was a winery, as there were large bins, some empty, some full of fermenting fruit, a platform with a stemmer/crusher on top, and a basket press, as well as hundreds of yellow fruit bins. This was the quintessential family winery. Page Mill at the time produced about eighteen hundred cases of wine, many of which were small-lot, vineyard-designated wines from the Santa Cruz Mountains.

As we drove up, I met Dick Stark and his son Dane. I was one of several people who had come up to watch the crush, and they were very busy, so I didn't get a chance to ask them any of the many questions I had. We helped to unload the fruit, and I watched as they used a forklift to raise the bins up to the stemmer/crusher. After the stems were removed and the fruit was crushed, it was immediately put through the basket press and then into large bins for fermentation. No time is spent on the skins when making white wine; the fermentation process begins with only the juice of the grapes.

When we finished watching the crush, we went back to Karen and Gary's house for a great meal and a party. I enjoyed every minute and every part of this day. It would stick with me and color my own thoughts about what harvest is about. But that was only part of the process. I didn't go back to Page Mill that season. I didn't see what happened to the fermenting grapes, the magic that turns grape juice into wine. But this was only the beginning of our vineyard journey.

In January 1993, another of those serendipitous, magical things happened to Denise and me. We were in the midst of planning to remodel the Fernhill house for the second time. This would be the big one, adding about two thousand square feet. It would also mean moving out of our house this time. We were in discussions with the Town of Los Altos Hills, which had arcane calculations for determining how much square footage a house can have, based on the amount of land and the slope of the property. It sounds relatively straightforward, but it wasn't at all. Our discussions revolved around getting a variance for an addition that would end up as a two-story, 4,400 square-foot house on our two-acre lot. It was frustrating, and we were making little progress.

This particular Sunday afternoon, we had asked the Campis to take us around to some of the brand-new, beautiful homes in the Hills so we could get ideas for everything from bathrooms to doorknobs. We were also interested in stairways, as we were trying to figure out what we could do in our own plans.

Gary and Karen set us up to see some beautiful properties. We saw rich woodwork and cabinetry, multiple colors of granite countertops, stunning fixtures, and everything you would expect in multi-million-dollar homes, homes that were well beyond our reach. Finally it was getting late in the afternoon, and as we got in the car, Gary said he thought there was one more property that had a grand staircase, but as it was getting late, he asked if we just wanted to go to dinner. Denise and I agreed that we should take a look. As we pulled into the driveway, we saw that it was lined with Italian cypress trees. The house itself was at the back of the property, with a hill rising up behind it. There were redwood trees and a row of old barns lining the street. The property was a long rectangle that was bisected by a small creek and several large, flat sections that we would later learn had been riding rings when the property was used to board and train horses. The setting was absolutely beautiful.

But the house itself was spectacular. It was done in a French Normandy style (ironic in that the Côté name originated in Deauville in Normandy, France). As we entered through large walnut doors, the entryway was exactly as I had envisioned one, with a grand circular staircase leading to the upper-floor landing, and impressive faux walls that rose two stories above the floor.

Radiating off this entryway were the library, the kitchen (which also led to a beautiful family room with a vaulted ceiling), the dining room, and another hallway that led to a guest room, the laundry, and the back door, which opened onto a porte cochère and a three-car garage. The upper floor had a spacious master bedroom suite with a sitting room, a large bathroom, and two walk-in closets. There were another three bedrooms on the floor, and a hallway that led to a finished room over the garage.

The short version is that we both fell in love with the house and grounds, and with Gary's help, we were able to negotiate a great deal and then sell the Fernhill house within three weeks. This meant we didn't need to go through a long remodeling and make compromises on plans based on the town's whims. The house was on two flat acres, with several large sections that would be perfect for vineyards. There were also the barns, which had potential, and a beautiful pool site (already approved) right off the family room.

We were ecstatic!

After we settled in, we could hardly believe what we had. Not only was the house perfect, but we didn't have to wait for remodeling. It also meant that the vineyard could become our number-one priority. So we called Eddy and Nancy and asked them to come out and talk to us. They arrived one evening in the early summer of 1993, and the first thing they did after we said our hellos was to begin to try to talk us out of putting in a vineyard. It was a major, long-term commitment, they said. Even though they could take care of it, there was still upkeep we would have to do ourselves. Did we know that we would have to find a "home" for our grapes—each and every year? We would have to fence our yard to keep out the deer ... and on and on for about the first half hour.

We were totally unfazed. As they laid everything out, we just nodded and said to keep going. Finally they took a breath and then said that they always began a presentation trying to talk the potential client out of putting in a vineyard. They said that many people thought it was a romantic idea, but when faced with the reality of what it entailed, they often decided to just put in lawn or a tennis court. Eddy and Nancy had just met Denise and me, so how could they know that this was a dream we had been talking about for over fifteen years? Once they realized we weren't going to be dissuaded, they began to talk about what kind of grapes we'd like to plant and their process for putting in the vineyard.

Red wine! We wanted to grow red-wine grapes. At the time, we were discovering Pinot Noir, and we asked about that as a possibility for our site. Eddy and Nancy said that we didn't have the climate for Pinot, which needed some of the cooling ocean influence that parts of the Santa Cruz Mountains, Russian River, and Carneros regions of California get. So we asked what kind of red grapes we could grow. They said almost anything else—Cabernet, Merlot, Syrah, Zinfandel, Sangiovese, and many others. We said we would talk about it, as the decision didn't need to be made right then.

Next they talked about their process, which included installing the vineyard and training the vines for at least three growing seasons to get the structure that would carry the vines for the next forty or fifty years, maybe even a hundred!

First they would need to test our soil and add appropriate amendments to get it in shape. Next they would rototill the soil and put in the posts for the trellising system. Here we had a discussion about the kind of trellising we would use.

Most people don't notice the tremendous variety of trellising used in vineyards. Many of the old-vine Zinfandel vineyards throughout California don't have any trellising system at all. They are what are called "head-trained" vines, and the shoots just come out of the main vine, with fruit produced on year-old wood. Much of the Wine Country uses some form of either undivided or divided canopy structures, in either a vertical or horizontal formation. It's already too complicated, so I'll stick to what we decided.

We were on flat ground, with relatively easy access to ground water, as the vineyard would be near the creek bed. For these reasons, and the warm, protected weather of our little valley, we decided on a more aggressive trellising system, using a divided canopy structure with quadrilateral cordons. Cordons are the major branches that come off the trunk of the vine that, together with the trunk, form the main infrastructure of each vine. Quadrilateral trellising refers to having four major branches, two on each side, coming out of the trunk horizontally. If you took an aerial view of this, you would see an H shape. Each of the cordons is allowed to grow halfway down the guide wire until it reaches the cordon from the next vine growing out toward it.

But we wouldn't need any of this for the first year, just the posts. Also, in the first year, the vines are mostly putting down roots, so after the first year they are pruned nearly to the ground, so that energy is put into the root system, not just growth. After the first year, the T-bars are put on the posts that will house the guide wires and the canopy wires. The guide wires are the structure onto which the cordons are trained. The guide wires are also put on before the second growth year. Before the third growth year, the canopy wires are put in place. These wires are above the guide wires to hold the canes (green branches) and create the canopy that protects the developing grapes from too much heat. Because quadrilateral trellising requires more "infrastructure growth" than an undivided canopy, it would take an extra year to get our first harvest. The benefit would be that we would get between 75 and 100 percent more fruit.

When they finished the discussion, we got to the money part. They said that a good estimate would be twenty-five thousand dollars over the three- to four-year period to get the vineyard set up, with two-thirds of that amount in the first year, when most of the work is done. We thought this was a great deal, given the alternative of landscaping the approximate one-half acre we would be using for the vineyard. Also, grapes are quite drought tolerant, so we would need to water the vineyard via a drip system only two or three times per season when the vineyard was mature.

When Eddy and Nancy left, we were giddy. This was our dream, and we now had the land and the people to make it all happen. We just had the happy task of figuring out what kind of wine we would like to drink for the next fifty years—tough work, but we were up for it.

As we thought about it, we kept in mind that it would need to be a grape varietal that we would enjoy for a very long time. We thought about Cabernet Sauvignon, but we were concerned about it being just about the latest grape harvested, typically late October or even November. Also, a really big Cab, which was probably what we would have hoped for, takes a while to age to be really enjoyed. We never seriously considered any of the Rhones, like Syrah, because as much as I like a good Syrah, it wasn't what we would enjoy all the time. The same is true of Zinfandel. So, in the end, we chose Merlot, mostly because we liked it. There was the added benefit that it harvests earlier than Cabernet Sauvignon. In our eleven harvests, we have generally harvested in the first two weeks of October and have never lost any of our crops to rain. The other reason we chose Merlot is because St. Francis Merlot from Sonoma County was one of our favorite wines, and one we could drink by itself, or with a variety of food. So Merlot it was.

A great benefit of our discussion with Eddy and Nancy is that we were now clients, and as such, we were invited to the Family of Vineyards celebration that they held every summer at their home in the Santa Cruz Mountains. We attended with Karen and Gary Campi, who had been coming to the event for several years already. It was a casual barbecue for their clients. Everyone was encouraged to bring a bottle or two of their wine, some made by the growers themselves, others, like the Campis', were produced by commercial wineries. Eddy fired up a huge grill and barbecued tri-tip, while Nan produced all the side dishes. It was a beautiful day, made even more fun because everyone there grew grapes and made wine. Some of the wines were very good, and some were very bad, but it was great to try the different efforts and discuss with these growers what they were trying to do and how much fun they were having doing it. Denise and I were in heaven.

There were some Silicon Valley legends that came, A. C. "Mike" Markula, who was then vice chairman of Apple Computer, having founded the company with Steve Jobs and Steve Wozniak in the late seventies. Also in attendance was Vinod Khosla, the venture capital partner with Kleiner Perkins, one of the leading VC firms in the valley. They both had vineyards at their homes. In those days, Bill and Brenda Murphy, who went on to establish Clos La Chance Winery in San Martin, worked with Eddy and Nancy, so they attended as well.

It was a party we attended for many years as our vineyard was planted, grew, and began to bear fruit. It was quite a treat in 1999 to bring a few bottles of the 1997 Page Mill Côté Merlot to the party we had attended empty-handed for five years. Sadly, in the mid-2000s because their business had grown (which was a good thing), there were just too many people for Eddy and Nancy to host for this annual event. We miss it, but we have fond memories of those great afternoons when all anyone talked about was their grapes and the wine that came from them. This was a group of true wine enthusiasts, not wine snobs, and we learned from them.

Through the spring of 1994, preparations were under way. We had the yard fenced to keep out the deer. Our neighbor Tom, who was an executive with one of the large pharmaceutical companies, was also our self-proclaimed game warden. Now, Tom did have an arsenal at his house, and having grown up in Pennsylvania, he knew his way around when it came to hunting. But I believe his reasoning was simply to ensure a steady supply of the new wine next door. Between the fence and Tom, I believed we were safe from deer.

Soil amendments were added, and the whole area was rototilled. We had two sections, split by our driveway. One side had been the construction site for the house, and Eddy and his team had trouble "ripping" the soil. He was concerned that this side might grow a bit more slowly, as the soil on the other side was much easier to work with. But in the end, they laid out the vineyard, putting in the anchor posts at each end, placed in cement and at an angle to handle the tension of the wires. They also put in the posts that would ultimately hold the trellising system. The posts were also markers for where the vines would be planted.

By the time everything was ready to go and they had secured the vines from a nursery in Napa, it was early July. The vineyard was planted on July 8, 1994, probably one of the hottest days of that summer, at over 100 degrees.

I remember this distinctly because the next day was my fortieth birthday. Denise wanted the vineyard planted by my birthday for the party she had planned … and of which I was completely unaware. There were 148 Merlot vines planted on that day. As we looked over the vineyard, I happened to count the rows for the first time. Because there were rows on either side of the driveway, I hadn't really thought about it before. But the east side had five rows, and the west side had eight rows, for a total of thirteen rows, of course.

On July 9, 1994, Denise outdid herself and upped the ante on parties. I was awoken in my bed again, this time by several of my friends at 6:30 AM. Leading the charge was Gary with a megaphone, shouting, "Happy birthday" and telling me I had twenty minutes to get ready for golf. Now, I wasn't much of a golfer, but the opportunity to play golf with my friends on my birthday was quite a treat.

I asked Denise what was going on. She said, "You'll see," but then she added that we would have a barbeque with friends later to celebrate my birthday. She gave me just enough to make it credible. We had a great round of golf, but then Gary said we weren't finished. We were going to the Giants game. It was a beautiful summer day, even for San Francisco. In those days, baseball was played at Candlestick Park (now named for some Internet company—Monster, I think). We enjoyed the day, and I think the Giants even won. At least that's how I remember it.

We stopped off on the way home to play laser tag, which was fun, but I was getting tired. Unknown to me, it was all part of the plan to give Denise time to set up for the real party. As we pulled into our driveway, I expected to see a number of our friends in the backyard, with the grill going.

Instead, there was a huge tent on the asphalt pad beyond our newly planted vineyard, and there were a hundred or more people, all dressed very nicely. I was arriving in shorts and a beer-stained T-shirt. Everyone yelled, "Happy birthday!" I mingled for a few minutes, but then I was told to go take a shower and get dressed. Denise had even laid out a suggested outfit. (She never does that, but it was a big help.)

By the time I got back outside, the party was in full swing. My mother had come up from Southern California along with my oldest brother, Chris, and his wife, Diane. As I said, there were over a hundred people. It wasn't a party; it was an event. Denise had it catered, so we could all just enjoy ourselves. Even Eddy and Nancy were there, which was a godsend, as we began to run out of Chardonnay. They just happened to have a case in their car, which they happily donated to the cause.

After dinner, Denise showed a video commemorating my birthday. It used video footage from a review of 1954, interspersed with comments from many of our friends, including an old boss from high school and my father, who didn't make it to the party. Denise and Nicole, age ten, had gone to a video-editing company and put the whole thing together. It was quite a feat, as this was before the many video-editing tools available for the Mac. Even my kids offered their thoughts. Nicole's context was basketball, as I had helped coach her the year before. She'd made her shot in the three or four practice takes but then missed on the real take. Without blinking an eye, she said, "Well, maybe I still need to work on it."

Adam, age six, closed the video with the phrase, "You're the best dad I ever had!" It was unforgettable, as was the entire evening. Denise outdid herself, and everyone had a great time—no one more than me.

I know of at least two couples who claim to have conceived children that night, so it must have been a great party. I also received some of the finest bottles of wine I've ever had. I guess people knew what I liked. More related to the vineyard and the overall story, as a consequence of planting on the hottest day of the year, we lost eleven vines. Eddy told us that normally we would have lost a few vines, so it wasn't a big deal. And in fact, over the next few years, we lost and replanted a few more vines that were taken out by gophers. Our vineyard today has 148 strong and healthy vines, most of which are over fourteen years old.

AN ATTEMPT AT WINEMAKING

By the fall of 1995, we had two growing seasons under our belts. The trellising system had been completed, with T-bars on all the posts and wires in place to hold the cordons and guide wires above for the canopy. It really looked like a vineyard, and some of the vines had just taken off, growing to take the full H shape of the quadrilateral trellising system. Most were in some level of progress to this ultimate result, which was why it would take another two growing seasons to get our first harvest. Ironically, the most vigorous side was the side that had been the construction site, which surprised all of us. One day, we were talking about it with our neighbors, and they mentioned that there had been a huge manure pile on that side of the driveway the entire time our land had been a horse property. When I mentioned it to Eddy, he just laughed and said that piece of land was probably supercharged with nutrients from the years of horse poop. And sure enough, for the first few years, those vines outproduced the other side dramatically. Even today those vines are more vigorous than the other side, though not by much.

The previous year, Gary Campi had decided to graft Merlot vines onto the row of table grapes that formed the first row of his vineyard. He said the squirrels and birds got more of the grapes than he and his family did, and besides, he'd like to get a little red wine. Within a year, due to the age of the vines, the grafted Merlot vines were producing fruit. Gary and I decided to try our hand at making wine. To be fair, we needed fruit from both vine-yards. I actually found two small clusters that had not been removed from our vines. All fruit in those first few years was removed to focus the growth energy on the green canes, which would become the cordons. Nonetheless, I had my contribution, compared to about a hundred pounds of grapes from Gary. We crushed the grapes in his backyard and then put them into a five-gallon food-grade plastic bin for fermenting. We added yeast, given to us by Dane at Page Mill up the street. I brought the bucket home, as I was taking responsibility for fermentation and "punching down the cap."

Punching down the cap is an important step in making red wine. The cap is the mass of skins, stems, and seeds that float to the top of the vessel when making wine. Punching down this mass of mostly skins back into the fermenting grapes results in several benefits. Most importantly, it provides richer color and flavor to the wine. It also serves to mix the yeast around, especially in the first few days. Additionally, punching down the cap intro-duces more oxygen into the must ("must" is what this mass of fermenting grapes, skins, stems, and seeds is called). More oxygen means faster action for the yeast at this stage of the process. It also helps to keep harmful bacteria from forming on top of fermenting grapes. Punching down is typically done three times a day during fermentation.

So every day before work, I would go out and punch down the cap. I also did it when I got home, and again before I went to bed. I could smell the grapes fermenting. A very earthy, warm smell filled our small barn; it is a great fragrance that I have always loved. During this period, I measured both the Brix and the specific gravity of the wine to gauge fermentation.

Brix is a measure of the amount of sugar in a liquid. When deciding time for harvesting grapes, the Brix scale is one of the primary measures used. It gives an accurate approximation of alcohol content of the finished wine, as the sugar in wine is converted to alcohol during fermentation. In the fer-mentation process, Brix provides a measure of progress as the sugar is being converted to alcohol. A more accurate measurement is made with a hydrom-eter, which measures the specific gravity of the fermenting liquid. It is a measure of the relative density of the liquid as compared to water. At about 1.030 to 1.040, primary fermentation is complete, and it is time to press the wine. Even though it really doesn't taste that good at this point, it is wine.

With the little wine we had, we essentially pressed it with a colander—not very romantic, but it did the job.

The next step is secondary fermentation, which I did in a glass carboy. Commercial wineries would put the wine into oak barrels for reds, but the benefit of the glass was that we could watch the process of secondary fermentation. It is a slower process than the frenzied bubbling of primary fermentation and is done in a sealed container, without access to oxygen. The carboy is filled to the shoulder to provide room for bubbles, which still do occur, at a much slower pace. During this period, the secondary or malolactic fermentation takes place. All red wines go through this, and some white wines do too. The process converts tart malic acid into smoother lactic acid, giving the wine an overall smoother and silkier texture. In white wines that do not undergo this process, you can often taste a hint of apples from the malic acid, while those that have undergone malolactic fermentation have a buttery flavor.

The top of the carboy is fixed with a rubber bung that has a hole in it. An airlock is placed in this hole. It allows the carbon dioxide and other gases to escape but doesn't let air (oxygen) in. This process takes several months to complete, and I racked the wine several times, siphoning it into a clean carboy each time. When secondary fermentation was complete, it really looked and tasted like wine, though it was very young. Next, I added oak chips to simulate barrel aging and left it alone for another year. Gary, Karen, Denise, and I tried it a year or so later and thought it was fit to drink. It was a fine first effort. But 1996 would prove to be a different year.

By 1996, the east side of the vineyard (where the horse manure had been) was nearly complete in the development and growth of the cordons, so we decided to leave a little fruit on them to give me more to experiment with before a real harvest in 1997. When it was time to harvest, we chose a Friday afternoon to pick. First we picked Gary and Karen's Merlot, which took us about two hours. Then we went over to our house, where I was sure we had about the same amount. Gary asked if we should get some help, but I assured him that the four of us could do it, and then we'd sit down to a satisfying dinner. We lifted the nets on our vineyard, placed there to protect the fruit from birds and "critters," as Eddy called them. To my surprise, the clusters seemed to have grown and multiplied. As we began to pick, I realized we had much more fruit than I had thought. We began calling friends to come over to help, with the promise of good food and wine at the completion of the harvest. Amazingly, no one was home or available. In a panic, we picked until nine o'clock that evening and hadn't made a dent in the vineyard. Reluctantly I gave up, saying that Denise and I would finish it tomorrow, as Gary and Karen were busy that day.

More importantly, as we discussed it over dinner, there was significantly more fruit than we were prepared to deal with ourselves. I had met Dane, the winemaker at Page Mill Winery, several times by now, and he had tentatively agreed to take our fruit when we were ready to harvest in 1997. Calling him in the middle of his harvest, when his workload was at its peak, was not something I was looking forward to. And to be calling in a panic, with a load of fruit that I needed to crush the next day, made matters worse. But I really didn't know what else to do.

Dane answered the phone, and I told him our dilemma. Amazingly, he just laughed and said to bring it over the next day. What a relief. And then I began to get excited. This was going to be a real wine harvest of sorts. In the technology business, think of it as a release .9—not quite the real thing, but pretty close. By the end of the evening, I was pumped up full tilt.

The next morning, we drove up to Page Mill to get more of the yellow lug boxes. Later I found out that they actually went by a different name: FYBs, which stood for Fucking Yellow Boxes because of the hassle they were to load into the crusher. But I happily picked up a bunch more and went home to finish the harvest. I was in my glory, picking our Merlot, and it was beautiful. Our fruit has been gorgeous every year. There is little mold or raisining; it is simply beautiful, purple clusters of the sweetest, juiciest fruit imaginable. By the time Denise and I finished, it was early afternoon, and between what we had done that day and the fruit we'd picked with Karen and Gary the day before, we had over forty boxes. Each holds between thirty and forty pounds of fruit, so we had around three-quarters of a ton of fruit—that's fifteen hundred pounds. It was amazing.

As we pulled into the driveway at Page Mill, I was quite proud of what Denise and I were delivering. Dane thought the fruit looked great. I'm not sure what he was doing at the time, but he dropped whatever it was, and we began to crush and destem the grapes and collect them in a fiberglass bin. Dane took over from there. I visited the winery several times over the next weeks, punching down the cap a few times but letting Dane work his magic.

When it was bottled twenty months later, it was labeled Page Mill 1996 Merlot Côté Campi Vineyards. It was great to be drinking the first fruits of our labors, and it was pretty good wine. It was much better than the wine that Gary and I had made, but then I was starting to learn something very important. There is an art and a skill to making fine wine, and Dane Stark knew what he is doing.

I will never forget Dane's immediate willingness to help. He is a gracious man, a person of great talent and heart, and someone who has become a great friend to me.

For Christmas that year, Denise's parents gave us a small plaque for the front of our house that said Chateau Côté. It was meant to be a fun gift and not pretentious, but later, as Nicole became a teenager, the plaque apparently did intimidate a few of her friends, but then they just made good-natured fun of her for it. We have enjoyed it, and we do call our home Chateau Côté these days.

Harvest Celebration

As the summer of 1997 came to a close, we were getting excited about our first full-fledged harvest. We had been talking with friends throughout the year, gauging their interest in coming to help with the harvest. The comments ranged from sheer joy at being asked to come harvest grapes to wondering how hard the work was—but saying they'd come to help us, no matter the work. Our goal was to get enough people helping that the work would move along quickly and we'd have them wanting more of the experience. Then we'd have a harvest meal with wine, and they'd be begging to come back next year. For me, it was like how Tom Sawyer got everyone to help him paint the fence, except that this really would be a fun day. The only problem was that it was difficult to predict just when we would harvest. We had planned to do it on a Sunday, but which Sunday? It all depended on the grapes. We told people we could only give them a few days' notice. We made a list of people that was much longer than we needed, but we figured we might need to call more people because of the timing.

I had received a gift from my family for my birthday that year. It was a portable refractometer. This was the tool that was used to measure Brix, the sugar in the grapes. It was a thing of beauty. You simply put a few drops of grape juice on the lens, held it in the light, and looked through it to see where a blue field representing the sugar content hit the scale that was centered vertically. It was very easy to use. I am sure that the first year I used it, I was out in the vineyard testing the grapes as soon as they turned red. The Brix was probably at 10, which is equivalent to 10 percent sugar. Most red-wine grapes are harvested between 23 and 26, depending on the varietal, so I had a long way to go. But this was my first year, and I dutifully went out every week and recorded the increase in Brix. I was excited when we had a hot spell and the Brix jumped a whole point in a week. As we got into September, the fruit was inching up into the high teens. As it got into the twenties, Dane came out to see how it looked and to test it himself. By the end of September, we were there. The Brix was about 23, which Dane felt was a good number for this young vineyard. He also tested the acid and thought it was just about right. So we decided that Sunday, September 28, 1997, would be the first official harvest and party at the Côté vineyard.

By the time we made the decision, it was Wednesday, so we began calling the list. As expected, we got enough people, about thirty-five, but we'd had to call about fifty to get there. So far, so good. Since this was our first time, and we didn't know how much preparation there would be for the harvest itself, we decided to cater the meal. All day Saturday, we made preparations. We told people to bring pruning shears or clippers, but we went out and bought about thirty clippers so that we'd be sure to have enough. Denise made a poster of rules for harvesting:

CHATEAU CÔTÉ
Harvesting Instructions

- Hold the cluster at the bottom, and cut with shears at the stem
- Do not cut the canes, as they are next year's fruit
- Do not cut your fingers … they are next year's harvesters
- Look over the clusters for:
  o Small green berries
  o Rotten or diseased fruit
  o Dead leaves
  … and remove
- Do not load bin over the top because we stack them — just grab a new one when it's full

---

Eleven years later, we still bring out the poster because some people need reminding, and we always seem to have a few new harvesters every year.

The day dawned beautifully. We had a perfect early fall day, with warm sunshine but not too hot. We had asked people to arrive at 11:00 AM, so we had work to do that morning. We set out tables with the shears and a first aid kit (hoping we wouldn't need it). We also set out snacks and drinks on ice. We bought balloons for the mailbox and a harvest cake from our local market, with the words "Côté Harvest 1997" on it. Our good friends Corky and Shelby came over early to help get ready. Shelby helped me to take the nets off the vines, something he has done with me every year before harvest, even the time he couldn't stay because he was coaching his son's basketball game. It is just one of our little traditions.

At about 10:30, Dane showed up with the bins and the truck, and we began to spread out the bins in the vineyard. By 11:00, people began to arrive. As this was our first harvest, I waited until most of the people had arrived before discussing the harvest instructions. People got a kick out of the line about cutting fingers, but it is something that happens often as people are trying to cut the bunch and can't quite see because of the foliage, so it is one of the more serious rules. By 11:30, we were ready to start. All of our friends spread out in the vineyard and began picking. After a short while, several of us began to run bins back to the truck, where Dane stacked them up. The work went even more quickly than we thought it would, and by 1:00 PM, we were finished. I think people were a bit disappointed, as they were really getting into it. But we thought it was perfect, as no one had to work too hard, and everyone seemed to have fun. We all grabbed a drink and headed to the backyard for food and wine.

I pulled off about two hundred pounds of grapes, which I mixed with the grapes from Gary and Karen's fifteen Merlot vines so we could try our hand at making wine again. A friend had given me a small hand crusher as a birthday gift, so before we ate, we crushed the grapes and put them into a larger food-grade plastic bin for fermentation. I won't go into the story, but this time I proved why I was not born to make wine. All I can say is that it did ferment and therefore could be called wine, but it tasted terrible. From this experience came one of my adages about wine. There are three parts to wine: (1) growing the grapes, (2) making the wine, and (3) drinking the wine. From that experience, I decided to stick with getting really good at 1 and 3.

We had a great meal set out for us, and for the only time, we served wine that was not from our vineyard. By the next year, we had the wine from our 1996 harvest that Page Mill had made for us. And from then on, we have served our wine at every harvest party.

At the end of the meal, before we served the cake, Denise and I got up to toast the harvest and our friends. We thanked them for being a part of this special day. We hoped they would come back to join us every year. We also thanked Dane for what he had done and for what he was about to do. Given the quantity of grapes, which we later found out was three and a half tons, Dane had decided to crush them the next morning, when it was cooler and he had more time. So he was able to join us for the harvest meal and celebration.

By late in the day, the vineyard was empty, the truck was gone, and we sat in the backyard with a few remaining friends, sipping wine and savoring the last warmth from the setting sun. It sounds a bit corny, but this was our dream come true. It also served to signal the fall of the year, a tradition that has kept many of our friends coming back year after year.

Somehow, I think, it also played to our roots as an agrarian society. There is something truly spiritual about harvesting the fruits of the land. As I said in the prologue, grapes touch me on so many levels that are both spiritual and earthly. This day every year, this harvest, is probably the most special day of the year. Denise and I are surrounded by our friends and family. We work together to harvest the grapes that will become wine, and we enjoy a meal together in celebration of the harvest, our friendships, and our love.

This first harvest was truly a blessing!

This may be a good point to explain how we worked with Dane. As growers, we were entitled to be paid for our grapes. Because Page Mill had worked with a number of small vineyards like ours, they had a system for those that preferred to take wine in trade. That was our preference, so we took a percentage of the production in trade for our grapes. This amounted to between twenty and twenty-five cases of wine per year. And the added benefit was that we could choose to take some of the cases in other Page Mill wines, such as their Livermore Sauvignon Blanc, Campi Chardonnay, and Bien Nacido Pinot Noir, and more recently we hope to tap into their Estate Petite Syrah and Livermore Cabernet, which are both tremendous.

This approach gave us plenty of wine to drink and share and to offer as donations to charitable events at our children's schools and organizations that Denise worked with.

This year, as we are about to get our 2006 vintage, we will have ten years of Côté Merlot in bottles. We are planning a ten-year vertical tasting in the early part of 2009 to see how the various vintages have faired. We only have a few bottles of the early years left, but it will be fun to see how they hold up.

The 1998 harvest was an interesting one. That year we had an El Niño condition in which we got very large quantities of rain very late in the season—June, in fact. We heard about several Pinot Noir vineyards in the Santa Cruz Mountains that got no fruit. We had a very light harvest that year, only about one and a half tons, so we took advantage of that and went up to Page Mill with a few friends to help with the crush and then have our harvest meal. Some of the Cabernet vineyards never ripened enough to be picked that year, so it ended up being a strange year. Our 1998 vintage was okay, as the wine was still fairly young, but it was the poorest of our vintages to date. Fortunately we had a good deal of the 1997 to enjoy through this period.

One of the true bright spots of that harvest was meeting Mike Sabina. Mike was a friend of Dane's who was working with him during that harvest. Mike was there when we harvested the 1998 Merlot, and he helped to crush it that afternoon. We enjoyed working with him, and at the time we didn't know that he was in the middle of remodeling his restaurant in Palo Alto. It was called St. Michael's Alley, and it had been named that long before Mike and his wife, Jenny, bought the place. As a result of working that harvest, when the 1998 Côté Merlot was released, Mike began to serve it by the glass and by the bottle at his newly reopened restaurant.

I don't remember the first time we had dinner there, but we have been back more times than I can count. It is our very favorite restaurant, not only for the company of Mike and Jenny; the food is always outstanding. Mike also has great taste in wines (of course, he serves ours), and we always ask him for a suggestion, which is usually both interesting and outstanding. Highlights of the restaurant include their special evenings, including Valentine's Day and New Year's Eve dinners, both of which we have attended many times. St. Mike's also teams with Page Mill, usually once a year, for a great food and wine pairing. For Denise and me, it's a real treat—great food, great wine, and great friends. What else is there?

Wine Cellars and Wine Barns

By 1999, we were well on our way, with a maturing vineyard, and with the backyard pool and landscaping complete. Denise and I had agreed to put our house on the St. Francis High School Annual "Christmas at Our House" Tour, a charitable event that featured several houses in a given area that were open for tours over three days. It began with a special event on Thursday evening, and we agreed that given the large area near our barns, we could have them set up the tent and have that special evening at our house, making it the last stop on the tour that night.

The house needed a little touching up with paint, carpeting, and some additional decorating by Denise. But in the midst of this, she gave me a wonderful present. The house had three wet bars; I'm not sure why anyone would need that many wet bars, but there they were. One of them was in the library, which was right off of the kitchen. Denise had the idea to turn it into a wine cellar in the house. It was a perfect idea. The room was in the center of the house and fairly cool already. It wasn't very large but could easily accommodate a 600-bottle wine cellar. The contractor went to work, clearing out the wet bar, putting in a stone floor, and ordering redwood racks for single-bottle storage, with a row of racks for magnums. The crowning feature was the door that Denise had come up with. She decided on a glass and wrought-iron door, and she designed a cursive "CC" in the center, which stood for Chateau Côté. It turned out beautifully. When the lights were on in the cellar, you could see the wines all lit up through the door. It was a hit at the tour, but more importantly, it was quite a special gift to me, as we now had a place to store and age our favorite wines. That winter and spring, we took several trips up to Napa and Sonoma to taste and buy wines to add to our cellar. We also kept a healthy amount of several vintages of Côté Merlot for ready access. It remains one of the most beautiful features of our house today.

By 2001, with the vineyard in and the backyard complete, we turned our attention to the last project on our property, the dilapidated barns that were a remnant of the old horse property. We had decided on three elements for the construction: a guesthouse, a large wine room, and a storage area for nets and other equipment. The barns ranged along the roadway, with a large twenty-foot-high barn with sheds running away on either side. As we began discussion with the Town of Los Altos Hills, they agreed to grandfather our structures, as they were technically in the setback, meaning they were too close to the roadway. This meant we could only use the footprint and heights of the existing structures for our remodeling. We began thinking about how we would situate the various elements we wanted to incorporate, and immediately we ran into a problem.

We wanted to put in a fairly complete guesthouse with a main room, a great kitchen, a bedroom with a full bath, and a half bath for guests. We imagined that our parents or children might need to use the space, so it had to be fully functional as a house. But most of the time, it would be used as an entertaining area. Denise also wanted a gourmet kitchen, as she imagined offering the space for charity events or other activities.

But the city required similar use in grandfathering the space. We could not definitely prove that there had been a bathroom, let alone a kitchen, in the current barn structures. We were sure there had been hands living in one end of the barn, but there was nothing obvious. This ended up being a very fortuitous problem. As we discussed the next step with our architect, he suggested building the guesthouse within our existing building envelope and offering to take out square footage from the grandfathered space to equal the amount we were adding. The city thought this was a great idea, so we ended up with a design that created three separate buildings: a thousand-square-foot guesthouse that could have all the amenities we wanted. We maintained the footprint of the main barn structure for our wine room and designed a large refrigerated wine storage room off of it. We then took the space removed for the guest house and turned that into a sunken garden between the wine room and the storage area. The result was that we created a plaza, with a road coming through the east side of the vineyard and entering an L-shaped set of buildings, with the guest house, storage, and wine barn all surrounding a round plaza with a beautiful bronze fountain I found online in Baltimore. Got to love the Internet!

We began construction in 2002 and completed it in 2003. It was sensational, and it completed what had become a stunning property. It truly was Chateau Côté. We inaugurated it with a dinner cooked in the guest-house kitchen and served in the large wine room. The large wine cellar off the wine room allowed us to take all of our Côté Merlot from Page Mill after it was bottled and not have to hold some of it at their distribution center. The room could hold thirty-two cases, and there was single-bottle storage for another fifteen hundred bottles.

The wine room was fabulous. The ceiling was nearly twenty feet high. Denise had found a wood salvage company in Berkeley, California, and secured beams for the ceiling that were from a hundred-year-old barn in Nova Scotia. They were hand-hewn, wormy chestnut beams.

The American chestnut tree covered much of the virgin forest in the eastern United States but was virtually extinct in the early part of the twentieth century due to chestnut blight, which was introduced from foreign lumber. The stands of devastated trees were harvested for fencing and outbuildings such as barns. In recent times, people have made a business out of reclaiming these beautiful wood beams and fencing from buildings that are torn down.

We had eleven-foot-high rounded doors that opened onto the plaza and fountain when the weather was warm. But one of the best features of the room was a ten-foot solid walnut table that we bought from Jan de Luz, a store in Carmel Valley that specialized in importing French furniture and fixtures. This table was built by an older man in France. He completed a limited number of tables per year, and each one was unique.

The previous summer, as part of our twenty-fifth wedding anniversary, we had spent a weekend in Carmel, where we bought the table and a stone Bacchus fountain that we put in the sunken garden after storing both pieces for about six months until we were ready for them.

Joseph Phelps Wines

August 2002 was the month of our twenty-fifth wedding anniversary. I mentioned the trip to Carmel, which occurred the weekend after our anniversary, which fell on a Tuesday that year. Our real celebration occurred the weekend before and included one of the most amazing wine experiences of our entire lives. But it all happened by luck.

We had planned to go up to Napa and Sonoma for a long weekend, beginning Thursday night and returning on Tuesday, which was our anniversary. A few weeks before we were to go, Gary and Karen Campi asked us to join them at a Joseph Phelps wine dinner that was held at Viognier Restaurant in the Draeger's store in San Mateo, California. We had attended other wine dinners there but had never experienced Phelps wines. They convinced us to leave for our weekend on Friday morning and join them for the dinner on Thursday night. It seemed like a small change of plans, and the hotel night we saved would more than pay for the dinner.

We arrived at the restaurant and stood around enjoying Joseph Phelps Sauvignon Blanc and passed hors d'oeuvres. Our host for the evening was Tom Shelton, who we discovered was the president and CEO of Phelps Vineyards. This dinner had been added late, and his regional sales manager was not available, so Tom had come instead. As we all sat down to dinner, I noticed that Tom was sitting alone nearby at a table for two. I turned to him and asked if someone was joining him. He looked a bit sad and said that his wife was supposed to join him, but at the least minute, she couldn't make it. I asked him if he'd like to join our table rather than eating alone. He smiled and said yes. We had the staff set another place for him, and we had the honor of having the president of one of the finest wineries in the world join us for dinner. We were entertained by his stories of his own career, the winery, and Joe Phelps, and of course we enjoyed the fabulous Joseph Phelps wines. For the first time, Denise and I tried their signature Bordeaux blend, Insignia. It is an incredible wine and has become a favorite of ours.

But the heart of the story began with an innocuous question to Tom. I knew that Joseph Phelps was not open for general tasting. I mentioned to him that the next day, Denise and I were going up to Napa Valley to celebrate our twenty-fifth wedding anniversary and would love to taste at Phelps. Could he let us know whom we might call to try to schedule a time? He said that he would have his hospitality manager call us the next day to schedule something over the weekend. After our wonderful evening of wine, food, and Tom's company, we were excited to go to the winery.

The next morning, as we were leaving town, there was already voicemail on my cell phone from the hospitality manager at Phelps. He suggested that we join them on Sunday at 11:00 AM for a tasting, and he asked us to join them for lunch afterward. We called back, told him that we would be there on Sunday, and thanked him.

The Joseph Phelps winery is set on a knoll overlooking Spring Valley, which is just off the Silverado Trail in Napa Valley. It is a beautiful setting, and the winery is a large redwood building with an impressive redwood timber trellis at the entrance to the winery. On the back terrace is a wonderful view down into Spring Valley and on to the Mayacamas Mountains on the west side of Napa Valley.

As we drove in, we were impressed with the beauty of the surroundings. We parked and walked into the hospitality center. The person at the desk asked for our name, found it, and said that Claude would join us in just a few moments. We could see a group of people tasting on the terrace, and we figured we were in the next group. A few minutes later, a tall, older gentleman introduced himself to us as Claude. He had a French accent, and when we asked where he was from originally, he said he grew up in Belgium. We knew we would hit it off with him when Denise mentioned that her grandmother had also grown up in Belgium, in the city of Bruges, where her family owned a chocolate factory.

He walked us into the winery and said that he was to be our host that day for a private tasting and lunch. He congratulated us on our twenty-fifth wedding anniversary and said he was looking forward to sharing his love of wine with us. Unknown to us, we were about to embark on an amazing afternoon as we got to know Claude and the wines of Joseph Phelps. Claude was an accomplished sommelier, having worked at the Kahala Hilton in Hawaii in the sixties and seventies. He was semiretired at this point and worked part time for Phelps doing tastings and seminars. He flattered us by acknowledging that we probably knew something about wine but saying that if we didn't mind, he would treat our tasting as a seminar, imparting some of his ideas and thoughts about wine in general and, of course, the wines of Joseph Phelps. For the next two hours, we learned how to first look at the colors of the wine, smell the aroma and bouquet, and then taste the wine, all in an effort to get the most out of the experience and best understand what we were drinking. All of this was done as we talked about our lives and drank some of the finest wines that Phelps had to offer—their Ovation Chardonnay; Mistral, which is a Rhone blend; and of course, Insignia.

Next Claude asked if we'd like to have lunch, and again, we thought we would be part of a larger group. But Claude went inside and returned with a basket of food that was clearly just for us. He set out the food and asked which wines we'd like to enjoy with our lunch. We chose the Ovation Chardonnay and the Insignia. We enjoyed a wonderful lunch overlooking the valley on a beautiful summer day, talking with Claude about his life experiences and his love of wine. At about 2:00 PM, Claude said that he was sorry, but he had to meet another group. We asked if we needed to move for the next group, but he said he would simply meet them inside and that we should enjoy the afternoon along with dessert and wine for as long as we wanted. He also brought out a chilled bottle of Delice, a Semillon dessert wine that was produced intermittently by the winery when the fruit was judged to be right. It was a wonderful wine to have with our dessert as we sat on our picnic bench on the terrace. As Claude stepped away, he said that if we wanted to buy any wines today, we should mention his name and get a 20 percent discount. And his parting words were to ask that we make sure to say goodbye to him, even if it meant interrupting him, as he had so enjoyed our time together.

We sat there for another hour or so, enjoying the experience. We then purchased our first Phelps wines and later joined their wine club. As we left, we did end up interrupting Claude, but he graciously broke away to give us a hug and thank us for joining him. Of course, we were the ones that were thankful, and we told him so.

This was one of the most amazing wine experiences of our lives, and we will always remember it. When we returned from our anniversary, our daughter, Nicole, had prepared a wonderful meal for us, and we told her about the awesome experience at Phelps. Shortly after that, Denise put together baskets of goodies for both Tom Shelton and Claude and sent them as a thank-you for the wonderful hospitality that we had experienced. We heard back right away from Tom with his thanks and his pleasure that we had had such a great time. It was a month or so later when we heard from Claude.

He sent a wonderful note reflecting that he had been thinking about the world on the first anniversary of September 11, as this was 2002. He was in a sour mood, thinking about how hurtful the world could be. For some reason he found himself reading the note that Denise and I had sent to him, and it reminded him of the day we spent together. He was encouraged by that experience and the joy of people in his life, and he sent those thoughts to us in his note. It made such an impression on us. Every time we have visited Phelps in the years since, we have always looked for Claude, and often he is there. Since that time, he has battled and beat cancer, and he continues to offer tastings and seminars at Phelps. We were there for the Insignia weekend in May 2008 (more on that later), and we had a great conversation catching up with Claude.

While writing this, I was looking at the Phelps Web site and didn't see Tom Shelton's name as president and CEO, but there was no replacement either. I googled Tom and sadly found an article from the *Napa Register*, dated a few weeks earlier, saying that Tom had died after a battle with brain cancer. After remembering his generosity, it struck me how important it is to appreciate and enjoy the many wonderful people that we come across in our lives. They touch us in ways they can't imagine and make our lives so much fuller.

Our Children Begin Their Own Adventures

In the summer of 2003, we celebrated Gary and Karen's fiftieth birthdays with a trip to Sonoma in the area around Healdsburg. We stayed just north of Santa Rosa at the Vintner's Inn, which is also home to the John Ash & Co. restaurant. During the days, we toured the Dry Creek area and visited A. Rafanelli for a private tasting. Unlike at Phelps, this meant walking through the caves with Dave Rafanelli, the owner, and sitting in their office, trying their wonderful Zinfandel, Merlot, Cabernet, and even their Terrace Select. We bought the limit of what we could buy, which was two bottles of each of their wines. We also visited Pezzi King Winery, a producer of Zinfandels in Dry Creek Valley. While we enjoyed their wines, the most notable part of that experience was that they had a giant crystal glass on display. As a bit of a joke, we asked them if they sold them. They said they did, and Gary bought one for each of the couples as a thank-you for the trip and something to remember it by. We even celebrated on our return by having a dinner in our wine room, and we drank out of the big glasses. Our glass is now firmly ensconced on the bar in our family room.

Our children, Adam and Nicole, were both growing up and becoming young adults. While they had certainly been around wine and grapes all their lives and would have a small glass here or there at Christmas or

Thanksgiving, they hadn't particularly warmed to the harvest day. They were busy with their young lives. But in their late teens and into their twenties, they both began to appreciate and enjoy wine. In the last several years, they have joined in the harvest, beginning to see the tradition that it has become and how important it is to our family.

Several years ago, after we had harvested the grapes and were ending our meal, we were about to toast the harvest and thank our friends. Adam came up to me and said that we should toast the harvest this year by drinking out of the huge wineglass. I agreed that it would be fun, so we poured an entire bottle of Côté Merlot into the glass, barely making a small pool in the bottom. We proceeded to toast the harvest, not just Denise and me, but also Nicole and Adam, beginning a new tradition that has continued today, whether they are coming home from college or living nearby. I think the harvest, for them, has come to mean much the same as it does to Denise and me—celebration of the completion of the harvest and the beginning of fall, but more importantly the love of family and friends, sharing an experience together.

As a side note on the huge glass, we decided to see just how much wine the glass would hold. We filled a wine bottle with water and began filling the glass. It turns out it holds thirteen bottles of wine, of course. But that's how big it is.

On the Friday after Thanksgiving in 2004, we had a real treat as parents. Our good friends Jim and Marcie's daughter Allison had been friends with Nicole since they were three, and she had turned twenty-one in August, just a month before our daughter turned twenty-one. Since both of the girls were away at school, we decided that we would take them wine tasting over the Thanksgiving holiday when they were both at home. Since everyone was busy, we decided to take a trip into the Santa Cruz Mountains. The Santa Cruz Mountains produce some of the best Chardonnay and Pinot Noir in California, though the appellation has only begun to be appreciated in the last several years. Fortunately this worked, as both Nicole and Allison liked those wines.

We chose four wineries that were open that day. We started at Savannah-Chanelle Winery in the hills above Saratoga, California. The winery was founded in 1892 by Pierre Pourroy, a French immigrant. He and his wife ran the winery until their deaths in the fifties. The land languished until 1971, when Vic Erickson bought the property and restored it as a winery and vineyard, calling it Congress Springs Winery. In 1996, the current owners purchased the winery and renamed it Savannah-Chanelle. The winery is named for the owners' two daughters and is noted for its small-lot Pinot Noir. It was a great place to start with the girls. The staff was very friendly and helpful and was very excited to have the girls at the winery for their first wine tasting experience. At each of the wineries, we bought Nicole and Allison a bottle of their favorite wine.

Next we went to Testarossa Winery. The winery is housed in what was once the Novitiate Winery, which was operated by the Jesuits from 1888 to 1986, producing some wine commercially but primarily producing sacramental wines, particularly during Prohibition. Testarossa had made a name for itself as a producer of exceptional Pinot Noir wines from various areas of California. The tasting room was a stone building and part of the original Novitiate Winery. The girls loved the space, and the young staff member was more than pleased to share his knowledge of wine and tasting with these two neophytes. We all had a great time.

After Testarossa, we headed up into the mountains, stopping first at David Bruce, also known for their Pinot, and then continuing up the hill to Byington Winery, a beautiful winery set on a hilltop at the summit of the Santa Cruz Mountains. I had been there for offsite meetings with Apple and other companies, and Denise and I had been there for a Valentine's dinner. It was a beautiful setting, and they offered a variety of nice wines. It was a beautiful final stop, and the girls really enjoyed their day. We completed our day with dinner in Saratoga. It was a pleasure to enjoy beautiful wineries and great wines just moments from our home.

In fact, in the next few years, we participated with Nicole and some of her friends in Passport Weekend. We had done this a few times before. This event is held four times a year and is sponsored by the Santa Cruz Mountains Winegrowers Association. Many wineries that are not open to the public are open on these days, and wineries that are open have special tastings for Passport members. Passport members simply buy a "passport" at any participating winery, and it is good for a visit to each of the listed wineries.

THE BEACH HOUSE

In late 2004, Denise and I realized another dream we had been think-ing about for a long time. Both of us love the ocean, and we had been thinking about getting a beach house for many years and had looked up and down the coast, from Half Moon Bay to Carmel. We vacillated on the idea because as the kids were growing up, it wasn't clear that we'd have the time to visit very often, with their busy schedules. But in 2004, we seemed to become more determined. We had ruled out Half Moon Bay as just too cold a climate. Having grown up in Southern California, I had no illusions that we would have the kind of weather I enjoyed, but we needed more sun-shine. We loved Carmel, but it was far away and very expensive. We looked at Pajaro Dunes, an isolated enclave west of Watsonville with homes right on a secluded beach. But it was also cold and far from any town. We looked at Seascape, a resort we had visited and where I'd had sales meetings, but we found out that their units didn't allow dogs, and we were not going to have a place where we couldn't bring Chloe, our black Labrador, and Ted, our puffball of a Bichon Frisé.

Once again, Gary and Karen set the pace. In 2001, they bought a house on a street that overlooked the ocean just west of Capitola, a cute little beach town near Santa Cruz. We had taken the kids to Capitola many times through the years, as it had a nice, protected swimming beach and was a quaint little town. Somewhat earlier, in the seventies and early eighties, the town had been a bit seedier, but it had really turned around. We hadn't really thought about that area, but as we visited the Campis at their house, we began to

77

see the benefits. It was a walk into the town of Capitola. The weather was the best in the Monterey area. If it was sunny anywhere, it was sunny here; in fact, some people called it the Banana Belt. In the summer of 2004, we were at the Campis' beach house to watch the Wharf to Wharf race, a 10k race that ran from the Santa Cruz wharf to the Capitola wharf and ran right down their street. We sat out in front of their house and watched the runners go by. The race was famous for the many bands that lined the streets. This past year (2008) there were forty bands along the race route. It's a great event.

After it was over, we were talking about how much fun it was and what a great house and area they had found. We had talked on and off about our own interest in a beach house, and Gary, true to his real estate background, but mostly because he wanted us around, just happened to mention that there was a house coming on the market that was a probate sale. Within two weeks he had scheduled an appointment for us to see the house. Our timing was perfect. The house hadn't been on the market that long. It was a great little three-bedroom, two-bath home with a beautiful yard overlooking Monterey Bay. We could stand at the fence and look across to Monterey and Pacific Grove. The house had a view of Capitola, its wharf, and the sailboats in the harbor. It was even closer to Capitola than Gary and Karen's, which we thought was great. Obviously we put in an offer on the house, went back and forth once more, and had a deal that worked for everyone.

Through the next few weeks, we remodeled the kitchen and one bathroom, painted the inside of the house, and restored the beautiful hardwood floors. Denise decorated with a Pottery Barn/TJ Maxx 'n' More motif that worked beautifully. That little house has become our getaway from the valley. We drive forty-five minutes from our house, and we might as well be miles away. We park the car and walk or ride our bikes the entire weekend. Our kids love it and join us or bring a few friends over to enjoy the beach.

It also has allowed us an introduction to the other side of the Santa Cruz Mountains and their wineries. We have done Passport Days "over the hill" to places like Corralitos, home to Windy Oaks' fine Pinot, and Alfaro Family Winery, for great Chardonnay and Pinot. Just up the hill from us in Soquel are several other fun wineries. Bargetto Winery is one of the oldest family-owned wineries in California. Farther up the hill is Soquel Vineyards, established in 1987 by twin brothers Peter and Paul Bargetto and their friend

Jon Morgan. They had left the family business founded by their grandfather to start their own venture. They are producing fine Pinot Noir, Chardonnay, Syrah, and a Cabernet Sauvignon from vineyards in Napa among other wines. Also in this area is Hunter Hill, with a variety of wines from Pinot to Merlot. All of these wineries have the feel of small, family-operated businesses with a welcoming attitude and easygoing charm. They remind us of Napa in the mid-seventies.

Another favorite of ours in the town of Santa Cruz is a wine shop called VinoCruz that was opened by two friends of ours, JP and Jeffrey. This shop specializes in Santa Cruz Mountain wines. They always have a flight of five wines to try for a small fee that is reimbursed upon purchase. But the real treat is that on most Saturdays and Sundays, they feature wineries from the area, often smaller wineries that aren't open for tasting except on Passport Days. We have enjoyed Chardonnays from Fernwood, Silver Mountain, and Trout Gulch. We met Richard Alfaro, owner and winemaker of Alfaro Family Winery. Richard had built a successful restaurant and bakery business. He sold the brand to Sara Lee, which continues to produce breads under the Alfaro label. He traded in this business for an old apple orchard in Corralitos that he turned into the Alfaro Family Winery. He is producing some very fine Chardonnay and Pinot Noir. The opportunity to meet and talk with people like Richard, Jerold O'Brien (the owner and winemaker at Silver Mountain), and the Bargetto brothers, Peter and Paul, is one of the real joys of discovering these smaller wineries.

Big Changes at Page Mill Winery

While all this was happening, there were major changes under way at Page Mill Winery in Los Altos Hills. Dane had joined his father, Dick, at the winery in 1992 as the winemaker, after studying at Fresno State and working for a chateau in France. By the late nineties, Dick was thinking about retiring, and in the early 2000s, he did it. He and Ome moved permanently to their home in Twainharte in the Sierra foothills. Though Dick did come back to work the harvest, the winery was Dane's baby now. Also in this time, Dane married Angela, and they were living in the family home. For a variety of reasons, they made the decision to leave the peninsula to start a new winery in Livermore Valley, which is one of the oldest wine-producing regions in California and has seen a renaissance in the last ten years.

In 2005 they purchased several acres and a wine storage building on Livermore Avenue, right at the beginning of the Livermore Wine Trail. It was a great location, but besides the wine storage building, it needed a lot of work. Dane held a barn raising of sorts. He invited a number of friends out to the new winery to work on cleaning up the place and get it ready for business. There was an old horse shed on the property that a group of us re-roofed and cleaned out to make a storage area for equipment, and later a lab for testing grape and wine samples. The center of the building is now a great space for parties and events that evoke a rustic, cozy feel.

For the first time, Page Mill was open on weekends for wine tasting, and the winery began a transformation to becoming one of the "new" wineries in Livermore. Dane and Angela have embraced their new home. They have two beautiful little girls, Stella and Lola. They contribute to various charities in the community and are building a wonderful life for themselves. Last year on the Fourth of July, they had an impromptu barbecue at the winery, which happens to be a quarter mile away from Robertson Park, where the fireworks show is done. So after dinner, we all just set out chairs and had the best seats in town for the fireworks show. I am told it is to be an annual event at the winery.

A Birthday of Tuscan Wines

In 2004, I turned fifty. Denise and I had discussed it and decided that with all that was going on in our lives, we should do something low-key for our birthdays. She still managed to surprise me, by picking me up at work in a limo with Adam, and the three of us went to the airport, where I found out that we were going to New York. I had been there many times on business, but never really as a tourist. The rest of the family had never been there at all. And to add to the surprise, Nicole met us in New York, having flown in from San Diego, where she was working and going to UC San Diego. We had a wonderful long weekend with dinners out, we saw *Wicked* on Broadway, and we spent an afternoon sightseeing and another in Central Park and visiting the Natural History Museum.

By the spring of 2006, as I began to think about Denise's fiftieth birthday, we talked about taking a trip to Italy. We had spent a few days in Venice and Florence back in 1993 after a business meeting, and we had always meant to get back for a longer visit, particularly to the wine regions of Tuscany. So, while it wasn't a surprise, it was my trip to plan. Early on, we discussed going on the trip with Karen and Gary, who jumped at the chance to go, particularly as I was planning the whole thing. We settled pretty quickly on three places to visit: Cinqe Terra, the five towns on the Ligurian Coast; Tuscany; and finally Lake Como for Denise's birthday celebration. As I began to look into destinations, I was overwhelmed. Fortunately, my assistant, Linda, connected me to a travel agent she used to set up our President's Club, which was the reward club for salespeople who made quota at our company. These were very nice events, and Linda assured me that Yannette had done extensive travel planning in Italy. And she was right.

Yannette helped us to find a wonderful hotel in Monterosso, the northernmost town of Cinque Terre, and we decided to stay at the famed Villa D'Este on Lake Como. But she found us the most amazing hotel in a small town at the southern end of the Chianti region of Tuscany, the Castelleto di Montebenichi. It dated from the twelfth century and had been an outpost of Firenze (Florence) in its ongoing battle with Sienna. In fact, when we arrived, the proprietor pointed out a similar structure several miles away on the hillside that was its Siennese counterpart, now also a small hotel—though nothing like ours.

We flew into Florence and rented a car for the drive to Cinque Terre. Denise and I had packed way too much, as we were going on to a business meeting in Ireland after the trip, so we jammed the car pretty full. But we all made it and headed out for the coast. When we arrived in the little town of Monterosso, we parked the car and took a taxi to the Hotel Porto Roca, which sat perched on the hillside a little out of town. The ride up the hill was so narrow that walkers had to climb up the hill to get out of the way of the taxi. The view was spectacular. As it was late, we enjoyed dinner at the hotel with a wonderful Barbera d'Alba from the Piedmont area, the first of many bottles of excellent Italian wine.

We discovered that most Italian wines are consumed in Italy and Europe, with very little getting to the United States, and often not the best Italy had to offer. So this trip was a treat because of the many Italian wines we tried.

The next day we hiked the Cinque Terre coastline between the five towns, from Monterosso to Vernazza (the most picturesque), to Corniglia, Manarola, and Riomaggiore. We returned by ferry and had dinner at the local Ristorante Miky, where we tried the local white wine that they simply called Cinque Terre, and the local red wine called Sciacchetra. Both were fine, but as we finished our stay in Cinque Terre, we were sure that the wines of Tuscany would outshine these.

We left for Tuscany, stopping to visit the walled city of Lucca before continuing on to our hotel. We arrived at the Castelletto di Montebenichi late in the day. It was a spectacular place with a wonderful collection of antiques, from Etruscan pottery to sixth-century chairs and an abundance of Renaissance furnishing. We stayed in the main castelletto, in the Pope Innocent III Room; he was pope during the thirteenth century, of course. The proprietor of the hotel was Marco, a retired pediatric oncologist from Milan who, along with his partner, had completely remodeled the castle with all of the period pieces. He was a gracious host with great suggestions for dining and trips into the Chianti region. At breakfast that first morning, he mentioned that across the valley were the Lands of Campi. He suggested we might like to visit the site and said he could give us directions that would take us there on our way into Chianti for the day. Of course, the Campis wanted to see their "Lands." As we got directions, Marco uttered my favorite quote of the trip. He told us that no matter what happened, not to worry: "You're never lost in Tuscany. You're just exploring."

After a bit of driving, we did find the Lands of Campi, but they were actually an archeological dig, and the only building standing was an old bar, which, given Gary's penchant for parties, was very appropriate. We took some pictures and made our way into Chianti, stopping at the first winery we found. It was Villa a Sesta, where we tried several of the red wines served by a sommelier named Ghenjian, who was actually Armenian. He told us about a restaurant he worked at, in the town of Villa a Sesta up ahead, called Bottega a Treinte, and suggested that we try it one evening. We bought some wine, thanked him, and went on our way.

We visited a famous Chianti producer, Badia a Coltibuono, for lunch and wine.

We toured the Castello di Brolio, owned by the Ricasoli family, who are credited with creating the formula for Chianti Classico in the mid-1800s. The castle is a historic landmark and has a beautiful tour.

The next day we visited San Gimignano, the City of Towers, and enjoyed the local white wine from the Vernaccia area; it was the best white wine we had during the trip. We went on to Sienna, and by the time we returned, we just grabbed some bruschetta and antipasto and went to the roof of the *castelletto*, where we enjoyed the food and the evening along with two bottles of Villa a Sesta wines, their Chianti Classico and their Super Tuscan. So much for taking wine home—this would become the pattern as the trip went on.

The next day was our foray into southern Tuscany to visit Montalcino, home of the Brunello wines, and Montepulciana, home of Vino Nobile.

Both wines are produced primarily from Sangiovese grapes, as are Chianti and Chianti Classico, but they are both grown only in the isolated areas around the two towns, not unlike an appellation in California or a region in France. As a result, the wines take on a specific character of the area, or *terroir*.

In Montalcino, we toured la Fortezza di Montalcino, which was the last stand of the Siennese in their battle with Florence before they were conquered. Inside of the fortress was an *enoteca* (wine bar) that served a sampling of local Brunellos. We sat on benches and had antipasti and sampled eight different Brunellos. They were good but very expensive.

As we were driving to Montepulciano, we drove through Pienze, which is best known for producing pecorino, the famous sheep's milk cheeses of Tuscany. In Pienze we bought three different kinds of cheese and *salame di cinghiale*—hard salami.

We then arrived in Montepulciano, another beautiful walled city in the southern Tuscan countryside. We stopped at the *enoteca* run by the Vino Nobile consortium and tasted three Vino Nobile—and bought two of them. They were our favorite wines of the trip, and while they are hard to find in the States, when I have found them, I have always enjoyed them.

That evening, both because of our conversation with Ghenjian two days before and at the further suggestion of Marco, our host, we celebrated Karen's birthday at la Bottega a Treinte. The chef was a French woman who, along with her Italian husband, ran the only Michelin one-star restaurant in Chianti. We were treated to a fixed menu, with wines chosen by Ghenjian to complement the meal. We began with a Prosecca, the lightly sparkling Italian wine, followed by Felsina Chianti Classico and a Vin Santo dessert wine that was incredible, from a winery called Rocca di Montegrossi. It was by far the best meal of our trip, and it was one of the best meals we've ever had.

Our entire trip was blessed with beautiful weather, and the next day was no exception. We were on a mission that day to explore Chianti and find the Rocca de Montegrossi winery and that wonderful Vin Santo we'd had the night before. And what started as a search for the winery turned into one of our best days.

As we drove into Chianti, we passed Castello Brolio and saw the sign for Rocca di Montegrossi, but it was completely unclear which way we should turn. We went back a few hundred yards, and I went inside the tasting room at Castello di Brolio just to ask for directions. Instead, I walked into a beautiful tasting room and immediately went out to get the others so that we could try their wines. We spent the better part of an hour there. The whole process of tasting in Italy is more relaxed and conversational. The staff was happy to talk about the wines, their vineyards, and the history of the place, which was extensive. We even saw the current *barone*, Francesco Ricasoli, the thirty-second *Barone* Ricasoli. In 1993 he led the complete renovation of the Brolio brand, taking back control from a multinational that had marketed their wines for a number of years.

We tasted a broad range of their wines and bought their 2001 Chianti Classico, a wonderful 2001 Super Tuscan called Casalferro, and Vin Santo, all to be shipped home. That was the only wine that made it home, as we drank every other bottle of wine we bought on the trip.

An interesting side note is that when our shipments arrived in the United States several months after our trip, both our case shipment and the Campis' had label damage on the bottles. It didn't appear that the wines themselves were bad, just that the labels were nearly destroyed. I contacted the winery, and they asked us to send pictures, which we did. They immediately apologized and sent new shipments to both of us. It was a great example of customer service, and to our delight, the original bottles looked bad, but the wine was just as we had remembered it—a bonus, to be sure!

The people at Brolio were also kind enough to give us directions to Rocca di Montegrossi, which was just up the hill. We discovered that the winery was run by Marco Ricasoli, one of the members of the family who started his own winery on lands that had been part of the overall Ricasoli holdings. We met a very knowledgeable woman from Sienna that talked to us about the winery and brought out some of their red wines for tasting. But the real treat was to stand in the room where they air-dried the Trebbianno grapes used to make their delicious Vin Santo, and take pictures. She described how the "wine angel" would come through the room and individually pick out any grapes that became diseased. Through our discussions, we found out that they distributed their wines through K&L Wine Merchants right in Redwood City, just up the road from Los Altos Hills.

Afterward, she gave us a great recommendation for lunch, but when we arrived, they were just closing. Gary went inside and came back out with the owner, who agreed to serve us. He was a great old gentleman who chatted with us through our meal as we sat on a terrace that overlooked the back of the Castello di Brolio, a truly memorable vista.

Our last stop was Fattoria di Felsina, which was home to the great wine we'd enjoyed at Bottega a Treinte the evening before. Again we bought wine, thinking we might bring it home with us. The evening ended back at the little trattoria at the bottom of the hill, below the *castelletto*, for a casual meal with more Chianti Classico.

On our last full day in the area, we took a drive to nearby Umbria, to the town of Deruta, which was famous for *ceramica*. There were hundreds of shops throughout the town, and it was overwhelming. We went from shop to shop and couldn't make any decisions. We decided to break for lunch, and we happened upon a great little restaurant, where the proprietor served us a bottle of the local Umbrian wine called Montefalco, which is made from a grape called Sagrantino. Sagrantino is a grape that is high in polyphenols, which add body and character to red wine through the high amount of tannins. It is produced in the small Montefalco region of Umbria and is becoming the new cult wine of Italy.

From Deruta, we drove to Assisi, where it happened to be the celebration of the feast day of St. Francis, so the city was bustling with people and activity. The city is perched on a hilltop, as are so many of the ancient cities in Italy. The walls gleamed pink in the afternoon sunlight as we approached the city. We visited the Basilica of St. Francis and his tomb. We didn't stay long, as it was getting dark, but it was a nice ending to our day, our visit to Tuscany, and this little taste of Umbria.

That night, we drove back to the *castelletto* and went up on the roof to eat our cheese and salami with bread and the Vino Nobile we'd bought a few days before. It was another beautiful night and our last in Tuscany.

The next day, we drove from Tuscany to Milan, where we boarded a train for Lake Como. This was a fairly long day of driving, and it included rather uneventful stops in Modena and Parma, though we did have a nice lunch of prosciutto di Parma and chunks of Parmigiano-Reggiano in Parma.

The excitement for the day came when we discovered a flat tire on our rental car within two hundred meters of the drop-off.

The train trip to Como was uneventful, but on our way to the hotel, our driver told us that there would be a Hollywood wedding after the hotel closed for the season. When pressed, he said it was rumored to be Tom Cruise and Katie Holmes; more on this later.

The Villa D'Este was a beautiful hotel, and Lake Como was a very beautiful lake, but after the joys of exploring Tuscany, Lake Como paled in comparison for us. It was just a very fancy hotel. We did celebrate Denise's birthday at Navedano, a beautiful restaurant in Como. We started with an Asti Spumante, followed by a wonderful Chianti Classico Riserva. And then our server suggested we try a Montepulciano d'Abruzzo; this is a grape from southern Italy that is made in Abruzzo, not the Vino Nobile from Montepulciano, but the wine was great.

The next day, Karen saw Katie Holmes, with her mother, sister, and bodyguard, walking through the hotel, lending credence to what the driver had said (though we found out later they did get married in Italy, just not at the Villa d'Este). The weather cleared, and we sat outside and then in the lobby, watching all the people going to a wedding between children of a Swiss diplomat and a wealthy Italian. The U.S. ambassador to Italy attended as well.

That evening, we had a quiet but great meal that included pasta with a chestnut sauce and a killer Barbera d'Alba—three bottles worth.

The next day, we left for Milan and our flights from Italy. For the Campis, it was home to California. For Denise and me, it was a return to semi-reality, with a business meeting in Ireland. Italy had been a wonderful experience, and we particularly enjoyed our time in Tuscany. It is a magical place because of the people, the natural surroundings, the sights, the food, and of course, the wine. Our stay in Italy lasted thirteen days, of course, and during that time, the four of us drank fifty-four bottles of wine. I counted. So that means each of us drank about thirteen bottles of wine, of course.

Back to Napa

Ith so much going on in our lives, by 2007 we hadn't been to Napa Valley since our trip in 2002. We were fortunate to be invited, through a friend of Denise's brother Emory, on a trip to Napa put together by a woman who had been doing this for several years. She would select an area of Napa or Sonoma and then search for highly rated red-wine producers that were small or interesting. She would then set up a day of tasting for eight to ten couples that were all friends of theirs, rent a limo van, and find a suggested hotel nearby. This trip was to be in the southern portion of Napa Valley, so we stayed at the Silverado Country Club.

We arrived on a Friday night in late March with unseasonably warm weather. We had drinks on the terrace of the hotel and met our hosts, Chrissy and Charlie, and their friends. Together with Denise's brother and his girlfriend, Annette, and George and Natalie, whom we already knew, it was a great group. We all had dinner in Yountville that night and agreed to meet at nine o'clock the next morning. The first stop on the trip was up a winding hill to a winery that had been built into the hill. We were met by one of the Buoncristiani brothers. These were four young brothers who handled all aspects of their small winery, from procuring the grapes to winemaking, to label art, to marketing and sales. They were producing some great red wines, their Cabernet and Syrah and a blend they call OPC, which I believe is a tribute to their father—Old Pa Claret. The winery was named a "Rising Star" by the *Wine Spectator* in 2004. Their wines weren't cheap, but we were given a nice discount, so we bought a number of their reds.

Next we visited a winery I can't remember because we simply sat outside on the terrace and tasted wines from Peter Franus, another small producer making Sauvignon Blanc from Carneros, Zinfandel from the Mt. Veeder area up in the Mayacamas Mountains, and Cabernet from the Stag's Leap area. Not only did we enjoy his wines, but we also had lunch on the beautiful terrace. Denise and I particularly liked his Brandlin Zinfandel. This was a wine produced from "old vine" Zinfandel grown on the hillside of Mt. Veeder, with the very intense fruit characteristic of great "old vine" Zins. We bought a half case and still have a few bottles to enjoy.

The next two wineries were great, but they were not small like the wineries we had started with. One of the members of the group had an "in" at Groth, a well-established winery in Napa founded in 1985 by Dennis Groth, who had made his fortune helping to build Atari into a $2 billion company. He lived the dream of how to make a little money in the wine business: start with a lot of money. But Groth made wonderful Cabernet Sauvignon, among other varietals, and we were in for a nice treat with a private tasting at the winery. Needless to say, we left there with several bottles of Groth Cabernet.

Our last planned stop was the Darioush winery. Founded by Darioush Khaledi, an immigrant from Iran, the winery focused on creating red wines. But the visitor center was something to behold. It was modeled after the Persian architecture of Khaledi's homeland.

A couple named Joe and Michele, friends of Denise's brother, met us the next day, and the six of us went up to Joseph Phelps, where we hosted them for a tasting and got a chance to speak to Claude, our friend from our anniversary celebration. As usual, it was a treat. Joe and Michele were also club members at Pine Ridge, one of our early favorites from the eighties. The winery had changed quite a bit, owing to their success. We tasted in a special area for club members in one of their caves. They were also members at Trefethen Vineyards, so we had a chance to do a reserve tasting there. Trefethen was another of our earlier finds from the eighties that we just hadn't been to in a while. It was fun to see that the winery hadn't changed much. Trefethen had its own rich history. It was founded by John and Janet Trefethen in 1973 at the old Eschol Winery that John's father had bought in 1968, in a very sad state. In the last forty years, they've come a long way, and they are making very nice wines.

In the fall of 2007, we again returned to Napa, this time with our daughter, Nicole. This was Nicole's first trip to Napa, so we visited a few of our favorites, including Joseph Phelps. On the way into Napa, we stopped for a champagne tasting in Carneros, at Domaine Carneros. We sat outside on the terrace and sipped several different champagnes, as if we were French royalty. Then we were able to participate in a private tasting at Etude Winery, also in Carneros and a favorite Pinot producer of ours. We were part of a group of about a dozen people trying a number of their different Pinots from all over the Carneros region, as well as their Chardonnay.

The next day was a beautiful November day, with warm, crisp air and the beautiful foliage of the vineyards. In California, it is the vineyards that provide us some of the vibrant colors that are so common in the forests of the Midwest and East Coast. The treat for today was a return to Duckhorn. We had met Dan Duckhorn many years before, and we viewed his Merlot, along with St. Francis Merlot, as some of the very best. We used to pick up wine at his small ranch-style home on the Silverado Trail in those days. Founded in 1976, Duckhorn was one of the first wineries in Napa to produce a premium Merlot, and today they still produce several of the greatest examples of Merlot wines anywhere. In the past ten years, the winery has grown to become three wineries: Duckhorn; Paraduxx, which produces a blend from Napa Valley Zinfandel, Cab, and Merlot; and Goldeneye, their Pinot vineyard in Anderson Valley, the valley we drove through in the seventies and eighties to get to Gram's.

As we sat in their beautiful visitors' center, we were given tastings of their Sauvignon Blanc, Napa Cabernet and Merlot, and the Goldeneye Pinot Noir. As we sat there and enjoyed these wines, we began to tell Nicole about meeting Dan Duckhorn and discussing Goldeneye and Anderson Valley with him. We were also talking about how we hoped our Merlot could taste like his Merlots. Overhearing us, the tasting room manager came over to join in. Pretty soon we were tasting all three of their premium Merlots—Estate, Three Palms, and Howell Mountain—as well as several of their vineyard-designated Cabernets. We were there for over an hour, and we had a great time. The staff couldn't have been friendlier or more helpful, and as they probably expected, we left with quite a bit of Duckhorn wine.

We went through the valley and got back onto Highway 29, finding our way to Beringer. We have always enjoyed the Beringer Private Reserve

Cabernet, so we went right back to the reserve section for a tasting. While there, we made a great discovery. The tasting staff had just gotten a new tool. It was called a Vinturi, and it was an aerator. You simply held it over the glass as you poured in wine, and it was immediately aerated, improving the overall flavor of the wine. As you might expect, we were skeptical, but the staff member opened a brand-new bottle of 2004 Private Reserve Cab and let us try it first, and then again after being put through the Vinturi. The difference was incredible. We bought several of them on the spot, and we use them often to open up that first glass of wine without needing to decant it.

After Beringer, we again crossed the valley to ZD Vineyards. This had long been a favorite of ours for their Chardonnay. The winery had been started by two aerospace engineers from Sacramento, Gino Zepponi and Norman de Leuze—hence the name ZD. In the late eighties when we visited, we were told that the ZD also stood for "zero defects," the kind of quality these two engineers were striving for. Their Chardonnay is a favorite of ours at our local restaurant, Los Altos Grill.

Our final stop was at Robert Sinskey Winery, which was largely built into the hillside along the Silverado Trail. They had a unique approach to tasting, in that they charged a twenty-dollar fee for a food pairing and tasting, which is a fun way to try their wines. We have had their Pinot Noir and other red wines, but we enjoyed a Pinot Blanc and a Cabernet Franc, one of the blending grapes from the Bordeaux region that isn't often made as a standalone wine. Both of these wines were different and very tasty. The Pinot Blanc surprisingly came only in half-bottles or magnums, in the long, slender Hoch style typically used for German or Alsatian wines. It was beautiful, and we decided to serve it at Thanksgiving that year, which was a big hit.

It was a great weekend, showing our daughter where we'd learned about wine for the first time, and visiting some of our old favorites. Though Napa Valley has become a celebrated and crowded place, it is still one of the most beautiful valleys in the world.

TO THE PRESENT

In 2008, we again got the opportunity to join the group for a weekend wine tour. This time Chrissy chose Alexander Valley in Sonoma. She again chose several small, unique wineries. We had our lunch at Medlock Ames. This winery was set back in the hills at the southwest end of Alexander Valley. The two founders, Christopher Medlock James and Ames Morison, were committed to a green winery, and they had worked extensively to achieve their goals. Staff members rode mountain bikes all over the vineyard. They used cattle and goats to clear the weeds, and much of their production facility used gravity as its main force. After a great tour and a lesson in pruning from their marketing director, we sat down to a tasting and then lunch on picnic tables near the winery. They offered us their Chardonnay, Merlot, and Cabernet to taste, as well as a new rosé that was due to be released in a few months.

Our next stop had an interesting connection for me. When I received the list of wineries to visit, I had looked them up on the Web immediately. As I looked through the Web site of Joseph Family Vineyards, I noticed that a photo of the owner looked familiar. When I found his name, Jon Joseph, I remembered that he had been the financial analyst covering one of the companies I had worked for; we had met a number of times for briefings on our company and its prospects. I looked forward to reconnecting with Jon. When we arrived and I reintroduced myself, we remembered each other and spent a little extra time during our visit catching up on our lives over the past several years. We discussed how we had both found ways to enjoy more than just drinking wine, and to enjoy the experience of winemaking and farming, something we both felt strongly about.

The tasting was held at their home on the hillside, among their vines in the Alexander Valley. He and his wife had laid out a wonderful outdoor table of meats, cheeses, crackers, breads, nuts, and dried fruit for us to enjoy with their wines. As a small producer of Cabernet, they treated us to a vertical of their Alexander Valley Cabernet Sauvignon—2003, 2004, and the 2005, which was the only one available for sale. The wines were great big, fruity California Cabernet that we all liked immediately. The label on the bottle has a large mountain lion on it. When I asked Jon why the mountain lion was used, he said that he had seen it walk down through his vineyard many times when they first put in the vines, so he thought it was fitting to honor the big cat on the label.

The next day began with a visit to Ferrari-Carano at the top of Dry Creek Valley. While I am not a huge fan of their wines, I enjoy the chance to visit their beautiful tasting center and gardens, and I do enjoy their Chardonnay and Fumé Blanc. On our way up to the winery, I had noticed a sign for Zichichi Winery. That was the name of one of the "old vine" Zinfandel vineyards that St. Francis produced, so we made the decision to try it out. Sure enough, it was a new, little winery. The family had decided to start making their own wine, so St. Francis would no longer be getting their fruit. We tried some barrel samples and decided to buy a few futures of the new vintage to be released in the fall.

On a previous trip to the area, two couples in our group from New Jersey had visited the Wilson Family Winery, which was noted for its Zinfandels. They had arranged a private tasting for us, and as both Denise and I love Zinfandel, we were looking forward to this stop. When we arrived, we were ushered into a room in the back, where at least ten bottles of wine were set up. The winery, founded by Ken and Diane Wilson, produces a number of red wines, all from Dry Creek area fruit, including Cabernet, Merlot, Syrah, Petite Syrah, Cabernet Franc, and of course, a number of Zinfandels. When we got to the Zinfandels, we were told that each of the main vineyards was named for one of the three Wilson children, Tori, Sawyer, and Carl, and the Old Vine Vineyard was named for Ellie, their grandmother. The person serving the wines tried to relate the flavors in the wines to the personalities of the children. Maybe Diane Wilson could make the connections, but for us, they were all big, jammy Dry Creek Zinfandels, different in subtle ways, but great wines. I also enjoyed their Petite Sirah. It seems that Petite Sirah was often grown in these older Zinfandel vineyards in the Dry Creek area, but good Petite Sirah is hard to find. Wilson produces a very nice one, so we left with several bottles and a number of Zinfandels with various children's names.

For the past several years, May has been a particularly busy time for me. It always seemed that I was traveling all over the world in the month of May. As a result, we had never been able to attend one of the best events at Joseph Phelps Winery: Insignia Weekend, a special celebration for members of their wine club. This year marked the tenth Insignia weekend, and in the five years we had been members of their wine club, we never had been able to attend. This year was different. Not only was I not on the road, but also we were in the final throes of completing the transaction to sell the company I had led for five and a half years. We were simply waiting for the deal to close. Denise and I took a long weekend and went up to stay in Yountville. As Phelps "preferred members," we could choose one of three days over the weekend. We chose Sunday, which turned out to be the best of the three days. Friday and Saturday were two of the hottest days of the year, at over 100 degrees. By the time Sunday rolled around, it was a pleasant 85 degrees.

As we drove up to the winery, we were met by valets and invited to take a shuttle up to the winery. When we arrived, we saw that they had set up a huge tent in the front of the winery and were meeting each of their guests with a glass of Sauvignon Blanc. Inside the tent was a variety of food stations and tasting stations with several of their wines, including the Cabernet, Merlot, and Syrah. As it was near noon, we stopped by the food stations for a quick bite and then began to stroll around the tent and grounds. Another station featured the new Freestone Winery, located on the Sonoma coast. This winery featured Pinot Noir and Chardonnay from that region and had only just begun to produce its wines in the last few years. This is where the Ovation Chardonnay is now produced; this is a blend of several Chardonnay vineyards from Sonoma. We went back to this station a number of times during the day. As we strolled between the winery building to the back terrace, we stopped at the first of the Insignia stations. Here we were able to try the recently released 2004 Insignia, as well as the soon-to-be-released 2005 Insignia wines. Insignia Weekend had been set up as a celebration for wine club members but also as a "futures" event for the upcoming Insignia release. At this event, we were able to secure 2006 Insignia futures, for release in fall 2009.

Later, as we were wandering along the terrace and enjoying the view, Bill Phelps, chairman of the board and son of Joe Phelps, came by with a decanter of wine. He asked us if we'd like to try the 1986 Insignia that he had just decanted from a six-liter bottle, or an imperiale. It was missing the big fruit of typical younger California reds, but it had enough fruit, and there was a smoothness to it that was a real treat. Here was a wine that was over twenty years old and tasted wonderful. Later he came by with both a 1989 and a 1994 Insignia for all of us to try. The 1994 was excellent, with a great balance of fruit and tannins, an example of just how good these wines could be when aged. We stayed about three hours and enjoyed the great food, chatting with other fans, and of course enjoying the Phelps wines. It was a special event, and it's one that we won't miss next year.

When we got back to our hotel in Yountville, it was still sunny, so we decided to go out to the pool. It was a beautiful late spring afternoon. We swam and enjoyed the sun. As I settled into my lounge chair, I struck up a conversation with the couple next to us. Alain and Penina Sotto were from Toronto, Canada, and came at least once each year to Napa or Sonoma. Because of the import laws in Canada, they could only bring home two bottles of wine each. They tasted and bought much more than that, so they drank great wine while they were on their trips. I explained that we had a Merlot vineyard, and Alain said I had to try a Reserve Merlot from Chateau St. Jean that they had just bought. He went up to their room and returned with the bottle. It was a wonderful wine: great fruit, oak, good tannins, and a long, lingering finish. It reminded me of our favorite Sonoma Merlots from St. Francis, just up Highway 12 from Chateau St. Jean. I had Denise try it as well, and she too enjoyed it. As we were talking, we learned that Alain had been an emergency room doctor but was now in charge of the wellness program for Ontario Power. They asked us to join them for dinner, and as we had made no plans of our own and enjoyed talking with them, we agreed.

We met up an hour or two later, each of us bringing wines for the dinner. We enjoyed a great meal at Bouchon in Yountville, but we enjoyed their company a great deal more. Both Alain and Penina were lively, friendly, intelligent people, and we all talked together easily. We told each other about how we, as couples, had met, and Alain entertained us with interesting anecdotes and remedies from his work as a doctor. As we contemplated dessert, Alain asked if we enjoyed bourbon. I said that I did but that I didn't know much about it. His eyes lit up, and he proceeded to tell me about his favorite bourbon, Pappy Van Winkle. It was the smoothest he had ever tasted. It was very hard to find. They had actually found two bottles of it in Sonoma on one of their trips. He'd bought them both and used his allotment to get them home to Toronto. As a result of this discussion, we each had a different whiskey at the restaurant, but neither one was "Pappy". Alain explained that a small amount of bourbon whiskey was a digestif, so we all felt better having been prescribed the whiskey we were drinking by the good doctor.

I began to look for Pappy over the next few weeks. I held the final executive staff dinner at Alexander's Steakhouse in Cupertino, just before our deal closed. This was a restaurant favored by our Japanese clients, who loved red meat and red wine, so we decided to go there as a final dinner together. After the meal, as a bit of a joke, I asked our waiter if they had any Pappy Van Winkle, and he said yes. I laughed and ordered it. When it arrived, I breathed in the aroma deeply and took a taste. It was great! I let several of my staff members try it. The following week, my vice president of product management, gave me a bottle of Pappy Van Winkle, as a thank-you. What a special treat. He had found it at Beltramo's, a wine and liquor store in Atherton. I have since found it at a local liquor store in Capitola, where we have our beach house. I will forever be in debt to Alain for this wonderful find, and we hope to see them in California on one of their trips west.

But back to wine and Napa.

The next day, after a big day of wine tasting, we decided to simply drive around the valley to see how it had changed in the over thirty years that Denise and I had been coming to visit. It was a Monday and therefore not very crowded. We crisscrossed the valley, stopping at a couple of places to taste olive oil. As we were coming across from the Silverado Trail above St. Helena, we reached Highway 29 and turned left. Without thinking about it, we had come out just north of the Charles Krug Winery.

Earlier this spring I had read Julia Flynn Siler's book *The House of Mondavi: The Rise and Fall of an American Wine Dynasty*. Denise and I had been discovering Napa Valley as the Robert Mondavi Winery was becoming famous, and there were clouds brewing at Charles Krug. The book is interesting, and I'm sure there are many opinions about the veracity of the story, but it did lay out the tremendous influence of Robert Mondavi on the California wine industry, and the all-too-human events that affect families. With Napa as a backdrop, it's a fun read.

Ironically, two days before we came to Napa for the Insignia Weekend, May 16, 2008, Robert Mondavi died at the age of ninety-four.

With this news and the book fresh on my mind, I suggested that we stop at Charles Krug for the first time in a long time. As we pulled up, the buildings hadn't changed much, though there were signs apologizing for their "dust," as they were renovating the winery. The flag at the winery also hung at half-mast in remembrance of their brother Robert. We went inside and spent a very pleasant hour trying a number of their reserve and limited-release wines. We ended up buying a couple bottles of their Carneros Chardonnay and two of their high-end red wines. The 2004 Family Reserve Generations is a blend, primarily of Bordeaux varietals (Cabernet Sauvignon, Merlot, Cabernet Franc, and Petit Verdot), with a touch a Syrah and Malbec. The other wine we bought was the 2003 Limited Release IX Clones, from Napa Valley. This wine is a Cabernet Sauvignon blend from nine of their unique vineyard blocks, with only 190 cases produced. We look forward to drinking these wines in a few years.

It is clear that the Peter Mondavi family has made a tremendous effort to bring back the Charles Krug Winery from the financial difficulties of the seventies and eighties and restore it to its former place in Napa Valley. Whether or not they will ultimately accomplish this remains to be seen. But they have also done it as a family, enabling Peter Mondavi to leave the legacy of his estate winery within his family, a challenge that Robert, though the more famous brother, couldn't accomplish.

This last trip to Napa, and our visit to the Charles Krug Winery, seems a fitting end to this preamble to the harvest of 2008, just as these two places formed such a significant beginning to my understanding and love of wine. I hope that what you read in these pages help you to understand the joy that wine has brought to our lives.

PART 2
HARVEST 2008

JULY

JULY 1, 2008

I spent a few hours this morning doing canopy management in our Merlot vineyard.

Bud break was the second week of April, and this simply means that the dormant vines develop beautiful little pink and green buds of new growth. They're not flowers, just the subtle colors of the new canes as they emerge from the "buds" that set along the horizontal cordons, or branches, of the vines. By early June, we were in full flower. Grape flowers aren't particularly impressive, just little bunches of tiny, white flowers that will turn quickly into grapes once they have self-pollinated.

So by today, we had extensive cane growth—the green branches that grow out of the cordons, each with two clusters of small, green grapes, which will be our harvest in a few short months.

Canopy management, which sounds impressive, is the process of making sure the canes are properly placed through upper guide wires, to insure that they create the appropriate canopy of green for the growing grapes. We have a special trellising system called quadrilateral, in which we essentially have four cordons extending from the trunk of each grape vine, two on each side. They are about two feet apart on lower guide wires, with two sets of higher guide wires on each side to accommodate the canes. This trellising system enables us to get nearly twice as much production from our vines as a traditional bilateral system.

Since we are on a flat piece of land with a creek on one side, we decided that the vines could handle the additional stress of quadrilateral trellising. It has proven to be quite effective, as we get wonderful fruit. It does take a bit more care in canopy management, but is well worth it.

Today was an incredibly beautiful day. We had had a tremendous number of wildfires in Northern California. At one point over the last weekend, the news reported upwards of fourteen hundred fires being battled by Cal Fire and others. These fires caused the air quality to be terrible during the last two weeks of June. But today we had a little fog in the morning, which cleared quickly to reveal a beautiful blue sky. I never tire of working this way in the vineyard—blue sky, bright green new foliage, and the small clusters of grapes peeking out from under the canes. The magic is here, too. Just three months ago, these vines looked dead. Now they were fully alive and bursting with growth and life. Within three to four months more, they would produce three to four tons of the most beautiful Merlot fruit on the planet, and then the vines would be spent, yielding leaves with the beautiful fall colors that would grace our Thanksgiving table.

But for now, they were in the full fever of summer growth. So it was appropriate that I got a call back from Gary Brink, the assistant winemaker at Page Mill Winery, while I was working in the vineyard. I had known Gary for many years. He had been involved in Page Mill for twenty years, and more recently he had been managing the tasting room, along with his wine-making duties. He had also been the face of Page Mill at our harvest for the last five years or so, and he was a good friend.

It was fitting that this call, in the vineyard, should signal the beginning of the harvest of 2008. It was a simple call, just to say hello and to return my call, saying that he looked forward to working with me for the harvest and that, among other things, I would learn to drive a forklift. This was apparently a key piece of machinery at the winery; there will be more on this later.

I had sent email to Dane Stark, the winemaker at Page Mill Winery, where our Merlot has been made for twelve years. This year would mark the thirteenth year that Dane Stark made Merlot from Côté Vineyards. Given that thirteen is our lucky number, it was fitting that this was the year that I would work with him, not only to harvest our Merlot, but to work the entire season with him and Gary to harvest all of the grapes and assist in making the wonderful variety of wines that are made at Page Mill. In fact, a few weeks earlier, when I first broached the subject with Dane, he was excited to have my help and stated that I would be the highest-priced, lowest-paid labor he had ever had at the winery. And that was my goal.

It was a simple start to the harvest season: a phone call in the vineyard.

JULY 7, 2008

I received the below email message from Dane in answer to my email about working the harvest:

Hey Dave,

We would love to have you for harvest ... in any capacity, as much or as little as you like.

We will begin getting ready in earnest around August 15, although we're working on equipment even now.... Just had the seals replaced on the bin dumper for the forklift..... installing a hot water system for tartrates.. etc.....

The crush goes from late August through late October, and sometimes into November.... during that time the work ebbs and flows, ten days of hectic non-stop, a couple days relax and recover, etc....

I'd love to talk live with you about it.

Hope you had a great 4th, we missed you this year, and the weather was perfect!!!!

Cheers,
Dane Stark
Page Mill Winery

JULY 24, 2008

I drove out to Page Mill Winery at around 9:30 for a meeting with Dane and Gary. It was a beautiful morning drive out of Santa Clara Valley on Highway 680, up and over the Sunol grade (in the opposite direction of traffic), and then east on Highway 84, driving through the golden California hills that form the southern side of Livermore Valley. After a few miles, I came through a newly finished stretch of highway overlooking Livermore Valley. As you look on the valley, it is a unique collection of vineyard land, rolling hills, and housing. But in the years that I have lived in the Bay Area (now more than thirty), Livermore Valley has seen a significant increase in the amount of land under cultivation, though still small compared to Sonoma and Napa.

Livermore Valley was one of the original winegrowing regions in California. The first vineyard was planted by Robert Livermore in 1846. In the late 1800s, Carl Heinrich Wente and James Concannon both created wineries in the Livermore area. Today, Wente and Concannon are still the big names in Livermore. But Livermore Valley fell victim to what many early agricultural regions suffered from: the building of homes. Just as early vineyards on the peninsula of the Bay Area and San Bernardino County were replaced by the suburbs, the same thing happened to Livermore through much of the 1900s. As premium wine has become more popular in the last twenty years, Livermore has seen a resurgence. According to the Livermore Valley Winegrowers Association, there are over forty wineries and over sixty growers in the valley today. About ten years ago, there were only fifteen wineries.

As I mentioned earlier, Page Mill Winery is a relative newcomer to Livermore Valley, having moved to their current location three years ago. And just three years ago, Page Mill was winery number twenty-five, and now there are forty-seven wineries in Livermore Valley. It is a very unassuming winery, with the tasting and barrel storage building, the crush pad, and the other storage building all at the back of the property. Most of the three acres of land is given to an Estate Petite Sirah vineyard. Dane won a double gold medal at the San Francisco Wine Competition last year for his 2005 Estate Petite Sirah, his first vintage since buying the vineyard and winery. I am looking forward to making this wine, among others, this year.

As I drove into the winery driveway, I noticed that veraison was starting on some of the Petite Sirah vines. Veraison is a French term that has been adopted by the wine industry. It represents the point at which the grape berries begin to change color. It is most notable in red-wine varietals as they change from green to red. But it is also noticeable in white-wine grapes as they shift from a dull green to a more translucent color. The change signals the increase in sugars, and also a shift from berry growth to berry maturity.

Particularly in a red-wine vineyard, it is a beautiful and exciting time. Just as bud break, flowering, and the formation of clusters all signal progress in the vineyard, veraison is the final signal that we're headed to harvest. When veraison is complete, all of the clusters of berries in this vineyard will be red. I was seeing the very beginning of the process.

When I arrived, Dane was driving a small tractor, mowing weeds in an adjacent vineyard, and Gary was cleaning out a storage room—glamorous beginnings. I also met Michael Curran, who was working at the winery during his self-proclaimed midlife crisis (maybe that's what I'm doing). Michael was spending two days a week at the winery. He worked at Oakland Children's Hospital as an emergency room nurse. He was a wizard with all things mechanical. I would come to find that he had built or fixed most of the machinery and tools at Page Mill. I would also learn that he was a very compassionate man when it came to wine and, more importantly, to people.

I mentioned the beginnings of veraison to Gary, and he agreed that he had just seen it that morning himself. I mentioned that we were probably a bit behind them in Los Altos Hills, as I had not seen any signs in our vineyard.

Dane waved from the tractor as Gary and I walked over to the neighbor's Syrah vineyard. Dane was mowing between the vines, helping his neighbor because he would be taking fruit from this vineyard in 2008. There were a number of barrels outside the storage room that were empty and waiting to be cleaned. That was part of the project Michael was working on today. Dane had purchased a pressure cleaner that produced very hot water. If it was hot enough, this water could be used in the new barrel washer not just to clean the barrels, but also to remove tartrates that build up inside barrels as wine is stored before bottling.

Tartrates are actually crystals of potassium bitartrate that form when the tartaric acid found in grapes precipitates out of the wine before it is bottled. Many white and rosé wines go through a process called cold stabilization, which enhances the precipitation of tartrates. You may have seen this harmless, tasteless substance as a small amount of clear sediment in the bottom of a bottle of white wine. It has no effect on the taste or quality of the wine, but as you might imagine, winemakers want to minimize this.

Michael measured the temperature of the water coming out of the pressure washer at 185 degrees, which was enough to "melt" away the tartrates inside the barrels; 160 degrees is all that's required.

Next Dane and I went in to update his "sophisticated" barrel inventory, "Dane's Brain on Wine." It consisted of a whiteboard with a numbering scheme for the barrel positions in the storage room. Because there was a fair amount of movement of barrels during the year as new wines were brought in and mature wines are bottled, the actual barrels were numbered with a six-character code, which was written on the board as well, to provide a snapshot of the barrel inventory and position. The code was straightforward. The first two digits were the year, the second two characters were the varietal, and the final two characters were the source vineyard. An example would be 07MECO, which means 2007 Merlot from the Côté Vineyard—and yes, I wrote it on the board with the circumflex (or "hat," as Dane calls it, even though he studied in France). Therefore, my rendering of the example above was 07MECÔ.

The board was a simple and flexible tool that allowed Dane to easily see what and where his wines were, so he could best strategize how to move barrels when he needed to.

Gary and I then went off to UDS, which was a local warehouse in town that stored Page Mill Wines. We picked up several cases of Zinfandel, Sauvignon Blanc, and Angela's Cuvee—a rosé you'll learn more about—and then we stopped off for sandwiches.

Lunch was the most important part of the day. We sat down to discuss the upcoming harvest, among other things. Gary brought out a bottle of the soon-to-be-released 2006 Napa Valley Zinfandel for me to try. This fruit, from the Balyeat Vineyard in Napa, was one of Page Mill's oldest fruit sources, dating back over twenty years to the time when Dick Stark, Dane's dad, was the winemaker. Dane and Gary had been a little worried about the wine, as it had shown quite a bit of bottle shock after bottling. Bottle shock is a fairly typical temporary condition that affects wine immediately after bottling, and sometimes after being shaken during traveling. The wine will tend to be muted in its flavors.

The wine we were drinking showed no signs of bottle shock. It was a nice, big, fruity Zinfandel and a perfect wine with food. As we were talking, Gary went into the tasting room and returned with a bottle of the 2005 Page Mill

Côté Merlot. He told me that they had sent it out to their wine club members in a recent shipping. He had decided to keep a bottle open on weekends for wine club members, and he mentioned that he had sold about a case and a half in the last few weeks. It was drinking very well, already showing signs of nice maturity in both the fruit and the tannins. Our vineyard produces some of the most beautiful fruit I have ever seen, but Dane can really make wine, and that makes all the difference.

As we enjoyed his wines, Dane talked about the upcoming harvest. He suggested that I call him at the beginning of the week, and he would tell me what was happening for sure, and what the "potentials" might be. The potentials were typically about when a particular vineyard might be ready to pick, which could vary over the course of a week. Based on that, we would discuss where he could use me best. And that was it. Oh, except he did mention that I would take a very active role in the making of the Côté Merlot this year. We would see!

Before I drove home that day, Gary told me about an alternate way to get back to Highway 84 that took me through more of the countryside. As I began to climb up into the foothills, I was amazed by the beautiful green of the vines in contrast to the golden grasses on the hillsides. This was going to be quite an experience, and I was thankful to be able to do it.

After returning home, I took a stroll through our vineyard to see how the vines and grape clusters were doing. It's a beautiful, relaxing walk among our vines, and I never tire of it. It is also a subtly changing, living space, so every walk through the vineyard brings new insights into the formation of the year's crop. I had been in the vineyard only a few days before, but sure enough, we were also showing small signs of veraison as I went through the vineyard—not as much as the vineyard out in Livermore, but a red berry among the green here and there. It seemed a bit early this year, as I recalled seeing the early stages in the first week of August most years. But we were only a week away, and maybe I was more conscious of things this year. Over the next few weeks, I would get a better sense of the development this year. But somehow seeing those first red berries made me excited about the weeks ahead.

JULY 30, 2008

Veraison was in full swing throughout our vineyard. The team from DeVine Consultants was out in the vineyard, so I asked them about netting the vines. They said they would be in the area the next day and could get the nets on the vines. As I said earlier, veraison is a sign that the sugars are increasing in the grapes. That signal is not lost on the critters. Everyone from birds to raccoons to squirrels would love to get a crack at our ripening fruit, so we net the vineyards. This is a common practice in small vineyards like ours. A single raccoon or a small flock of birds could devastate a small vineyard.

We heard a story of a vineyard in Southern California that was netted and still got wiped out. It seems there is a small finch that migrates through the area every fall. Usually the vineyard has been harvested by the time they come through the area. It was a very late harvest that year, and the birds came through while there was still fruit on the vines. The birds were so small that they were able to get to the grapes through the small holes in the nets. An entire flock came through, and before the people had noticed or had time to do anything, the vineyard was devastated.

While we are not in this kind of danger, even with the nets on, I need to constantly check the vineyard as the raccoons in particular will come through and chew holes in the nets to get to the vines. In years past, I have gone through the vineyard and found a whole vine stripped of its fruit, and a big hole in the net where a raccoon has gotten through. So I patrol the vineyards regularly during this period of ripening to try to stay ahead of the birds and the beasts.

AUGUST

AUGUST 20, 2008

Today I tested the first samples for sugar content. I knew it was very early, but I wanted to get a gauge of the changes in the vineyard and how they tasted. I only used single berries (grapes) at this point, as I only want to know in what direction the vineyard was headed. As the season progressed and the vineyard was closer to harvesting, I would pull samples of entire clusters from around the vineyard to get a more accurate measure.

I use a handheld refractometer to measure the sugar content of the grapes. Sugar translates to alcohol content through fermentation, as I mentioned earlier. Refractometers use lenses and prisms to measure the different refractive index of liquids, with water as the reference point. Drops of grape juice are placed on the external lens and then covered. I then look through the eyepiece at a graduated scale that measures the Brix of the liquid on the lens. That liquid can come from a single grape in the vineyard, or from a sample of juice from an entire cluster that I have crushed in a plastic bag.

I pulled berries from all over the vineyard and tested them in the field. They ranged from a low of 15 Brix to a high of 19, with most in the 17–18 range. We would harvest at somewhere around 24–25 Brix, so there was clearly a long way to go. But it was a good first test, and I could easily distinguish the sugar content by taste between the 15 Brix grapes and the 19 Brix grapes.

I also checked the netting at the same time. I didn't see any places where the animals had gotten in, though with the Brix this low, the grapes might not have been as enticing yet. I did find a number of places where I needed to repair the nets. This means simply using a cable tie, or zip tie, to close the frayed holes in the nets. With everything looking good, I thought I would go up to my neighbor's vineyard to check their sugars just for fun.

Four years ago, our friends and neighbors Russ and JJ Harris put in a Cabernet Sauvignon vineyard that Dane from Page Mill managed for them. This year would be their first harvest. Their vineyard was south-facing, on a sloping hillside that got plenty of drainage. This was very different from our vineyard, which was slightly below their vineyard on a flat stretch next to a creek. Russ and JJ's vineyard had enough stress, so they used a bilateral trellising system, which means they had two cordons off of each vine, as opposed to our four. (Remember, we used a quadrilateral trellising system.)

Their vines were very young, and this was the first year that Dane had left fruit on them. The clusters were small, given the age of the vines. I tested several berries from around the vineyard and found the Brix to be between 20 and 22, which is high for this time of year. I talked to JJ, and she said that veraison started in mid-July for them. So I sent an email message off to Dane, letting him know the situation. He replied with thanks and also told me that next Monday (August 25) he expected things to begin to heat up at the winery. He sent me the message below:

Hey Dave,

Got your voicemail! Glad you are back … I thought we had cured you of your desire. ;)
We have a small bottling for a friend on Sunday. I'll be there while Gary runs the tasting room. He's bottling only about thirty gallons.
We crushed chard today and put it in the tank for settling. We'll rack and begin fermentation tomorrow. We're also tearing up the crush pad and trying to extend it with a flat dirt area for fermentation tanks. Michael will be there most Wednesdays and Thursdays. We decided that we'll change the "barbe-cue" day from Friday to Wednesday so that we can have Michael there. For the rest of harvest, we'll have a standing barbecue lunch on Wednesdays with various and sundry characters coming and going. You're always welcome.

I haven't done any numbers, but I suspect we'll have SB coming in first. Perhaps next week?

I have to rack some more stuff in barrels and do one more organization of the cellar before the onslaught.

Also, I'd like to bottle by hand the Côté Merlot and the Petite Sirah in the next couple weeks … hopefully next week. I'm sure you'd like to be involved in the Merlot, eh?

Do you have time next week for that? I'd like for it to not be off-the-charts hot, but I can make do in a pinch if necessary.

Look forward to seeing you.

Dane

When I read this email, I was a bit perplexed. I had told Dane that I was available throughout the harvest, and his message seemed to suggest that I might like to come out and help with the bottling of the Côté Merlot and the Petite Sirah. I wasn't quite sure what to make of it; did he want my help or not? When I showed it to Denise, she provided a very insightful viewpoint.

I was first and foremost one of Dane's growers, and a friend. I was older than Dane by at least fifteen years. He had known me as a CEO and president, and I know he respected both Denise and me very much. He knew that I loved all things related to grapes and wine, but when I told him I wanted to work the harvest, how could he know that I meant to truly work the harvest? And further, for all the reasons above, he wasn't about to order me around. I thought Denise had it right, and I was determined to make sure that Dane knew I was there for the entire harvest and was available to do anything to help.

AUGUST 25, 2008

This day signaled the start of school for many in the Bay Area, and for my son, Adam, as he started his third year at Loyola Marymount University in Los Angeles. It also signaled the first day of work at Apple for my daughter, Nicole, and she called Denise and me to say how excited she was, and what a great first day she'd had. She was the second-generation Côté at Apple, as

I spent eight and a half years there, from early 1983 to mid-1991. It was a special place to work, and I wished her great success.

But back to the harvest. With all the kids going off to school, many with mom and dad in tow for the first day, it took me twenty minutes to get out of Los Altos on my way to Page Mill, for what was the run-up to the real crush (pun intended) of harvest.

When I arrived at the winery, Dane was inside the combination tasting room and barrel storage room, doing paperwork. It is amazing to me that the tasting room gets used for so many things during the week, and then Gary pulls it all together into a quaint little space that is great for tasting Page Mill's wines on the weekend.

I brought up the subject of my working the harvest and explained to Dane that, other than a few days on which I might have appointments, it was my intention to work the entire harvest. I was willing to do whatever needed doing and was confident that I would get exposure to all the interesting stuff while doing the grunt work as well. It was a good conversation, and I think Denise was right on the mark. Dane was not going to be presumptuous about my time or what I wanted to do. But now he understood, and I could tell he was pleased, and so was I!

To get started, he showed me his to-do list. While he had gotten in a small lot of Dry Creek Chardonnay through Michael for his first-ever sparkling wine, the main onslaught of grapes had not begun, and so the tasks were still about preparation for the upcoming harvest.

I began my day by tying "bird tape" to the poles and wires in the two-acre Petite Sirah vineyard at the winery. This was the wine that in its first vintage (2005) made by Dane had won a gold medal at the San Francisco Chronicle Wine Competition earlier this year. Bird tape is metallic strips of material that are very lightweight. They flutter in the slightest breeze, scaring the birds with their shiny movement throughout the vineyard. We used netting in our small home vineyard. Netting is very impractical for larger vineyards. The key to the bird tape is to use it as late in the season as possible, so the birds don't get used to it. With the vineyard ripening and the birds just starting to get active, now was the time to strike. So I spent the morning tying the tape throughout about half of the vineyard.

This was one of those tasks that I'm sure Dane thought of as mundane, and if I had to do it for days and days, I'm sure it would be. But, it was a beautiful morning, and the fruit in the vineyard was gorgeous. Like our Merlot, the Petite was tightly clustered, but even more so. The fruit was a beautiful deep purple color. This, coupled with the sense of contributing, made the task easy. And though I never got back to finishing that job, it would be on my plate the next morning to complete.

As I was coming back toward the storage room, Dane called me over from the top of his large stainless steel tank, which was used for fermenting and settling white wines. He was coming down off the ladder with a pitcher of what frankly looked like beer. But it was the fermenting Chardonnay that would become his first sparkling wine, done in partnership with Michael, who had made sparkling wines before. In fact, the fruit came from a vineyard where Michael got his fruit for the co-op winery he ran out of his house. Dane was measuring the specific gravity of the juice to see how far along fermentation had gone. As I tried it, the juice was still sweet, so there was a way to go.

Sparkling wines are picked at a Brix of only 18 or 19, and thus sparkling-wine producers are the first to harvest. This base wine is fermented dry. All sparkling wines have sugar added for a second fermentation that creates bubbles, but only the exact amount needed to achieve pressure, not sweetness. More sugar means more pressure. The amount of sugar defines the type of champagne, from savage (no sugar) to brut, extra dry, Sec, and demi-sec. You can check out this site for a short piece on how champagne is made: *http://www.wineintro.com/making/champagne.html*.

After he tested the juice, he had me climb up the ladder and get a whiff of the fermenting juice. It gives off a tremendous amount of CO_2, so you have to be careful breathing it in. It is a great smell, though.

We took a break for lunch; Dane brought out a chilled bottle of the 2007 Chardonnay to have with barbecued chicken and grilled vegetables, leftovers from last night's barbecue at Dane's. It was a treat. This brought up the subject of Wednesday barbecues. I guess it was a tradition at Page Mill that during harvest, there was a designated day when someone barbecued and all manner of people showed up to help, or just to eat. Wednesday would be that day. In addition, Michael would bring his guitar, and I was encouraged to bring mine, so we could play music as a part of the lunchtime festivities.

As we were finishing lunch, the new air-conditioning unit for the barrel storage room arrived. I hadn't known he needed one, but with the arrival, I learned that the air-conditioning unit had gone out last Friday, and this was the earliest that Dane could get a replacement. Fortunately it hadn't been too hot over the weekend, but the forecast called for increasing heat—into the hundreds, possibly, later in the week. So this was an absolute necessity as soon as possible.

We cleared up lunch, and went around back to help remove the old unit and bring in the new one. The whole process was uneventful, and within a few hours, we could feel a noticeable difference in the barrel room—mission accomplished.

The task for the afternoon was to rack a Cabernet Sauvignon from a barrel into a topping barrel. Racking a wine simply means to transfer it from one container to another, in this case from a barrel to a topping barrel made from stainless steel and used to top off other barrels as the wine evaporated. Without topping off, oxygen gets into the barrels, and wine and oxygen do not get along at all.

This process was also an opportunity for Dane to show off the new barrel washer. When I had visited the winery several weeks earlier, Michael was finishing up the new system, which included a pressure washer to heat the water to above 165 degrees, and an old water heater as a holding tank. The holding tank fed the barrel washer, which could now easily clean the tartrates out of the barrels, using the hot water to dissolve them, rather than Dane (or probably me) scraping out the tartrates and not doing anywhere near as good a job as the 165+ degree water was capable of.

The next step was to clean the hoses that would be used for racking. First they were rinsed with a solution of percarbonate as a cleaner, and then with a solution of citric acid to neutralize the percarbonate. Finally they were rinsed with water, which completed the process.

The hoses were hooked up and the wine transferred between the two barrels in a matter of a few minutes. When this was done, I asked Dane what was next, and he said we needed to rinse out the hoses. He then told me one of the truths of winemaking: it is 90 percent cleaning and 10 percent winemaking. He was right. It had taken us at least thirty minutes to clean the hoses, and only a few to rack the wine. Then we needed to rinse the hoses so they were ready for the next time. All of these steps contributed to the quality of the wine that Dane would be making. In fact, Dane observed that the barrel washer, while a great timesaver, more importantly meant that his wines would be of a higher quality, as he was able to clean the barrels much more effectively. Many winemakers use a combination of both new and used oak barrels, so the cleanliness of those being used again was critical to the process.

The other important aspect of this simple racking process involved my first forklift experience. Dane gave me a quick lesson, explaining what the various levers did. He told me that as long as I didn't hurt myself or anyone else, I would be a success. I slowly drove the forklift toward where I needed to lift the barrel stand and the stainless steel barrel. I slid the fork under the stand, gradually eased up the fork, and promptly saw the barrel fall off the stand onto the ground. Dane, who had been nearby, asked if everyone was okay, and since we were, he deemed my first experience, while not a success, not a failure either.

I lowered the fork and placed the barrel back on the stand. I had inadvertently raised the fork as I was backing up and had literally knocked the barrel off the stand with the fork. This time I was more careful, and I succeeded in bringing the barrel to the storage room for racking, and then returning the forklift to its place; I was on my way to being a forklift expert. My brother Kevin would be so jealous—eh, Kev? He had always wanted to drive a forklift, and he'd even said so a few weeks earlier when we saw each other at my mom's house in Huntington Beach.

Dane and I discussed my testing sugars on a couple of Chardonnay vineyards near my home that afternoon, the Campi vineyard (our great friends) and that of their neighbor Lorene Arey. If the random berries from around the vineyard averaged above 22, I was to bring several random clusters back to the lab for acid and sugar testing.

Just before I left for the day, Dane got a call; the Livermore Valley Sauvignon Blanc might be ready by the end of the week. That would truly signal the beginning of the season, so for me, it was an exciting call.

I arrived home, grabbed my refractometer (which I would start to keep in my car), and went to test both vineyards. With only slight variations, they both came in around 18 or 19 Brix. With the heat forecast through the rest of the week, those numbers could change rapidly, so I was sure that I'd be testing them again soon.

AUGUST 26, 2008

I arrived a bit before 9:00 AM and said hello to Dane, who was topping off barrels in the storage room. My job this morning was to finish putting bird tape in the Petite Sirah vineyard. While I thought I had completed half of it yesterday, let's just say I misjudged how big the other "half" of the vineyard was.

I brought along my broad-brimmed hat, as I had sunburned the back of my neck yesterday—all part of getting used to the routines and activities. It was definitely going to be a hot day today.

After a short period of time in the vineyard, I heard a truck pulling out of the parking area around the winery, and I noticed it coming along the driveway toward me. I didn't recognize the woman driving, but she was clearly staring at me. Finally she stopped the truck, got out, and began walking into the vineyard toward me. I came out along the row, and when we met up, she was laughing. She told me she'd thought Dane had gotten himself a great scarecrow, but then she saw me move and was a bit freaked out, until she realized it was a person. We laughed, and she told me that her name was Lynn and that she ran the lab at the winery. I had heard of Lynn. She ran Buster's lab, having gotten space from Dane in trade for the testing of his samples. It worked great for both of them.

Lynn had worked for a number of years at Concannon Winery, in their lab, and she was enjoying having her own smaller operation. I mentioned that I was interested in the science as well as the process of winemaking, having taken a number of chemistry classes in college on my way to a degree in zoology. She said that she'd be happy to show me some of the testing she did, if I was going to be around. I said that I would be, and I thanked her.

She drove away, and I went back to bird tape, or bird scare tape, as it was called on the Internet when I looked it up the previous night. We would see how it did. I would take it personally whenever I saw clusters that had been eaten. Similarly, if there was less bird damage than last year, I would demand a few bottles of this Petite Sirah for my extraordinary efforts. The fact that it won the gold medal at the San Francisco Chronicle Wine Competition and should be even better by the time the 2008 vintage came out was not lost on me either.

By the time I finished the vineyard, it was 1:30, so Dane and I drove into Livermore and had sushi at his favorite place. The food was good, but more importantly, Dane and I just talked about his winery, his wines, and the fruit that went into them. We discussed the upcoming days—four tons of Chardonnay to process for someone tomorrow, and the Sauvignon Blanc, all seven tons of it, arriving Friday for processing. It would be a couple of very busy days ahead, and the weather was due to get even warmer.

I sat there thinking that harvest was really about to hit full force.

When we got back to the winery, I helped Dane pack up a few cases and bottles for shipment. He laughed and said to me, "Now this is winemaking."

I chuckled and said, "No, this is the revenue part, and that's very important as well." He agreed with me.

When we were finished, I left for the day, knowing that the next few days would be the beginning of a very busy season, and I was ready for it.

AUGUST 27, 2008

After a relatively quiet day yesterday, today exploded with activity. When I arrived at around 9:15 (I was still trying to figure out traffic and coffee), Dane, Michael, Gary, and Lynn were all there. Dane greeted me with a phrase I thought I would hear more than once in the weeks ahead: "Makin' the wine." We were due to get four tons of Chardonnay today. This was not fruit destined to become a Page Mill wine; rather, it was a job he did for a local winemaker, Tom Doczy, of Jonathan Christopher Cellars. We would simply process the fruit, meaning we would press the whole fruit and then transfer it to a stainless steel tank overnight. Tomorrow we would pump it into barrels, and Tom would pick it up.

This job meant that we needed to move the Chardonnay for Dane and Michael's sparkling wine that was fermenting in the large stainless tank. Michael and I cleaned two stainless steel barrels using a solution of peracetic acid, which is a strong antimicrobial, and then rinsed out the tanks. Before we transferred the fermenting juice, I released argon gas into the tank. Argon is heavier than air, so as we transferred the juice, it created a barrier between the juice and the oxygen in the air. Argon was used extensively for this very purpose. When Dane finished with the topping tank, he gave it a shot of argon to create the same barrier in the tank. After the transfer, the smell of the fermenting fruit was great—very earthy. If you stuck your nose too far into the tank or barrel, you got a strong whiff of CO_2, which burned your nostrils.

While we were waiting for the fruit to arrive, Dane asked me to sort through a "field blend" from an old high-school friend of his. Some of the fruit was probably table grapes, but he had promised to make the wine for this friend. This was a typical example of Dane's generosity. He always had side projects that he did to help a friend or fellow winemaker. He met people easily and was very giving of himself.

The challenge here was that about six of the twenty-four lug boxes had either rotted fruit or very perfumed table grapes—possibly Concord, I thought. I tossed these grapes but kept the other boxes. Dane had mentioned this batch of grapes at lunch the prior day. He thought the fruit wasn't that good, but he felt committed to helping his friend. He went so far as to say that he would probably dump all of the grapes and give his friend thirty gallons of his wine, so as not to disappoint his buddy. I thought that might cause him more grief, as his friend might think he had great grapes, given the quality of Dane's wines, but that was for Dane to sort out. I had sorted out the bad grapes, so my job was done.

The fruit arrived at about 11:30. Gary used the forklift to unload the half-ton bins, and we finished readying the membrane press.

Dane had bought this press a couple of years ago, and it was far and away the most expensive single piece of equipment at the winery, costing thirty thousand dollars. But Dane said it would pay for itself in about three years because the press delivered about 20 percent more juice, and juice of better quality, than the manual one-ton basket press he had been using for years. And while the cycle time to complete a pressing was about the same as the basket press, he could do other things around the winery as the press worked, instead of having to operate the basket press the entire time. The basket press was very hard on the operator's back, so the longevity of the winemaker was also improved with the membrane press.

The press looked like a giant stainless steel cylinder with sliding doors to load the fruit. Inside the press was a membrane that was slowly inflated to press the fruit in a fully programmable system. You could vary the pressure and the timing of the pressure to get the results you wanted.

Once we were ready, we slid the hopper over the doors of the press. Gary drove the forklift with the box loader attachment. This allowed him to pick up the half-ton boxes and dump them into the overhead hopper that fed the press. I had a very important job. I stood upon the hopper, and as the box was being dumped, I used a cultivator to help get all of the fruit out of the boxes.

It turned out that there were just over three tons of fruit, so we loaded up the press with half the fruit and then turned it on. It would take about two or three hours to press all of the juice out of the grapes and pump them into the stainless steel tank that was already cooling the juice.

The timing was perfect, as this was barbecue Wednesday, and it was time to eat. I learned that "barbecue" was a bit of a euphemism. While it was true that last week Lynn, of Buster's lab, had barbecued ribs, this week, Dane had prepared a chicken tagine, with olives and onions in a wonderful sauce. A tagine is a traditional Moroccan recipe that essentially bakes in a heavy dish. This was Dane's first attempt at the recipe his wife, Angela, usually made. He served it with couscous and sliced tomatoes that an older Italian stonecutter named Filippo had brought from his garden. He was a neighbor of Dane's who brought garden veggies throughout the summer and made small amounts of wine for himself every year.

Lunch was served with a 2006 Bien Nacido Vineyard Chardonnay that was excellent (and there were only a few bottles left). We had to move to the 2007 California Chardonnay, which had some Bien Nacido fruit but also fruit from a number of the small peninsula vineyards, like Campi and Arey. Dane made his Chardonnay in a French style, and served chilled, it was a great complement to the chicken dish. Gary and I sat chatting about the Harvest Festival on the upcoming weekend, a Livermore Valley Winery Association event held on Labor Day weekend. There was no doubt that it would be busy. The real question was how hot it would be. It was over 100 degrees today, but it was supposed to cool down by Sunday, in time for the festival on Sunday and Monday. For Gary's sake, I hoped for a cooling trend.

Earlier Dane had asked me if I was coming out to the winery tomorrow. I knew that seven tons of SB, or Sauvignon Blanc, was due to arrive. I said yes, just as I said yes every time he asked me that question. After lunch, Gary, seemingly innocently, asked me the same question. I answered yes, further telling him that in general I would be out at the winery during the week, but probably not on weekends. Before the day was done, I realized that they all must have gotten together to annoy me, as Dane, Gary, and even Michael had to ask me several times during the rest of the day whether I was coming out tomorrow. I finally got it, and they all had a good laugh. My guess was that I might hear the question again before harvest was through.

After lunch, we cleaned out the press and readied it for the second batch of fruit. As a part of this process, we emptied the press into low bins, and then Gary used the forklift to take it out to the end of the vineyard and dump the pressings, which would later be strewn in the vineyard as good organic additives. As we were getting the last bin ready to go, Gary had stepped away, and Dane asked me if I'd like to drive the forklift. Of course I jumped into the driver's seat just as Gary came back. With a big smile on his face, he asked if I was taking his job. I told him that Dane only trusted me with forklift jobs that didn't require great skills, as I was just a novice. Going out into the vineyard and dumping a bin of pressings represented one of these unskilled opportunities.

Meanwhile, Michael, who was a builder and tinkerer by nature, had put in an outdoor shower and named it "The Full Monty." Dane had mentioned it, and Michael built it. That was a pattern that I had heard about and would probably see again. Shortly after it was installed, I soaked my head under it, at Gary's urging. It felt very cool and refreshing … for about two minutes, and then my head was dry in the 100+ degree heat.

We pressed the second batch of fruit in much the same way we'd done the first. This time, as we let it press for the next two hours, Dane, Michael, and I went into the tasting room, and Dane and Michael brought guitars. We sat down and played a couple of tunes together, with Michael and me on acoustic guitars and Dane on acoustic bass. We didn't play that long, as there was still work to do, but we agreed that we would do it again as the season progressed. It was a nice break, and it was quite cool—literally, as the tasting room was the front section of the barrel storage room, so it remained very cool in the Livermore Valley heat.

By now it was after 6:00 PM, and both Gary and Michael, who had arrived earlier than I did, needed to head for home. I stayed with Dane to finish the pressing and cleanup. When the pressing was done, we unhooked the pump and hoses and rinsed the hoses. We rolled out the large pan that collected the juice from the press and hosed that out. Dane loaded pressings into the bins, and I drove the forklift and dumped them at the back of the property. When we had everything cleaned up, Dane looked at me and said, "You get an A+, not an A++, today." When I asked why, he said that whenever you finish using a forklift (or any hydraulic equipment), everything must be at its lowest position. Even with the engine off, if you touch the levers, gravity takes over and drops the fork hard and fast. That could hurt someone or ruin the equipment. Great lesson.

As I drove home that night, the sun was just setting over the East Bay hills. It was a beautiful time of day. On the way home, listening to the radio, I heard Bo Biden introduce his father, Joe Biden, at the Democratic National Convention, as he was to give his acceptance speech for vice president. Bo was very well-spoken, and clearly he made his father proud. Joe delivered a lively speech largely in support of Barack Obama, and when it was over, Joe Biden was surprised by an appearance from Obama, who came on stage and gave him a big hug and then briefly went on to thank all of the speakers and all of the delegates at the convention. It was an uplifting ending to an uplifting day. No matter your politics, I felt we were going to see change for America, no matter who was elected—and that could not come too soon.

AUGUST 28, 2008

As I drove into Livermore Valley, it was already hot. Today it was supposed to get above 100 degrees, and it was on its way. As I arrived, Dane was finishing filling the barrels with the Chardonnay we had pressed yesterday. He filled the barrels about three quarters full, as the wine would ferment in these barrels and need space for the fermentation process. As he was finishing up, he asked me to load the barrels onto his truck because we were going to deliver them to Charles R Winery, where the fermenting wines would be stored and cared for. Each rack held two barrels. I carefully picked up the first rack and drove it over to the truck. I loaded them on, and just before I was pulling back, Dane came over and had me shift them to butt up against the front of the truck bed, so we could fit all ten barrels into the truck. The forklift was incredibly maneuverable, and with its various features, it was extremely versatile. This made it just about the most important piece of non-winemaking machinery at the winery—though according to Michael, everything was part of the winemaking process, even the Full Monty, our new shower.

After we loaded the truck, we drove up to Charles R, where we met the winemaker Randy. I had been to the facility before in 2005, when we did the barn raising when Dane first moved to Livermore. Charles R Winery looked different, as Randy and his father had added more square footage to the barrel storage facility. Randy was storing barrels and finished wine for Bent Creek Winery, as well as his own. When we arrived, Dane hadn't seen these new changes before, and he remarked, "What are you building, the Winchester Mystery Winery?" I don't think Randy thought it was funny, but they both delighted in giving each other shit constantly, so it was part of the game.

Randy offloaded the wine, and we headed back to Page Mill. Dane had a very important meeting that morning: Lola's first-year checkup. So I took the half-ton bins from the Chardonnay delivered yesterday back up to Charles R Winery, while Gary started on pressure washing Dane's half-ton bins that we would deliver to the Sauvignon Blanc vineyard later that day. When I returned, Gary was in the midst of the job, but he hadn't counted on all the wasp nests in the bins, which hadn't been used for a year. The wasps weren't too happy, and they just flew all around us as we pulled the rest out and began cleaning them. The undersides of each bin had several wasp nests, so no wonder the wasps were unhappy at us destroying their homes. I took over, both to give Gary a break and to try my hand at yet another aspect of winemaking (remember, 90 percent cleaning, 10 percent actual winemaking), and I saw what looked like a black ball come out of one of the bins. As it landed, it sprung open to reveal a very large black widow spider, one of the few things I truly detest in the world. Without even thinking, I simply stepped on it with my boot. They still unnerve me.

The rest of the work was uneventful. When Dane returned, the three of us went into the tasting room to escape the heat and eat lunch. Gary opened a wonderful Fleming Jenkins Victories Rosé. This was from the winery of Peggy Fleming, the famous figure skater, and her husband, Greg Jenkins. Dane got it from Peggy at a trade tasting, where he said that many of the winemakers swapped wines to try them out. It was a very dry but very fruity rosé. It went well with the leftover cold chicken and couscous from yesterday. I was beginning to really look forward to lunch every day, and though the food was great, the wine was even better.

It was hard to leave the cool 70 degrees of the tasting room and go outside, where it was over 100, but we had to deliver the bins to the Sauvignon Blanc vineyard. Gary drove the forklift, and Dane and I loaded and arranged the bins once they were in the truck. Dane and I took off in the truck to deliver the bins, while Gary got the remaining bins ready for us. The vineyard was only about ten minutes away and was owned by a Livermore developer named Jim Ghielmetti, who had developed the vineyard property as an offset for a housing or commercial development project closer to the town of Livermore. Livermore, along with several other communities in the area, created the Tri-Valley Conservancy as a means of fostering the resurgence of an agricultural economy in Livermore Valley. It was primarily aimed at growing grapes, but there were olive orchards and even a pistachio orchard within the conservancy lands.

Sauvignon Blanc was the backbone of Page Mill Winery. Up until Dane had secured this Livermore Valley fruit, he was sourcing his Sauvignon Blanc from the French Camp vineyard near Paso Robles. Not only was this a more economical choice, the fruit was wonderful, and his Sauvignon Blanc was even better than before. I always traded a case of my Merlot allotment for a case of Dane's Sauvignon Blanc.

We dropped off the half-ton bins near another set of bins. As we were pulling away to get the rest of the bins, the new winemaker from Fenestra, Brent Amos, was unloading bins for the Sauvignon Blanc harvest tomorrow as well. Fenestra was owned by Lanny and Fran Replogle, and Lanny just recently had turned over the winemaking reins to Brent, who had been his assistant winemaker. Dane told me that there was an interesting Page Mill connection to Lanny. Back in the seventies, Lanny had been a chemistry professor at San Jose State. He taught a course he had created called the Chemistry of Winemaking. Dane's father, Dick Stark, who founded Page Mill in 1976, took Lanny's course as a part of his own winemaking education.

When we got back to Page Mill, Gary had the bins all teed up, so after we loaded them, Gary said his goodbyes. He needed to go home and pack, as he was staying out at the winery for the next few days. Gary ran the tasting room, and as I said earlier, this Labor Day weekend (Sunday and Monday) was the annual Harvest Festival. Page Mill, like many of the local wineries, would have food and a band as well as wine tasting, and Gary would be in the middle of all of it. Additionally we had seven tons of Sauvignon Blanc grapes coming tomorrow.

Dane and I drove back up to Ghielmetti Vineyard to drop off the rest of the bins. On the way, we were following a truck with two pallets of what looked like tarpaper. The tie-downs on one of the pallets had come loose, and the rolls were beginning to slide. We noticed this just as the truck began to turn left off the road to the vineyard. Dane quickly said, "Shall we tell him?" We agreed and made the same left, with Dane honking and me flailing arms out the window. We couldn't get the driver's attention. We followed him for about a mile, and finally he slowed down to turn. He made a left, and we followed, still honking and waving. He turned right into an industrial park, and we finally gave up. He never heard us or saw us. We had attempted to do a good deed, but I think we only got half credit because we never actually made contact with the driver.

The rest of the trip was uneventful, and by the time we dropped off the last bins, there were additional bins for Garré Vineyard and Wente Vineyard. This was going to be quite a harvest—and quite a crush at Page Mill tomorrow. This would be the first real Page Mill wine of the 2008 harvest season.

Dane and I said our goodbyes for the day. I was having the time of my life. Dane and Gary were both such a pleasure to work with. They were quick to share their knowledge and more then appreciative of any help I gave them.

For me, the dream of working a harvest was coming true, and the actual experience was beyond anything I had ever hoped. First and foremost, it fed my love of wine and my genuine interest in learning more about how it's made. But the work also tapped into so many other interests and joys of mine. It was about chemistry, which had always fascinated me. I had a chemistry lab in my garage during high school, and I took two years of chemistry in college. This was chemistry applied to something I loved, and it was all amazing. It was working outdoors and doing things that had direct, measurable, and meaningful results nearly immediately. Working in marketing for much of my career, and being a general manager and CEO for the last 9 years meant that the results of what you did were often seen months later, if you could ever tie what you did to the outcome. At Page Mill, every day I saw the results of my work in many small ways. And as we worked through the harvest season, I would see it in bigger ways, through the wines of Page Mill's 2008 harvest ... and that was what this was all about.

AUGUST 29, 2008

It was Friday, the last day of my first full week at Page Mill. Today we would destem and press seven tons of Sauvignon Blanc grapes from the Ghielmetti vineyard right up the road in Livermore. When I crested Pigeon Pass on Highway 84 and entered Livermore Valley, it was about 9:00 AM and already 85 degrees. It was going to be a very hot day.

When I arrived, Gary was getting the destemmer ready, and Dane was working in the office. He would be gone most of the morning, so when the fruit arrived, Gary and I would begin to destem the fruit and fill the press. The fruit was due to arrive at about 11:00 AM. Dane had made the decision to destem the fruit before putting it into the press. Removing the stems would save space in the press and hopefully enable us to do only two pressings, saving time. We had simply put the whole clusters into the press when we processed the Chardonnay on Wednesday, and we had needed two pressings to get it done. This extra step added some time, but saving a cycle of pressing meant saving four hours or so.

The first of the fruit arrived at 10:00 AM; it was eight half-ton bins on a flatbed truck. These came from a particular block, and the driver said that the other seven bins were at the weighing station. The truck was weighed with empty bins and then weighed again with the fruit on it, yielding the weight of the grapes. This is the weight that would be used when paying the grower and to understand yield by calculating the number of gallons of juice per ton of grapes.

Gary offloaded the fruit and put it in the shade. We went back to preparing the destemmer, and just as we were finished, the second load arrived. We were given the weight sheets from the Wente weighing station showing the two lots at 3.715 tons and 3.240 tons, for a total of 6.955 tons of Sauvignon Blanc fruit.

As Gary continued the last preparatory steps, I used the forklift to get all of the fruit into the shade, except the first bin we were processing. As we prepared to process the first bin, the destemmer and the press were lined up on the crush pad. The crush pad is a concrete pad with drains where all the work of processing the grapes takes place. Above the destemmer, we had situated the receiving chute, or hopper. I turned on the destemmer, and Gary grabbed the first bin with the bin-dumper attachment on the forklift. This device adds a frame on three sides around the fork. After using the fork to lift the bin, the bin-dumper can be closed on the remaining end, holding in the bin. In this way the attachment enables the operator to tilt the bins, emptying them into the chute. Gary then raised the bin to the chute above the destemmer and dumped in the grapes.

I stood up on the chute and helped guide Gary in. Once situated, I used a cultivator to remove the grapes and ensure that we had emptied the bin. Then, as Gary went off to get the next bin, I made sure that the grapes flowed into the destemmer, until all of them had been processed. This meant that underneath the destemmer was another half-ton bin collecting single berries, and out the back of the destemmer, we collected the stems in a bin.

When the destemming was complete, I used a pallet jack to pull out the bin of fruit so that Gary could grab it and dump it into the press. A pallet jack is essentially a fork on wheels that can be raised or lowered hydraulically by pumping on the handle. Before Gary dumped the bin into the press, we also had to move the chute over the opening of the press, which we did. Now Gary again lifted the bin and dumped it into the chute. My job was easier this time, as I simply needed to guide Gary and clean out any few remaining grapes that didn't slide into the press.

We were about to start our second bin when Dane arrived. This enabled Gary to continually drive the forklift, getting another bin and transferring the loads into the destemmer and then into the press. I spent all of my time up on the chute, making sure that the destemmer had a smooth flow of grapes and that the press received each load. Dane alternated in moving the chute from destemmer to press and back again with me, and beginning to operate the press and pumping juice into the 750-gallon chilled stainless-steel tank. Even as we were filling the press, juice was already draining out.

We had processed six bins, and our goal was to get eight into the press for the first round of pressing. Dane looked inside the press and asked my opinion from up on the chute. I told him we could do one more for sure, and then we'd need to check. Sure enough, after the seventh was processed, we looked again. It was going to be close, but Dane said optimistically, "Let's do it!" As Gary brought that last bin of destemmed fruit to the chute and began to pour it in, I wasn't so sure. But we went ahead, and it all fit inside. We knew we would be able to get the seven remaining bins into the other pressing, saving ourselves a nice chunk of time.

The press began to operate, and we took turns watching the pump, increasing or decreasing speed as the juice flowed. The press went through several cycles of inflating the membrane inside the press to squeeze out the juice, creating a strong flow of juice into the large pan underneath the press. At this point, the pump was on high. As the press finished a cycle, the membrane would deflate, and the press would rotate several times, shaking up the increasingly dry fruit. This cycle went on for several hours, with a goal of getting around 140 gallons per ton of grapes.

While the press was working, Dane went off to an appointment, and Gary and I watched over the process. By now it was also 103 degrees in the shade, so we were drinking water regularly and hoping the weather would break a bit for the upcoming Harvest Festival.

I went for sandwiches in the middle of the cycle, and when Dane returned, we took a break and had beer and sandwiches.

After lunch, we set about doing a quick cleaning of the press and pan underneath, removing the dry skins into a bin and emptying them at the end of the property. Later these and the stems would be spread throughout the vineyard to add their nutrients back to the soil. With that done, we were ready for the second pressing. For the rest of the afternoon and into the evening, we finished the other seven half-ton bins and loaded the press for the second time. As expected, we got all of the grapes in the press. Dane set the program on the press, and we began to clean up.

Gary opened up the destemmer and then used the forklift to remove the bin of stems, as I began to clean the destemmer. By now it was nearly 8:00 PM, and the temperature was still 90 degrees. The next day, Denise and I had guests coming to stay for the weekend, and she had been home, preparing everything for the weekend. I wanted to be home to help with the final preparations, so I told Dane that I felt bad about leaving, but that I needed to leave then. He looked at me and said he was surprised that I had stayed this long. He told me that no matter what we were doing, or what we were in the middle of, I should feel comfortable leaving if I needed to leave or just wanted to. Then he said that he would be here until the job was done tonight, and that was what he signed up for in this business. That was not what I needed to sign up for. I thanked him for understanding and said my goodbyes. He asked when I would be out again. With the Harvest Festival on Sunday and Monday, and our guests for the weekend, I told him that I would be out on Tuesday.

I still thought he hadn't figured out that I would be there for the entire harvest—that the hard work was not intimidating, and that I was getting as much out of this as he was gaining through my help. If not for our guests arriving tomorrow, I would have been there as long as it took to finish the cleanup. As it was, the three of us had processed seven tons of fruit today that was now cooling and settling in the large tank. We would get it into barrels and begin the fermentation process next week.

As I drove out of the Page Mill Winery driveway in the gathering dark, I noticed Angela (Dane's wife) with a friend and their two little girls walking up the street, about to come into the winery. I waved as I drove on. I'm sure they were coming to check on Dane (and the kittens Cinderella and Belle— now, who do you think named those kittens?). Harvest was the hardest part of the year, and it had only just begun, but Dane seemed to relish this time. I guess that as a winemaker, this was your time, and Dane seemed always to have a smile on his face.

September

September 2, 2008

Dane and I spoke first thing in the morning. I asked how the Harvest Festival had gone, and he was very pleased. The weather had cooperated, with both days in the eighties. Coming off the week before, when temperatures were well over 100 degrees on most days, this must have made the organizers very pleased. Dane said that there were fewer people this year, a sign of the economic times. But he had almost broken even on wine sales, which was a plus.

I asked him what was on tap for the day, and he said that he needed to pick up grapes at two small vineyards on the peninsula that day, and that by the time he got back to the winery in the early afternoon, there would only be a couple of hours before he left for band practice. He was taking a course in which he and several other people formed a band and practiced five songs for eight weeks and then put on a concert. It was a great outlet for him, and it fed our desire to play music at the winery when we got a break.

With his shortened day, and with his visit to the peninsula in late morning, we agreed that I would check sugars at several vineyards and take some samples if it was warranted. I would then meet up with him so he could take back the samples for lab tests.

First I went right up the street to our friends the Harrises. This year, their Cabernet Sauvignon vineyard was going to be picked for the first time. I had checked the fruit nearly two weeks ago and found that the berries were in the mid-twenties, so I took a few samples for Dane to test later. This vineyard would probably need to be picked in the next week.

Next, I went over to the Kennedy Merlot vineyard, which was near the Los Altos Country Club. Dane had told me that he thought this might be the next vineyard we picked. I first checked a few berries from various parts of the vineyard, and I found them to also be in the mid-twenties. Again, I took a number of samples for Dane to test. Given the layout and shade versus sun of the vineyard, I took a few more samples to ensure that he got a representation of the vineyard.

Finally, I went back to the other end of Los Altos Hills and tested sugars at the Campi and Arey Chardonnay vineyards. Both vineyards had Brix in the low twenties. I talked to Dane, and we decided to test again next week before we began to take samples. While I was sampling the Arey vineyard, I saw a sparrow stuck in the netting. I raised up the net and was able to shoo the bird out from under the netting. I noticed there was a large, orange cat nearby, so I imagined that any birds that got stuck in the nets wouldn't last too long.

With the samples from Harris and Kennedy, I headed for home. I began to do some sampling in our Merlot vineyard and found the Brix to generally be in the low twenties as well, and the fruit looked beautiful. Dane arrived a few minutes later, having picked up the fruit from the two small vineyards. I gave him the samples, and we talked about the rest of the week. With all the heat, it seemed like a number of the vineyards were starting to come in.

By the time Dane left and I finished testing our vineyard, it was about 12:30. It was a short day, but I knew that the rest of the week would be busy.

SEPTEMBER 3, 2008

Today was also a less hectic day, except it was barbecue Wednesday, and Gary was cooking kebabs. But before that, we had a custom crush job. These jobs provided a bit of cash flow and filled in the dead spots as the harvest was getting under way. The fruit was Pinot Gris, which is probably better known by its Italian name, Pinot Grigio. It is a white variant of Pinot Noir, though the grapes are light bluish, or pinkish brown. It is made in the style of a white wine, meaning it is pressed immediately off the skins. Due to the color of the grapes, the juice can have a tinge of pink color, even though it spends no time on the skins.

We processed just about half a ton of fruit. As a result, like the Chardonnay last week, the clustered fruit went right into the press. This time, yours truly drove the forklift. I had the box-dumper attachment on the forklift but had to turn it around to get the first bin. As I maneuvered on the crush pad, there was a stack of gray boxes that were drying.

These had contained the fruit I had sorted last week. And just as Gary and I had thought, Dane had waited until the fruit had gone totally bad, so Gary had dumped it that morning. Now the dilemma was that Dane would feel obligated to his friend and would give him Page Mill wine instead. He had done that last year, not telling his buddy that he had dumped his fruit. His friend had remarked upon how good the wine from his grapes was becoming. This would serve to further his belief in his own fruit. The saving grace, according to Gary, was that Dane's friend had sold the house and moved, so there wouldn't be any more fruit from this backyard vineyard.

Back to the forklift. As I maneuvered it around, I was trying to avoid the boxes, but of course I hit them and toppled a number of them all over the crush pad. As I shut off the power and stepped down from the forklift to pick them up, I noticed a big grin on Gary's face up on the chute. He was having fun with my "quality" driving skills. I asked him what he would have done, and he calmly replied that he would have raised the box-dumper higher to avoid the boxes. I thanked him for sharing his wisdom after the fact. Again he just grinned.

With the boxes restacked, I again mounted the forklift and this time picked up the bin uneventfully. I raised it up, aligning with the chute above the press, with Gary guiding me in this time. Over the chute, I tipped the bin and dumped the grapes into the press. I then lowered the bin for Dane to wash it out. I set it down at one end of the crush pad and went over to get the second bin. Dane and Gary were sorting the fruit, as there were a few bad bunches. Dane had me grab the bin and tip it about halfway, so they could finish going through the fruit. After they had finished, I dumped the remaining bin into the press, rinsed the bin, and stacked it on top of the other bin. Dane turned on the press, and it began to do its work.

Dane asked me if I'd mind running an errand. I was to add an additional thirty-five yellow bins to the truck, strap them down, and take the truck to the public scales on the other side of Livermore to get a tare sheet (which I thought was a tear sheet) on the truck's unladen weight. It turns out that the word "tare" means the weight of an unladen container, which is compared with the gross weight to provide the net weight of the cargo—grapes, in our case. I was doing this to get the unladen weight, or tare, of the truck that Dane had used yesterday to pick up the fruit at the two small vineyards on the peninsula. Obviously he had returned to Livermore and had the truck weighed for its gross weight.

When I returned, Gary had finished cooking the kebabs and rice pilaf, and he had just sat down with Dane and Michael. With them was a friend of Dane's named Richard, who worked up the street at Wente. He brought along a bottle of Wente 2005 Livermore Valley Chardonnay that was very crisp. As I sat down, Michael looked up and said, "Hey, are you coming out tomorrow?"

Dane raised an eyebrow and smiled, so I said, "I'm not sure. Probably." Later we finished off partial bottles of Angela's Cuvée, Dane's rosé in tribute to his wife, and his Livermore Valley Sauvignon Blanc, both 2007s, and both probably left over from the Harvest Festival. It was a great lunch. I had agreed to make lunch next week and was already working on my menu, with Denise's help—Italian, I told them.

After lunch, Dane checked the press. He had about fifty gallons of juice and was hoping to get a bit more to be able fill a barrel. With that Dane, Gary, and I discussed the plan for tomorrow. Dane would drive out to Lodi at 4:00 AM to pick up Zinfandel fruit, with the pickers arriving at 6:00 AM. Hopefully he would be back by 11:00. Gary and I decided to drive together tomorrow, arriving around 9:00 AM to set up for the arrival of the fruit. It would be a busy day tomorrow, so we said our goodbyes and headed for home.

SEPTEMBER 4, 2008

Gary picked me up at 8:00 AM for the ride to Livermore. I didn't get a chance to make coffee, which I had promised Gary the evening before, so I told him that I'd buy him a coffee as we left Los Altos. He suggested that we stop in downtown Livermore, as he needed to get gas anyway. We drove into Livermore Valley and headed for Panama Red Coffee in downtown Livermore. I bought him coffee, and we ran into Randy, the winemaker at Charles R Winery, who was having coffee with friends and said hello. We also got a text from Dane, saying that he would be leaving Lodi around noon, as the picking was going more slowly than he had anticipated.

As we drove into the winery, Michael was already there. He was working on the sparkling wine that he and Dane were making. The wine was essentially fermented to dryness, and he was figuring out the sulfite needed so that he could consolidate the wine into smaller containers.

Gary and I began to prepare for the Zinfandel fruit that would soon be on its way. I started by pressure washing three one-ton fermenting bins. We got out the destemmer and set it up with a half-ton bin underneath. I was becoming an expert in driving the forklift (or at least an expert in my own mind). I grabbed a couple of pallets with the forklift. We needed to elevate the fermenters so that the chute would be inside the fermenter when we poured in the destemmed fruit, lessening the spillage.

Next I used the forklift to move the fermenting bins into place, one on the pallets, and two nearby, where we could easily move them into position. We were ready. All we needed was the Zinfandel!

As we waited, I helped Gary wash and box glassware for the tasting room, as well as other odds and ends that needed doing as we waited for Dane and the fruit. It was about noon when Dane called and said that he would be there in about an hour, but he also said that the fruit was beautiful.

Gary, Michael, and I took a break for lunch and had sandwiches left over from the Harvest Festival. Michael brought out a 2006 Cabernet that he had made from fruit in Dry Creek Valley, which had also been his source for the Chardonnay that was now fermenting for their sparkling wine. The wine was young, with moderate fruit, but it had a good amount of tannins. It could be a very nice wine in a few years, but I was certainly no judge. The main thing that Michael was concerned about was that he had submitted this wine to the California State Fair for judging. One judge made mention of the smell of "Brett."

This smell is named for *Brettanomyces,* which is a unicellular yeast that is actually a fungus, not a bacterium. The presence of high amounts of "Brett" is noticed by the barnyard smell some wines get—or is it wet dog, or wet newspaper? None of it sounds very appealing, and generally no one wants it in their wine. Neither Gary nor I noticed any hint of "Brett" in the wine. It was actually fairly fruit-forward and clean tasting. The real test, though, should have been done by letting Denise try the wine.

She has one of the finest and most sensitive palates I have ever seen. Claude, our sommelier friend from Joseph Phelps, told us that, in general, women have better palates than men. This is indisputable in our house. Denise can always pick out the subtle flavors in wine, both good and bad, while my system is simply whether I like it or I don't. So, when I open a bottle of wine, if it isn't very good, or even great, I'll have Denise taste it to pass judgment. Sometimes she'll suggest we wait a bit, and the wine gets better, though these days we can run that test quickly by putting the wine through a Vinturi for a quick bit of oxygenation. This system provides me with foolproof good-to-great wine every time, and Denise is the gold standard in the Côté view that "life is too short to drink bad wine."

Back to the day. Dane arrived with the Zinfandel. It was incredible. As I have said before, our fruit was beautiful, but this Zinfandel rivaled ours. The clusters were big and a beautiful deep purple in color. Dane said that part of the reason he was late was that he was able to hand select the fruit as it went into the bins, which contributed to how uniformly beautiful the fruit was. We unloaded the bins, and Gary and I began to process the fruit. There were six half-ton bins to be destemmed.

I began up on the chute, as I had for the Sauvignon Blanc. This time, as the fruit was dumped in, it smelled incredibly sweet and, yes, jammy. It is amazing how much the fruit smelled like ripe blackberries. After the fruit went through the destemmer, we moved the chute over the fermenting bin and pulled out the destemmed fruit with a pallet jack, so that Gary could pick it up and dump it into the bin. We repeated the process with the next bin and then used the forklift to move the fermenting bin into the shade and position the next one.

I moved to forklift operator for the rest of the process, which we repeated twice more—two half-ton bins per fermenting bin. At this point, I was feeling pretty good about my forklift skills. But of course, just when you get cocky, God shows you the foolishness of your ways. I raised up a bin, positioning it (I thought) at the right point above the chute. I began to dump the bin, but was a bit too far forward. Before I could get the bin upright, I had dumped clusters all around three sides of the chute—clearly off target. I repositioned the bin and dumped the rest into the chute without incident. I then got out of the forklift and walked around the chute, picking up the clusters and tossing them into the destemmer. No harm was done to the grapes, just my own ego as a forklift operator.

After we finished processing the Zin, we cleaned up. I used the forklift to take two bins of stems out to the edge of the vineyard. All of the stems and pressings would ultimately go back into the Petite Sirah vineyard as soil nutrients, so nothing would be wasted. We finished cleaning up and went into the tasting room to say our goodbyes to Dane for the day. He was more than happy that we had processed the fruit while he was able to take care of other matters. I felt good knowing that I had given him some real extra time, as he would have been out there with Gary if I wasn't there. I was beginning to feel comfortable with a number of the operations of the winery, and as Dane always said, everything we did was about making wine, no matter what.

Sᴇᴘᴛᴇᴍʙᴇʀ 5, 2008

Today we didn't have any fruit to pick up or to process, so it was an opportunity to get caught up and to taste some wine. More on that after lunch. In the morning, I loaded the truck with seven empty bins and drove over to the public scales to get the tare weight, to figure out the net amount of Zinfandel grapes from yesterday. It was 6,120 pounds—pretty close to the three tons for which Dane had contracted.

When I got back, Dane suggested that I smell and taste the fermenting Sauvignon Blanc. As I was going up the ladder to get a look at the fermenting grapes, he warned me again about how strong the CO_2 would be that was coming off the wine. Even with that warning, as I carefully stuck my head down close to the opening, I couldn't help jumping a little with the stinging in my nose from the CO_2. I had smelled this before, but I had forgotten how strong it could be. The SB was just bubbling away happily in the tank. I had brought a glass with me, and I scooped out a taste of this new wine. The Brix was down to about 18 from the mid-twenties, but the taste was a wonderful, fizzy sweetness. I told Dane to stop right then and bottle it. He could make a fortune, and we wouldn't have to wait to drink it. He laughed and said that it was Vin Nouveau, or new wine, which was done in some parts of France and Italy (and probably other places). A famous form of this is the Gamay Beaujolais Nouveau in France, which is released just weeks after the harvest and shortly after fermentation. This wine was going to be great, even though we would have to wait!

My next job was to put together a tent that someone had given to the winery for free. It did not come with directions, just poles and nuts and bolts and canvas. Fortunately for me, a winemaker named Ramon from Tracy was there to get alcohol from Dane to fortify his port. This took the form of 37.5 percent alcohol Barbera wine that Dane was also using for his port. While Dane was getting out the barrels, Ramon and I took a look at the tent and figured out how it went together.

Dane had moved the Zinfandel into the stables to try to keep it cool during the extremely warm days we were having. While I was getting the truck weighed and building the tent, Gary went off to pick up 250 pounds of dry ice, which Dane would use to cool down the Zinfandel and an extra tank of Sauvignon Blanc; they were getting too warm, the Zin being near 80 degrees and the SB at 75 degrees. He wanted to get them both into the low seventies or high sixties as they went into strong fermentation, hopefully to slow it down somewhat. I also punched down the Zinfandel (you'll remember that from the earlier discussion of my short stint at winemaking). This time I used a long stainless steel tool designed for punching down wine. We would need to punch down these wines three times a day.

After punchdown, Dane added a red-wine enzyme to one of the Zinfandel tanks. In using the enzyme, he was essentially experimenting with this tank. Enzymes had been used for a number of years, primarily for enhancing the color of red wines, as well as the extraction of additional flavors from the skin. They work on the berries themselves, just as maceration does to break down the skins and the compounds in them. The skins provide all the color to grapes and much of the complexity and tannins. Dane had just begun to experiment with the enzymes to see if they improved the color and quality of his wines.

The interesting thing about experiments like these is that you can begin to see the results as the wine matures, but the result is in the final product, which was two years away. That's a long time to discover what works and what doesn't. Much of the wine business takes time to develop.

When we finished with the Zinfandel, Dane asked Gary and me if we'd like sushi for lunch. The answer was a resounding yes. We went to Sushi Sammy, where they knew Dane and Gary only too well. In fact, we sat at their table. It was a great break from all the tasks at the winery, and it gave us all a chance to relax and to discuss the upcoming vineyards and speculate about timing.

After lunch, I had the opportunity to do something you only dream about. We pulled samples from all of the 2006 Merlot barrels, including the '06 Côté, and we pulled samples of the '07 Côté Merlot. Dane was hoping to bottle the '06 California Merlot and Côté Vineyard Merlot the next week, so this was an opportunity to try all of the barrels in preparation for blending the final wines. We pulled the '07 samples because there were four barrels that Dane suspected were '06 Côté but were marked as '07. I also think he pulled them as a treat for me. Each sample had a number, but we didn't know which was which.

I started out by taking a sip of one of them, just as Dane was giving instructions to smell each of the glasses first and comment on the smell and color of each—good job, Dave! By tasting the wine, the smell of the next wine would be affected by the taste of the prior wine. All of the senses work together, so smelling each wine is an attempt to isolate one of the senses before more of them are put into play by drinking the wine.

I was watching Dane and Gary taking copious notes on the smells. I had a more limited set of comments. In general, many of them smelled great—lots of berry and spice, some oak. A couple of the samples had a more alcoholic smell. At one point, Dane said, "I know you'll think this is crazy, but it just hit me. Try number 512 and tell me what you smell?' He waited a bit and then said, "Chow mein?" Gary and I looked at each other, not getting it. Then he said, "I know! How about soy sauce?" Sure enough, with the suggestion, there was hint of soy sauce.

As we progressed, I found that I could distinguish broad categories, like berries, oak, spice, tannin, and what I called alcohol. I don't have a very sophisticated palate, but as I've said before, I know what I like, and this was part of the learning process. What a fun way to learn.

The colors of the wines all tended to be a fairly deep ruby red, but there were samples that clearly were darker red than others. Later, this would be telling.

Then we began to taste the wines. Dane and Gary would take a sip, swirl it around in their mouths, and then spit it out. As I tried this technique, I felt that I wasn't getting the true taste of the wine, which was more complete for me by swallowing. I was sure it was yet another technique that I would need to learn. But trying the wines, coupled with the aromas and our discussions of them, made it a more effective process. I thought this was particularly difficult, given the subtle differences, which in many cases were defined only by different barrels of the same wine. As we finished trying the wines, there were two samples that had a similar alcoholic taste—not bad, but not as smooth as many others.

Dane suggested that this wine (both samples were from the same small vineyard) might be high in VA. I asked what that was, and he explained that it stood for volatile acidity. A certain amount of this is in all wines, and it is primarily from the presence of acetic acid. Again, all wines have some amount of acetic acid, which is the primary acid in vinegar, and thus associated with spoilage in wine. When the amount gets too high, the senses can recognize the compound, and the perception is that the wine is bad. This is similar to *Brettanomyces,* where the "Brett" comes from too high a concentration of the fungus in a wine. This was another example of the complexity and art of winemaking. Nearly every bottle of wine possessed the ingredients to be good, or even great, as well as to be horrific. The winemaker, with both art and science, put it all together to make wine that was a pleasure to drink.

That said, we all agreed that one group of wines all had similar characteristics and represented the best of the lot. Their color was deeper, their smell was wonderful, with a great balance of fruit and oak, and each of us had rated them highly in their overall taste, flavor, and finish. When we looked up the number to the corresponding barrels, this was the '07 Côté Merlot. Both Gary and I thought it could be bottled now. As we revealed the various samples, we were able to distinguish between the Côte '06 and '07 and thus find the mismatched barrels. It was actually more obvious than I would have thought.

While I enjoyed the '06 Côté, the '07 was going to be spectacular. I know Dane was pleased. He commented that he might add a bit of Petite Sirah to the '06 to improve its complexity. It was late afternoon, and Dane needed to run an errand, so we covered up the samples and said our goodbyes. Dane would be back later to spend much more time on these samples, planning his blending and thinking about how to make his '06 Merlot the best it could be. I was looking forward to bottling the '06 Côté as well, and I would have to be patient in my wait for the '07.

But this had been a unique experience in my time at Page Mill, and it was a glimpse into the true art of winemaking.

SEPTEMBER 7, 2008

I received the following email when I checked late this evening:

Hey Dave,

Tomorrow we have a bit on tap ....

I need to pull barrels out of the cellar and organize for the new SB, etc. I need to filter a couple barrels. I may even get to consolidate the SB ....

However, all that goes around me running into San Jose and picking up cases, then delivering them to Los Altos Hills ... which means I'll be gone from something like 10:00 AM until 1:00 or so (maybe not that long).

If you want to take the day off, since I'll be gone throughout the middle, I would understand ....

On the other hand, there's lots to do, so if you feel like coming out and spending half the day alone, working on our task list, it'll be great to have you. Either way, your choice!

Hope you guys had a great weekend.

 Dane

Dane Stark

Owner/Winemaker

Page Mill Winery

1960 S. Livermore Ave Livermore, CA 94550

925-456-7676 www.PageMillWinery.com

 "… wine that fits your life"

since 1976

Here is my reply:

Dane

I'll be out tomorrow morning. Happy to do whatever needs doing.

Dave

Sent from my iPhone

SEPTEMBER 8, 2008

This week, it was noticeably cooler coming into Livermore Valley around 9:00 AM. There were even remnants of overcast still lingering in the sky. When I arrived, Dane was in the barrel room in a sweatshirt, so I knew it had been colder earlier in the morning. As he had mentioned in his email of the previous night, he had to make a delivery later, but we discussed my adding acid to several of the wines while he was gone.

But first, I went out and punched down the three tanks of Zinfandel and a small tank of Cab/Merlot. Then I measured the Brix of the fermenting Zin, Cab/Merlot, and a tank of the Sauvignon Blanc that was in addition to the 750-gallon stainless steel tank—and there were four more oak barrels of Sauvignon Blanc. But more on all that later.

The Zinfandel, which had only been fermenting for four days, was already well into fermentation. In fact, the Brix of the three bins ranged from 6.7 to 10. Just a couple of days earlier, they had all been around 24. Dane used the rest of the dry ice from last week to try to cool down the tanks some more in an attempt to slow fermentation just a bit (they ranged from 97 to 100 degrees). That's tough to do when the grapes are in the throes of converting sugar to alcohol. One of the key byproducts is heat. We also left the tanks uncovered to let some of the cool air into the tanks. At this point, they were putting off so much CO_2, another byproduct of the process, that there was no possibility of oxygen getting to the grapes—they were shrouded in CO_2.

I also took measurements on the tank of Sauvignon Blanc, which had a Brix of 1.9 and a temperature of 80 degrees. It was coming to the end of fermentation, as was the small bin of Cabernet/Merlot, which was at -.05 Brix.

I measured the Brix with a series of hydrometers that were calibrated to different ranges of Brix, rather than the one I had used when I was experimenting with winemaking thirteen years ago. That one measured specific gravity or relative density of a liquid. I was using Lynn's hydrometers. They operated by filling a graduated cylinder with the juice and setting the hydrometers down into the liquid, spinning it to make sure all of the air bubbles were released and the measurement was accurate. The hydrometer floated in the fermenting juice, and the Brix was measured at the point where the hydrometer broke the surface.

I have mentioned a set of hydrometers. That is because there are different calibrations on them for different points in the fermentation process. I used one that measured 0 to 12 Brix for the Zinfandel, and another that measured 5 to -5 for the SB and the small bin. When I was finished and shared the numbers with Dane, he was pleased, even though he wanted to slow down the Zinfandel. The Sauvignon Blanc smelled wonderful. I could really get a sense of the flavors that would be present in the finished wine. I did ask Dane why there was a negative indicator on the hydrometer. He said that he was looking for readings at the minus level to ensure that the wines were fermented completely dry; in other words, that all of the sugar had been converted to alcohol. When this occurred, because alcohol was lighter than water, which is the zero measurement on a Brix scale, the hydrometer had to be less than zero. It made perfect sense once Dane explained it.

Next we jumped into the truck, which still had the seven half-ton bins from my tare weight measurement last week. This was perfect, as we needed to deliver bins to a Chardonnay vineyard up the road. Dane had arranged for a crew to pick Chardonnay for delivery tonight or tomorrow. This was the first Page Mill Chardonnay that we would process. As we discussed the vineyard, I asked Dane about the quality of this fruit. He said it wasn't as good as the two premium peninsula vineyards, Campi and Arey, but it was solid. When I asked him why this was, he said that the vineyard had several issues. One was that it had quadrilateral cordons but didn't have the trellising system to support it, so the canopy was uneven. He also said the watering system was old and uneven in its application, so some fruit got more water while other parts got less. All in all, though, the fruit was good. We had a bottle of his recently released 2007 Chardonnay, which was a blend of all three vineyards' fruit, and it was outstanding.

One of the ways he could get the best from this vineyard was in how it was picked. There are two approaches to picking. A crew can be paid by the bin or by the hour. They are paid by the bin when the fruit is of uniformly high quality. When this is the case, the crew can move quickly, and filling bins is the right goal. When the fruit is a bit variable, the hourly approach works better for everyone. The bins may not be filled as fast, but they are filled with higher-quality fruit. The crewmembers are not penalized for being selective in their picking. Dane said that, all in all, it was a win-win situation, unless it was an Easter egg hunt. He said it very matter-of-factly, so I had to ask what that meant. He said that some vineyards had so many problems that finding the good fruit was like an Easter egg hunt—and then it probably wasn't such a great proposition.

When we returned, Dane made the calculations on adding acid to several of the wines. The wine industry uses tartaric acid as an additive to some wines to get the correct balance of sugar and acidity to optimize the wine. He made calculations based on the current acid levels and the various goal levels and sizes of containers. He made calculations for me to add acid to the large stainless-steel tank of Sauvignon Blanc, as well as the smaller tank and the four barrels. I also was to add acid to the fermenting Pinot Gris that was a "custom crush" for one of his clients.

After that, Dane thanked me for helping with these projects and told me to take a couple of bottles of the 2007 Angela's Cuvée when I left for the day. This was his rosé wine that was dedicated to his wife, Angela. It was very nice of him, and I know he wanted to give me something for all the work I was doing—no matter how many times I told him that he was giving me the experience of a lifetime. On the other hand, Angela's Cuvée very cold is quite a treat, so I didn't mind the offer at all.

After he left, I went to work adding the acid. First I sterilized two five-gallon buckets with peracetic acid and rinsed them out. Then I measured the tartaric acid, 100 grams for each of the barrels, 3.2 pounds for the stainless tank, 0.8 pounds for the other SB tank, and one pound for the Pinot Gris. In the case of the barrels, I mixed it with juice from each barrel and then added the mixture back into that barrel. In the case of the larger containers, I dipped out juice from each of them, mixed it with the tartaric acid, and poured it back into the respective container. All went well until I tackled the large stainless-steel tank. There was a valve near the bottom of the tank. I opened it a bit, and Sauvignon Blanc came hissing out. I filled the five-gallon bucket, ascended the ladder, and began to pour it in. I noticed that all of the tartaric had not dissolved, so I went back down and repeated the procedure. I had to do it four times in total to get the acid dissolved.

With this complete, I punched down the Zinfandel for the second time that day, locked up, and left with my two bottles of Angela's Cuvée to chill in our refrigerator at home. I felt good that I had been able to take on new tasks; my chemistry courses in high school and college certainly helped all day. But it also felt good to know that I was truly helping Dane that day, freeing him up to do other things, while getting important work done at the winery as well.

On the way home, I got a call from JJ Harris, our neighbor and good friend up the street. She had checked her vineyard and found some raisining starting to occur. I told her that I would stop by and get some samples to be tested at the winery tomorrow. When I got home, I grabbed a plastic bag and went up to their Cabernet Sauvignon vineyard. Sure enough, it was showing some signs of raisins at one end. But this was also a very young vineyard, as I said before, so it was due to be a bit uneven. I cut clusters from all around the vineyard and bagged them for testing.

SEPTEMBER 9, 2008

Today was overcast and in the mid-sixties when I left Los Altos Hills, and it was the same temperature as I arrived in Livermore. When I arrived, no one was around. I saw Michael's car, so I figured he and Dane must have gone to pick up the Chardonnay at the vineyard where we dropped off bins yesterday.

As I wandered onto the crush pad, Lynn came out of the lab. I gave her the samples I had taken from the Harris vineyard. After a brief chat, and a small skirmish with the kittens, who were trying to get into the lab, she went inside to test the grapes.

Dane and Michael pulled up a few minutes later with the fruit. I was still wearing shorts, even though it was a chilly morning. So were Dane and Michael. But both of them had on sweatshirts and hats, though Dane won the prize today because he had on a green knit ski cap, complete with ear covers and dangling ties in case he wanted to secure it tightly to his head. All in all, it was a very cute outfit for the winemaker set!

I was becoming much better with the forklift, and I set about removing the bins from the truck and readying them for the press. When I had finished this, Dane and I pushed the large, plastic 500-gallon tank onto the forklift, and I slowly drove it over to the barrel washer. With Dane guiding me, I set the tank's opening on top of the barrel washer. He turned on the washer and rinsed out the tank, readying it for the Chardonnay we were about to press. When that was done, I carefully lifted it off the barrel washer and moved it to a spot near the press, where we offloaded it onto a pallet and connected the hose from the pump to the tank.

At this point, Michael was ready with the chute and the press. I dumped three bins into the chute, with Michael ensuring that it all got in. I only spilled a couple of clusters on my first bin and none after that. I was improving and not losing the profits. After three bins, Michael closed up the press and set it for a single inflation of the membrane, which produced a large initial shot of juice but also made room for the remaining two bins. Once this cycle was done, I added the other two bins, and we began to press the juice.

On the pump, there was a valve that can be used to introduce argon gas. The hose from the gas tank could be screwed onto this valve; just like an intravenous line can introduce fluids or medication, this valve enabled the addition of argon gas. As it is heavier than oxygen but lighter than the juice, it will rise above the juice in the tank but seal out the oxygen. Michael had the argon line hooked up as the pump filled the tank.

When I was finished with each bin, I rinsed it out and put it back on the truck. When we had finished all the bins, I replaced all the stakes on the truck and took it to the public scales for the tare weight. The net was 4,320 pounds, just a few hundred pounds over two tons of Chardonnay grapes, which was about what Dane was hoping for.

When I returned, Dane had just given Lynn a sample of the estate Petite Sirah for testing. She walked out a few minutes later with a beaker full of juice. We each took a sip. It was very sweet. Dane had the idea to have each of us predict the test results. Dane went first, predicting Brix, TA (titratable acidity), and pH. Michael and I were thinking about it. I predicted a slightly higher Brix, but I hadn't had any experience with tasting for TA, let alone pH. Michael guessed a lower Brix and lower TA than Dane. The Brix had us all fooled, as it was a point higher than my guess. Dane was within .01 on pH, and the TA was higher than Dane's high score. What it meant was that Dane needed to plan to harvest the Petite Sirah very soon.

I also asked about the numbers for the Harris vineyard. Their numbers also indicated time to harvest, with Brix at 25.4. Dane called Russ Harris to discuss the timing of picking. They settled on a Saturday harvest. Russ and JJ were planning to have a harvest party, like we did. Unfortunately, we would be attending the christening of some friends' first baby, so we would be unable to come to their first harvest. I was actually disappointed, as I love to pick grapes. Oh, well, there was always next year. Oh, and our harvest in the coming weeks—I wouldn't be missing that.

I ran an errand for Dane to pick up some dry ice, which he used to cool down the Chardonnay, as a means of getting fermentation started a bit more slowly. Interestingly, Lucky Market sold dry ice. It was kept under lock and key, and it came in plastic bags, which were then double bagged in paper, and it was still too cold to handle for more than a few minutes. I also grabbed sandwiches for lunch before driving back to the winery.

I broke up the dry ice and put it into the tank. The minute the dry ice hit the liquid, it began to fog and boil. There was many a cackle and witch imitations from Dane and Michael in those first few minutes, but like the dry ice, it quickly died down, thankfully.

As we sat down for lunch, Dane brought out a wine in an unlabeled bottle. He opened it and set it before Michael and me, pouring us each a glass. He then asked us to tell him what it was. By looking at it and smelling it, I could tell that it was an older wine. The bottle was a burgundy bottle, so it was probably a Pinot Noir or a Syrah. As I looked at it and tasted it, there wasn't a great deal of fruit, but it wasn't a Syrah. I thought to myself that it was an older Pinot Noir, but kept it to myself. Michael thought about it and said he thought it was a Pinot. Dane said he was right. (I was right too, I thought.) It was a 2001 Bien Nacido Pinot Noir.

Bien Nacido was a huge vineyard in Santa Maria, California, and Dane had been getting Pinot Noir, Chardonnay, and Pinot Blanc from Bien Nacido for years. Only this year they had decided to stop doing business with their smaller wineries, and Page Mill was notified a few months ago that there would be no Bien Nacido fruit. It was disheartening, as Dick Stark, Dane's dad, had built the relationship when the vineyard was just getting started and helped put it on the map. To be left out like this was bad form, very bad form.

Back to the wine, though. It was browning at the edges, and the first smell told you that it was an older wine. The first sip had little fruit, but it was dry and interesting nonetheless. Dane told us that he had twenty-five cases of it, and it was his Quintessence Pinot Noir, named for fruit exclusively from the Q Block of Bien Nacido. He had never found the right time to release it, and he was wondering if he should. We got to give our opinions.

After a few minutes of the above explanation, I took another sip, and it had changed. The older smell was gone, replaced by some fruit and tannins. The taste was still very dry, but you could taste the flavors. It was a wine that I thought would go well with Brie and almonds—and dried fruit, Dane suggested. I agreed. He was thinking about including it in his wine club shipment. Both Michael and I thought it would be a very interesting wine, and that it would benefit from a description of what to expect and how to handle the wine. Dane just listened, so we would have to wait and see what would happen with it.

I helped clean up the press and left for the day.

SEPTEMBER 10, 2008

Gary and I carpooled to the winery today. It was overcast again, so I brought a sweatshirt (that never left the car). Today was barbecue Wednesday, and it was my turn to cook. I had prepared red sauce made from tomatoes from our garden, and I had added onions and mushrooms. I also brought along Italian sausage that I would grill, as well as zucchini marinated overnight in Italian dressing that I would also grill; thus barbecue Wednesday was being upheld. We stopped on the way in for bread, and I got a fresh-baked loaf of Pugliese bread.

When I arrived, Dane was again in the ski cap, except this time Michael had brought one as well; he asked if I hadn't gotten the memo on hats, and then he smiled. He showed Gary and me his latest refinement. There were two planks laid on either side of the press to hold the plastic chute in place as the grapes were dumped into the press. They had fallen out a day or so before, so Michael was bent on a new design that wouldn't fall out. What he showed us this morning was a major step forward. He had notched the wood and even carved out a groove, so now when they were placed on the press, they slid into place solidly. We would test them later today, as Dane informed us that we were getting a custom crush job of Viognier grapes from the young winemaker at Big White House Winery in Livermore Valley.

But first, I needed to clean out the grill so that I would be prepared for my lunch today. It appeared that at one time, the grill had been a propane grill. By now, briquettes were the mode of barbecuing, so the ash from several previous barbecues needed to be cleaned out. I dumped out the ash and cleaned the grate. I also made sure that I had the hotplate set up. With that, I was ready to cook!

But first we had to rack the Chardonnay from yesterday from the large plastic tank to a fermenting tank, and prepare the press for the incoming Viognier, which was due in about an hour. Gary and I worked together, first sterilizing the hoses with a peracetic acid solution and doing the same with the fermenting bin. Then we rinsed everything with water, set the racking wand in the tank, and turned on the pump. The racking wand is a curved stainless-steel pipe with an adjustable opening at the end. It enables the hose to stand on the bottom of a tank, allowing liquid to be pumped out of the tank to the point of being very nearly dry.

Once we had racked most of the juice, we put the tank on the forklift as Dane and I had done yesterday, this time with Gary driving and me directing him into the barrel washer. After it was cleaned, we moved it back out of the way, at just about the time the Viognier arrived. John, the winemaker at Big White House, unloaded the fruit.

It was nearly noon, so my part in the winemaking process was preparing lunch. Everything was about making wine, no matter what you were working on at Page Mill. I had fired up a pile of briquettes half an hour earlier, and they were covered with a thin coat of ash and ready to go. I began to heat up the pasta and extra sauce on the hot plate. Then I cooked the sausage and zucchini, and soon everything was ready.

Meanwhile, Gary and John had loaded the fruit into the press and had just started the cycle. The timing was good. I put the lunch on our table, and everyone sat down. Michael had brought a Barbera/Zinfandel blend from Shenandoah Valley, which is in California's Sierra foothills and overlaps with places like Amador County, known for its Zinfandels. Dane came out of the tasting room with Sauvignon Blanc and a half bottle of Syrah. This was a feast, and we all enjoyed the food and wines. The bread was also excellent for sopping up sauce, which Michael enjoyed.

After lunch, Gary and John went back to finish the pressing. John wanted to get an initial lot of fruit into one of his barrels, so they were carefully pumping this juice into the barrel. Meanwhile Dane brought out his guitar, and Dane, Michael, and I took turns playing songs. Both Michael and I were rusty; even as we remembered songs, we didn't have all the lyrics down, so it was a little hit-or-miss. Dane had his music with him, so he played several complete songs. We all joined in on each other's songs where we could. It was fun, and it energized Michael and me to do a little homework for next week.

Dane was finishing up a song when Gary and John walked up. Dane stopped, looked at them, and said, "I guess you're ready for the press, huh?" He looked a bit disappointed but jumped right up to help. I took my cue and began to clean up from lunch. I joined them at the press as John was filling the barrels on his truck. Dane, Gary, and I went into the barrel storage room and discussed the upcoming weekend's logistics. Dane confirmed that they would pick the estate Petite Sirah on Saturday. Gary and I would commute in together on Friday so that I could drive the truck home for the harvest at the Harrises' on Saturday.

After that, Dane said that he'd finish up the pressing and cleanup with John, and that Gary and I didn't need to wait around for the two hours it would take to complete the pressing, just to help clean up. So we said our goodbyes for the day, and I packed up my cooler with the remnants of lunch and headed home.

SEPTEMBER 11, 2008

I got going earlier today because I was leaving at around 12:30. When I arrived at the winery, the sun was just about breaking through the overcast.

Gary was watering the plants, and we both spent a few minutes watching the kittens playing. I commented that it was amazing that kittens were some of the most playful animals on the planet, and these two were right up there. They jumped and contorted their bodies for no apparent reason. They played with each other or played alone—it didn't seem to matter. What is interesting is that grown cats are among the most aloof animals. Our cat, Midnight, was a prime example. He was a great cat, but he really didn't have time for anyone. So I reflected on what happened from kitten to cat, while watching Cindy and Belle having a great time. I only hoped, for Dane and Gary, that the kittens would become great mousers and earn their keep at the winery. But Dane's girls loved them, so I guess they were in solid!

I went into the barrel room to say hello to Dane. He asked me to punch down and check Brix and temperatures of the fermenting bins of Zinfandel and the small tank of Cab/Merlot.

I got the punchdown tool and went into the stable to punch down the tanks. There was a noticeable difference from when I had punched down these same tanks on Monday. On Monday, there had been lots of activity in the bins, and as I punched down, there was obvious CO_2 being released and purple foam, which evidenced the fermentation frenzy. I could also sense the heat of the bins.

Today as I punched down, much of that energy was gone in all of the tanks. I had expected that in the small tank, as it was a week ahead of the Zinfandel. But the Zinfandel tanks had obviously calmed their fermentation as well. Also, there was definite separation between the skins and the juice. The skins formed a cap on top of the fermenting juice, whereas on Monday the grapes were somewhat more intact, so there wasn't as much free juice as there was today, a mere three days later.

As I checked Brix, all three Zin tanks were in the single digits, but fermentation clearly had slowed. The temperatures were also lower, in the high seventies and low eighties.

When I shared this with Dane, he told me that the fermentation had probably stopped and most of the natural yeast was dead. He decided to think about it a bit.

Gary and I drove off to UDS, which was the retail storage area for Page Mill. This was a warehouse in North Livermore that I had been to with Gary a month or so ago. He kept most recent vintages at this location and pulled from it for the tasting room or for online or phone orders. We picked up four cases of the recently released 2006 Zinfandel, two cases of the newly released 2007 Chardonnay, and a case of the 2007 Sauvignon Blanc.

When we returned, Dane had decided that we would press the Zinfandel and then add yeast, which would restart the fermentation and complete the process to the level Dane was looking for: no residual sugar, and a completely dry wine.

The process had changed from ten years earlier. In the past, Dane and other winemakers would add small amounts of sulfite to the must, which is the freshly crushed grapes with the skins and seeds. This would kill the natural yeast. The next day, the must would be inoculated with a specific strain of yeast designed to produce a fully dry product.

Since then, there had been a movement to allow the natural yeast to begin the fermentation process. These so-called wild yeasts add to the complexity and flavors of the wine, according to some people. Certainly not using even small quantities of sulfites in the early stages is nothing but good for wine-making flavors. Dane said that often the natural yeast died off before fully fermenting all of the sugar, so at that point he could judiciously add yeast to complete the fermentation process.

The Zinfandel had come to this point, where fermentation had slowed way down, yet there was still significant sugar, as evidenced by the single-digit Brix readings.

We began to prepare to press the Zinfandel. I worked the forklift. This was nothing but fun for me. In the two weeks since I had first driven the forklift, I had improved measurably, and I went about the various tasks of changing the fork and putting on the box-dumper like a champ.

First I needed to move several of the tanks out of the stable and move the three tanks of Zinfandel into position for processing. After I had gotten these tanks out and put the others back into the stable, I took off the heavy-duty fork and put on the box-dumper. This entailed moving the forklift into position to grab the attachment. Once I did that, I raised it up, changed the hydraulics so that the dumping action worked, and screwed on the plate that held it on the forklift. Over the past few weeks, I had observed and even helped in this process. Today I took all responsibility for the forklift, removing and adding attachments all by myself.

While I was doing this, Dane and Gary were rinsing and readying the press and pressure-washing the tanks into which the Zinfandel juice would be transferred.

When the tanks were in place, we first pumped the free juice into the tank. Gary inserted a four-inch piece of perforated PVC into the first Zinfandel tank. He then stuck the intake end of the hose into the PVC. This allowed us to pump the free juice into the new tank first, taking much of the weight out of the tank. When this was finished, I used the forklift with the box-dumper attachment to grab the tank, raise it up, and dump it into the chute that fed the press. If we attempted to pour a full tank into the press, it would have been awkward to dump the full bin, and I'm not sure how the forklift would have handled that much weight at the height required to dump it.

As it was, Dane gave me guidance on maneuvering the tank and positioning it to be dumped. I had the knack of the half-ton bins, but these were four feet tall. But owing to my newfound experience with the forklift and some hand signals from Dane, I dumped the tank into the press without spilling a drop of profits … I mean, juice.

Once this was done, Dane started the press, and even more juice began to fill the tank. At this point, it was after noon, and the press would take another two hours to finish its cycle. I said my goodbyes for the day. I had to go to a meeting on the peninsula, but I would take samples of the Campi and Arey Chardonnay vineyards later in the afternoon to bring to Lynn tomorrow morning.

After my meeting, I went up to the two vineyards, which were side by side, and took cluster samples from throughout each vineyard. I tasted the grapes in both vineyards and thought they tasted sweet. Additionally, the seeds were brown, which was a sign of ripeness. But I was anxious to find out how close these vineyards were to being ready to harvest. Also, we had crushed Livermore Valley Chardonnay earlier in the week, so I wanted to see how far behind the peninsula was. I guess I would just have to wait until tomorrow.

Even though I knew our vineyard wasn't close to ready, I decided to take a few clusters to Lynn tomorrow, just to see where we stood.

SEPTEMBER 12, 2008

Gary picked me up at 8:00 AM, just as I was out in our vineyard, grabbing a few clusters. There was a heavier than usual overcast this morning, but the weekend forecast was for a warming trend.

We arrived at the winery, and I gave my samples to Lynn for testing—Campi and Arey Chardonnay and our Merlot.

Steve, a vineyard manager who was a custom crush customer, dropped off two small lots of fruit—Malbec and Cab Franc. I unloaded it from his truck while Gary got the destemmer and a tank ready. I put the fermentation tank inline on the pallets, so we were ready to go.

I loaded the fruit into the destemmer in two quick trips. The destemmer made quick work of the fruit. Gary pulled out the bin of berries with a pallet jack, and I grabbed it with the box-dumper. Then we moved the chute over the fermentation tank, and I got back into the forklift and dumped the bin into the tank. We rinsed out the bin, as we'd done with the two bins in which Steve had delivered the fruit. All of this took about fifteen minutes. We then spent the next thirty minutes cleaning the destemmer in preparation for the estate Petite Sirah we would process next.

Dane had told me before that it was probably just as much work to make ten gallons of wine as it was to make a thousand gallons of wine. Given all of the steps required in cleaning and setup, I'm not sure this was far off.

Gary then took the truck loaded with two bins of Petite Sirah to get a weight. These bins had been picked that morning by Leopoldo and his crew. Leopoldo had worked for Dane for a number of years, mostly on the peninsula. He and his team helped care for the peninsula vineyards and harvested them. He had work in Livermore today, so he and his crew came out a few hours early to get a start on the harvest.

After Gary left, I put a "skin" of plastic over the tank with the Malbec and Cab Franc, and then I added a layer of CO_2 gas over the fruit. Then I moved it into the stable, where it was cooler, to allow it to settle overnight.

Lynn came out of the lab with the results for the samples I'd given her. The Chardonnay vineyards were both at 24 Brix, and the Côté Merlot was at 22.8, so I felt comfortable in assuming that we had another couple of weeks before harvest. I took the numbers in to where Dane was working. He looked at them and said that while the Brix were fine for the Chardonnay vineyards, the pH and TA (acidity) were too high. He mentioned that this was occurring in much of the fruit he had received thus far, and he had heard it was happening all over California as the harvest of 2008 began to take off.

His specific plan of attack was to let the sugars go higher and bring more balance to the pH and TA. Selfishly, I was interested in what he thought about our vineyard. Again he said that he would go for higher sugars to make sure that everything else was balanced, and that it would be three weeks or more before harvest, given a normal weather pattern for September and October.

I was beginning to think about what this might mean for the 2008 Côté Merlot—a subject I would enjoy discussing with Dane as it got closer. From earlier conversations, I knew that he was anxious to have me take a more active hand in making the Côté this year. When he had mentioned it a month ago, I had said that I would look over his shoulder. Now I was feeling like taking more of it on directly, which was what Dane wanted. Still, we'd see when the fruit came in.

Before Gary returned, I was able to prepare for processing the Petite Sirah. I finished cleaning the destemmer and set up for the Petite Sirah, putting the destemmer back together and running it to make sure that everything was working. I pressure-washed a fermentation tank and set it on the pallets, ready for the chute.

I finished all of this just as Gary pulled up with the truck. Gary jumped on the forklift and unloaded the fruit heading for the chute and the destemmer. I worked the chute this time, while Gary dumped the fruit. As I mentioned before, these were some of the darkest-colored grapes I had ever seen. The clusters were very tight and fairly large. The fruit was beautiful, without much, if any, raisining and no mold or other rot. When I mentioned this to Gary, he agreed but went on to say that the section that Leopoldo had picked was the poorest part of the vineyard. If this was representative of the poorest fruit in the vineyard, it would be a beautiful harvest, and this fruit would become a stellar wine. Remember, this was the Petite Sirah that had won a gold medal in San Francisco for the 2005, which was Dane's first vintage. I couldn't wait to taste what this fruit would deliver.

Gary and I finished up with the Petite, put a skin on the tank, and moved it into the shade of the stable. We then cleaned the destemmer and surrounding crush pad for the second time today.

Just as we finished, Dane came out of the barrel storage room and asked us if we were on strike for the rest of the day. We both looked at him, and he laughed. He asked us to move all of the equipment to one end of the pad which we did. He wanted to have room to wash barrels in preparation for receiving the Chardonnay we had processed earlier this week, and for upcoming wines.

I used the forklift to set the first two barrels on the barrel washer. I moved very cautiously, as this was more precise work than I was used to. Dane helped guide me in. Nonetheless, it took me five minutes from the time I picked up the rack of two barrels until Dane turned on the barrel washer.

I went off to grab sandwiches, and when I returned, Dane was working the barrel washer himself. He grabbed a rack of two barrels and set them on the washer, all in about thirty seconds. I guess practice does pay off.

Gary and I loaded up the truck that I would drive home. I was going to leave it at the Harrises' up the street for their harvest tomorrow morning. I am a big fan of picking grapes and always look forward to picking our vineyard. I am also happy to help anyone else who needs help harvesting. Denise and I were going to the christening of a friends' new baby tomorrow, so I couldn't help Russ and JJ Harris or Dane, who was picking the rest of the estate Petite Sirah tomorrow. I was sure there would be other opportunities, but I was disappointed that I couldn't help.

I was excited about going to the christening, though. George and Natalie were Russian, and we went to their wedding at the Russian Orthodox Church in Burlingame two years before. It was a beautiful ceremony, and there was a great party afterward, with a bottle of vodka for toasts at every table. The christening was to be held at the same church, so we were looking forward to the ceremony—and the celebration afterward.

Back to loading. We put two half-ton bins on the truck, as we expected less than a ton of fruit. This was Russ and JJ's first harvest of their three-year-old Cabernet Sauvignon vineyard. We also put in thirty FYBs (remember, effing yellow boxes) to be used by the harvesters. But we also loaded in 230 FYBs that a guy Dane knew wanted to buy from him here on the peninsula. He would be at Russ and JJ's tomorrow, so I was bringing him the bins. All of this filled the truck, and we strapped it all down.

Gary and I said our goodbyes to Dane, and Gary followed me to the gas station to fill the truck with diesel, using the winery's credit card, and then he headed for home. I got on the road and had an uneventful drive home, though it seemed that everyone was a little close to me on the freeway. I guess I just wasn't used to the length and width of the truck in traffic.

On the drive home, I realized that today had been a breakthrough day. Several times during the day, I had worked alone on tasks that three weeks ago I'd have had no clue about. I had removed the heavy fork and put the box-dumper attachment on the forklift with no assistance, which included removing a pair of the forklift hydraulic system hoses and replacing them with the box-dumper hydraulics. While Gary had gone to weigh the truck with the Petite Sirah and Dane was working in the barrel room, I cleaned and reassembled the destemmer, running it to make sure that everything was working. I had pressure-washed a fermentation tank and set it on the pallets, ready for the chute. I had put plastic skins on a fermentation tank and gassed it with CO_2. I was getting comfortable with a number of the tasks associated with making wine at Page Mill Winery. This was more than just Dane or Gary giving me tasks; I was contributing to the real work of the winery, without direction. It felt good, and we had only just begun the harvest.

I arrived on my street and drove past my house to the Harrises', parked the truck, and walked up to the house. JJ was home, so we discussed the plan for tomorrow and the logistics of everything going on.

SEPTEMBER 15, 2008

Today marked the beginning of my fourth week full time at the winery. As I went over Pigeon Pass and into Livermore Valley, the overcast was just beginning to burn off, and the vineyards looked green and lush in the brightening morning. As I pulled into the parking lot at Page Mill Winery, it was clear that the Petite Sirah vineyard had been picked. Obviously there were no grapes, but there was more to it. I realize that this is ascribing too much human emotion to a vineyard, but it looked exhausted. Canes seemed to droop. There was more browning of the leaves than I had noticed last week, and the vines just looked worn out. I remembered feeling the same way as I walked in my own vineyard after harvest. I had always thought it was just a reflection of how tired I felt after a long and wonderful harvest day, but here it was in Dane's Petite Sirah vineyard, and I was fresh and rested. The vineyard had clearly done its work and was ready for the long rest it was due. Dane would water the vineyard today, to refresh the vines after the rush of harvest.

Dane was in the stable when I arrived, so we took a minute to discuss the weekend's goings-on. He had received a good response to his request for help and had a good group of people to pick the Petite. He had barbecued, and then his band played music for everyone. In total, including the fruit that was picked and processed on Friday, he'd gotten about four tons of fruit. On Friday I had remarked how beautiful the fruit was, and he said that what they'd picked on Saturday was even more beautiful, if that was possible. He was very pleased.

We also discussed the Harrises' harvest. They had gotten about 750 pounds of fruit. Dane hoped that it would be enough for a barrel. He said the numbers were very good on their Cabernet, particularly for a young vineyard. I told him that Denise had spoken with Russ on Saturday evening, and they were excited. Both Denise and I remembered that feeling of the first harvest, so we could relate. But Russ and JJ would be pleased to hear that the numbers were good.

Then Dane and I discussed the tasks for the day. There wasn't any fruit coming in, so Dane was hoping to leave early to get to his band practice and class, which occurred every Monday. One of the tasks for the day was checking inventory for bottling later in the week. Dane talked about bottling our Merlot on Wednesday, which meant blending and filtering the final wine tomorrow for Wednesday. Dane also remembered that we were planning to do a few cases of magnums, so he made a note to pick some up for the bottling.

I began my morning by punching down the four bins of Petite Sirah, the Harrises' Cab, and the small lot of Malbec/Cab Franc from last Friday. I didn't take any measurements for sugar or temperature. When I opened each tank for punchdown, I smelled for CO_2 signaling the start of fermentation. None of the tanks had really started yet, so there was no sense in measuring the Brix, and it had been cool over the weekend, so temperature wasn't an imminent problem. After punchdown, I gassed each tank with a combination of argon and CO_2.

That completed, I jumped on the forklift to move the tanks to the covered patio next to the barrel room. As I picked up the first tank, Dane was getting something out of the tool room. I asked him to take a picture of me on the forklift. Next Sunday was my brother Kevin's birthday, and I planned to send him a copy of the picture, telling him that the next time he came up to visit, as a birthday gift, I'd give him forklift lessons. While this was true, I was really sending it to him to make him jealous of my good fortune!

As I finished moving the first of the tanks, Dane stopped me and said, "Come on, let's do some real work." We went into the barrel room, and he used a wine thief to pull a sample from the Pinot Gris to test for dryness. A wine thief is a glass tube with a bend in it that is used to draw a sample out of a barrel or a tank.

First we smelled and tasted the Pinot Gris. It tasted very good to me, and Dane seemed very pleased. This fruit had come in at very high Brix, and it seemed that Dane was coaxing the very best out of this fruit. Next he did a sugar pill test. This was a test that used pills made for diabetics to test their blood sugar at a very granular level. Dane and others had found it very useful for testing the dryness of wines that are at or near complete fermentation.

Dane put ten drops of the Pinot Gris into a test tube, added a pill, and swirled it all together. The pill began to foam and color the juice a bluish green. This color signaled a dry wine, and given Dane's satisfaction with the taste of the wine, the Pinot Gris was progressing nicely. I remember now seeing Lynn use the same test, and the color was orange, which I now knew meant that there was residual sugar in whatever sample she was testing.

I went back outside to finish moving the tanks and then went on an errand to drop off empty five-gallon water containers at the Culligan franchise in town and drop off a case of wine at UPS that was bound for a customer in Hawaii.

When I returned, Dane was in the lab, talking to Lynn. He had a glass of new white wine, which he handed to me. I could tell right away from the smell that it was the Sauvignon Blanc. It was now bone-dry, but you could smell and taste the fruit, tropical and citrus, already in this very young wine. It was going to be great. Dane was already getting excited about it.

That, in fact, was our next task for the day. We racked the extra tank of Sauvignon Blanc as well as the four barrels into the large, plastic 500-gallon tank, after thoroughly pressure-washing it and running it through the barrel washer. When this was done, Dane moved the four barrels out of the barrel storage room, and then I took over, washing each pair of barrels on the barrel washer and moving them just off the crush pad for later use.

When this was finished, I went back into the stable, where Dane was taking inventory on bottles, labels, corks, and foil for the bottling on Wednesday. Other than the magnum bottles, he had everything we would need. As it was nearly three, we both got ready to leave. I asked him if there was any fruit coming in this week. He thought about it and said that we should probably plan on the Campi and Arey Chardonnay vineyards for later in the week. I told him that I'd get samples when I got home today, so we could see where we were and make more definite plans. He agreed, and I was on my way home.

I stopped at home to pick up a couple of large plastic bags for samples, and I timed it perfectly, as Denise came home for a few minutes on her way to help her mother. We got a chance for a quick hello, a kiss, and a hug, and we were both on our way, agreeing to meet back home in a few hours.

I got both sets of samples. The fruit looked good, and the seeds were definitely turning brown: a key sign of ripeness. I suspected that the end of the week would be our target for these vineyards—but I'd learn more tomorrow.

SEPTEMBER 16, 2008

When I arrived at the winery, Dane was in the barrel storage room, working on paperwork. We said our hellos, and he showed me the task list for the day. There were the usual punchdowns, as well as the need to check Brix on some of the tanks. We needed to take samples of the Syrah vineyard next door as well. But the big task for the day was to decide the blend for the Côté 2006 Merlot that we would bottle tomorrow.

I had also brought in the samples of the Campi and Arey vineyards for testing, but Lynn wasn't due to arrive until 11:00 AM.

I set about doing the punchdown for the four tanks of estate Petite Sirah, the Harris Cabernet, and the small lot of Malbec/Cabernet Franc (for the Johnson vineyard, as I found out from Dane). The Petite was just getting started with fermentation, and I could smell the early signs of CO_2 gas. Also, when I punched down, there was purplish foam in the must, showing activity. The Harris Cab was also just getting started.

After this, I got out the hydrometer with the 5 to -5 scale to measure the Brix of the Zinfandel, the small lot of Cab/Merlot, and the Chardonnay, all of which were coming to the end of fermentation. The Zinfandels ranged from 2.6 to 3.3 Brix and smelled of CO_2. We had pressed the Zin last week, and Dane had added a finishing yeast, which seemed to have taken hold. The Cab/Merlot was at -1 Brix, so it was nearly finished, and the Chardonnay was at .6 Brix, so it too was nearly dry. In the next day or so, we'd perform the sugar pill test to get more accurate readings.

Dane had gone off to run an errand, so I finished up the tests and went next door to gather sample clusters from the Syrah vineyard. By the time I finished, Dane had returned and Lynn had arrived, so I gave her the samples of Syrah, and she went in to perform tests on these samples and several others that had been dropped off that morning.

Dane and I went back into the barrel room to prepare the samples for tasting the '06 Merlots, with an eye toward getting the blend we'd use in bottling the Côté tomorrow. I counted the number of '06 Merlot barrels in the storage room, and there were eight barrels of Côté and five barrels of other Merlots, for a total of thirteen barrels of '06 Merlot, of course.

Dane also wanted to taste the '06 estate Petite Sirah to decide any blending we might do next week when we planned to bottle it.

As I was setting out the glasses for the sampling and marking them with the various barrels, varietals, and vineyards, Dane and I began talking about the business. He was wondering aloud whether he should take on more custom crush clients. There was a growing number of small wineries, and even growers that had no capability to make their own wine and were coming to Dane and others for custom crush. The challenge that Dane outlined for me was that he had a capacity problem. He could store barrels for the production of three thousand cases of wine. In 2007, the winery had produced about 2,200 cases, and the plan for this year was to increase that to 2,500 cases on the way to 3,000 in the following year or two.

So for every custom crush customer that required production and storage all the way through bottling, Dane would soon be trading off his own production for the custom crush clients. He was having a hard time finding barrel storage space, and it was expensive. So if he took on clients, they would need to pay handsomely for the costs Dane would incur, to allow him to make as much profit as he would with his own wines.

We agreed that it was absolutely opportunity cost, but the other point we discussed was that often these custom crush customers had small lots, and as he had told me before, it takes as much work to process a small batch as a large batch, and that extends to punchdown, racking, and so on. Remember, 90 percent of winemaking is cleanup. Whether you do two hundred pounds or two tons, you still have to clean the destemmer and the press, put the fruit in a tank, and punch it down three times a day, among other tasks. We discussed his P&L, his overhead, and his variable costs. He really needed to get to the 3,000-case capacity to start making money, and the question was whether or not custom crush helped or hindered that.

After we discussed it, my observation was that Dane had a real dilemma. Small-lot producers might pay an exorbitant amount to have their small amounts of fruit show up in bottles with their own labels, so they might be willing to pay the equivalent of $250–$300 a case, a point at which Dane could make money. These small lots took too much time on a relative basis, even if people would pay. The larger customers were typically small, virtual wineries or people just getting started. Even though they might bring in enough fruit to make it more efficient, they would be unwilling to pay higher prices because they were in turn trying to sell their wines. Neither option made a lot of sense until such time as Dane had excess capacity and labor, so that he could truly use a marginal cost analysis to make the economics work.

The one thing that I suggested did make sense was using an idle asset during off times. The best example was his membrane press and opportunities like the Jonathan Christopher Chardonnay we had processed several weeks back. If the press was not already in use, Dane could make use of it to process fruit, pumping it into a tank for overnight settling, or right into the customer's barrels. In either case, he would be using his idle asset for a very limited time and not bearing the brunt of the other areas of a turn-key custom crush operation. He could generate cash with no downside to his scarce resources or time. These types of opportunities might make good sense, but custom crush in general distracted from the main work of building and growing the winery.

I told him that his energy would be better spent figuring out how to make an extra buck or two per bottle; more on that later. He said that this called into question all of his small custom crush business as a distraction, and he said he needed to think about whether or not to continue any of it.

For me it was an interesting discussion that drew on my understanding of running a business, but it also gave me insight into the unique aspects of the wine business, with its high fixed overhead and lower variable costs. It was also clear that if Dane could get more money for his wine, through quality products, marketing, or both, that would be a big lever.

When I looked at my iPhone to see what time it was, we had spent forty-five minutes discussing the business. I think Dane found the discussion helpful, and I found it fascinating. But we needed to get ready for bottling.

When we took a break and went out into the sun, Lynn had finished running the samples I had brought. The two Chardonnay vineyards, Campi and Arey, hadn't moved much in Brix over the past four days. Based on that and their higher acid numbers, Dane decided that I should get samples again in a week, and we'd assess the situation. The Syrah was only about 23 Brix, so it was a week or so away. When Dane called his neighbors with the news, he found out that they had been watering regularly. This will hold the Brix down in the grapes and require longer hang time until harvest. Given that this year had been progressing early in many cases, Dane felt that it was okay to give the Syrah more hang time. He did ask that they cut the watering in half.

We went back inside to begin blending. First, Dane went up into the barrels to get the samples with the wine thief. When we had all of the samples in front of us, Dane suggested that we focus first on the Côté. There were samples from the eight barrels of our '06 and we were selecting the two best barrels to be bottled as the Côté vineyard designated Merlot – about 50 cases. The other barrels would be blended with the remaining 5 barrels from small Merlot vineyards to create the '06 Page Mill California Merlot.

Interestingly, we narrowed them down to four, based on the smell and color alone. We were definitely dealing in degrees here, at least for me. I did notice differences in the samples we selected, but the other four were also good. We then tasted the four we had selected. It seemed that there were two pairs that tested similarly. Two had more oak, and two seemed to have more fruit in both the smell and the taste.

Dane then used a pipette to create a number of different blends among the four samples. We settled on a pair that we both liked best. As we had discussed a week or so ago when we had tried these wines, we felt they needed a little more complexity or breadth. We tried samples that had a small amount of Petite Sirah (2.5 percent), but even that small amount seemed to overwhelm the Merlot. Next we tried a 10 percent addition of Cabernet Sauvignon. This tasted better, but Dane thought maybe it was too much Cab. So he mixed up a sample with 5 percent Cabernet, which tasted better, keeping the fruit flavors of the Merlot while maintaining some of the tannins and breadth of the Cabernet. All along, we had been tasting samples of the two Merlot barrels alone as a control.

As we finished this last blend, Dane got a look in his eye that was half question and half "Watch this!" He dumped the control into the 5 percent sample; they were both about the same amount. Then he declared, "Let's try 2.5 percent!" We each tried this sample, looked at each other, and smiled. Dane said, "You like?" and I said yes. He went on to say that it added that little bit of breadth from the Cabernet Sauvignon while going a long way in preserving the wonderful fruit in the Merlot. He declared that we had our blend for the 2006 Côté Merlot from barrels 343 and 344, and Cabernet Sauvignon from barrel 113. He would later filter that blend and rack it into a tank for bottling tomorrow.

We then turned our attention to the estate Petite Sirah. We had samples from six barrels. Dane began to smell them, and he handed me one that he thought captured what he wanted in a Petite Sirah. It smelled like cherry pie—it was so ripe with fruit. As we went through the remaining samples, I found one that I thought was similar to his choice, and he agreed. There was one sample that he said had a higher level of VA. I could taste it slightly, and he said that it was not excessively high and might simply go away when blended with the other barrels and filtered. As an example, he poured together the four barrel samples, including the one with the slightly elevated VA. He took a sip and smiled, saying, "Added complexity," and sure enough, the sample did taste more interesting. That is the dilemma with these so-called imperfections. At high levels, they are just plain problems. At lower levels, they may add to the flavors of the wine, not unlike the arguments that go around and around on the subject of slight amounts of "Brett" in wines.

The discussion then turned to whether or not the two samples that were excellent should become a "Vintner's Select" and sell for a higher price. The marketer in me certainly argued for it. It would be an opportunity to make higher margin on the wine, and it would begin to create differentiation that Dane could use in the tasting room and other venues.

Obviously, Dane would think about it, and he wouldn't have to make a decision until next week, as we got ready to bottle the Estate Petite.

By this time, it was late afternoon. I had a dinner to attend that evening, so I helped him clean some hoses in preparation for racking, and then I headed for home. Today had been a very different and quite interesting day.

The discussion about his business and the economics of different aspects certainly fed my own interest in the mechanics of how businesses run and the levers available to improve revenues or margins, or both. But the opportunity to be a part of deciding the blend for the 2006 Côté Merlot was a special treat, and it was one I would savor in the bottles we would drink in the coming years. This experience was one of those that would change the way I thought about and drank wine—another incredible day in this incredible harvest season.

SEPTEMBER 17, 2008

When I arrived in the morning, the place was buzzing as everyone focused on setting up to bottle. With both Michael and Gary at the winery on Wednesdays, there was naturally more activity than on Monday and Tuesday, when it was just Dane and me, or sometimes just me. But today, there was also the energy around bottling and the Wednesday lunch.

Once again, Michael had built an interesting and very helpful tool: an inverse sparger. Sparging is the process of blowing gas into a wine bottle, typically nitrogen, which will help insulate the wine from the air (oxygen) for the brief period between filling and corking. The beauty of an inverse sparger is that while the air is being blown into the bottle, if it is upside down, there is an added benefit of blowing out any unwelcome particles or critters (such as a spider) that might have ended up in the bottle.

I went with Dane to set up the filter for the Côté Merlot that we would be bottling. From yesterday's blending, we would be taking the contents from barrels 343 and 344 to make the Côté, as well as three gallons of the Livermore Cabernet Sauvignon in barrel 113, which would make up the 2.5 percent addition we had decided on yesterday.

Because of the clarity of the wine, we were using what Dane called a "rock and frog" filter. This was a three-micron filter designed to take out only the larger particles; thus the name "rock and frog."

As we were bottling my wine, I got the honor of placing the hose into the barrel. I climbed up into the barrel stacks in the barrel room and placed the hose inside the first barrel.

When I got down, Dane showed me how the filter worked. Wine was delivered into the top of the filter via the pump. The wine was then distributed across a series of filter pads; through a combination of pressure and gravity, the wine was forced through the pads and into the receptors that captured the filtered wine and delivered it out the bottom, via a hose, into the clean tank from which we would bottle.

When we were set to go, Dane turned on the pump and began filtering the wine. Midway through the first barrel, Dane took samples from the top of the filter and the bottom to compare. There wasn't much difference, except the color of the filtered wine was just a bit clearer, as you might expect. But the wine coming out of the barrel was already beautiful.

When the barrel was empty, I turned off the pump, climbed back into the barrel stacks, placed the hose into the other barrel of Merlot, and turned on the pump. When this barrel was empty and filtered, we placed the hose in the Cabernet barrel for our three gallons. Dane was able to estimate this based on the pump speed and time, delivering three gallons to the two barrels of Merlot, completing the blend for the 2006 Côté Merlot. The wine was now ready to be bottled.

As Gary, Michael, and I set up the stations—sparger, filler, corker, spinner (for putting on the foils), and labeler—Dane brought the wine over to the stable where we were setting up to bottle. The tank was placed on a stack of pallets to enable gravity feed for the bottler. Before he lowered the tank, he placed blocks on three of the corners of the top pallet where the tank would sit, thus creating a single low point in the corner without a block. The hose was placed at the bottom in the corner that was the low point. Now we were ready to bottle.

We got into position at our stations, with Dane at the sparger and filler. Michael worked the corker, I would handle the foil with the spinner, and Gary was at the labeler.

I explained the sparger earlier. The filler was a four-bottle filler with a reservoir of wine coming from the tank that serviced the four bottling stations. Once full, a bottle was taken off the bottler and set on the manual corker, which is a very simple affair. The bottle sits on a metal plate. The operator puts a cork into the top of the device and pulls down on the handle. The handle causes the cork to get squeezed, and then a pin in the handle pushes the cork through a small opening into the bottle, where it re-expands. That bottle, with its cork, is handed to the next station, where metal foil is placed over the top of the bottle and the bottle top is pushed into the spinner, which has a series of spinning rollers that smooth the foil around the contours of the bottle. Once complete, the bottle is placed on the table for the labeler.

Before we got started, Dane needed a reading on SO2, which was a measure of sulfites in the wine. This was required as a final step to make sure there was enough—but not too much—sulfite to preserve the wine. Lynn, whose birthday we would celebrate at lunch today, took a bottle of the Merlot for testing, not tasting, which would happen shortly. She was back in a few minutes with a reading that Dane described as perfect!

We were ready to go.

We had just gotten started when it was clear that the spinner wasn't working. I was working that station, and of course I assumed it was operator error on my part, as the foil came out badly wrinkled and not fitting well on the bottle. Everyone laughed until Dane took the housing off the spinner and discovered that the rubber O-rings that kept the rollers in place were all worn out. Michael immediately began to make suggestions, including hair bands that we could get at the local drugstore, or replacement O-rings at the hardware store.

Dane got on the phone and reached Dick Bartlett, the owner of Charles R Vineyards and Randy's dad. Dick was quick to suggest that he bring his spinner down for Dane to borrow. We continued to bottle the wine, including labeling, just holding the bottles aside for foil when Dick brought the spinner. He was there within a few minutes, and we set up his spinner. Within about fifteen minutes, we had caught up on the cases that were awaiting foil, and we continued the overall bottling process.

After a while, Lynn's friend Nancy arrived and they came into the stable where we were bottling. As I said, it was Lynn's birthday today, and we were set to have a party at lunch in honor of Lynn. Michael was cooking and would soon leave the bottling line to begin preparing grilled salmon—pretty fancy, but it was a birthday celebration.

Nancy and Lynn began tasting the Merlot, which I think signaled the beginning of the party. Meanwhile, we were furiously bottling. The hardest part of my job was that the foils were in stacks, and separating the individual pieces could prove troublesome, but after a while and a handful of crumpled foils, I had it under control. If I got ahead of Gary at the labeler, I'd take a filled case box, seal it with tape, and place it on the growing pallet of Côté Merlot.

As lunchtime came around, Michael broke off from bottling to handle his chef duties for the day. We got some timely help from Filippo, Dane's neighbor who made wine for himself and his family but was a stonecutter by trade. Filippo was a classic older Italian gentleman who was quick to give help, and he also grew wonderful tomatoes that we had all enjoyed at lunch. He had come for lunch, but he got roped into manning the filler and corker, as Michael was otherwise occupied.

Michael would come into the stable every so often with a time check. Finally, he came in and asked if we could take a break in five minutes. We were all very happy to comply. We were about halfway finished, having bottled about twenty-five cases up to this point, so a break was welcome. Just as we were finishing up, Lynn's husband and son arrived for lunch.

Michael and Nancy had set up a table for us inside the stable, as it was breezy and in the mid-sixties outside. I was still wearing my sweatshirt, which has to be an indication of how cold it was because I never wore sweatshirts.

As we sat down, Gary arrived with a bottle of the 2007 Chardonnay, and Dane brought over a bottle of the new Merlot, fresh from the filler—the first of many. Michael had also brought a couple bottles of his sparkling wine, a savage (pronounced *sa vaj)* and a brut. The difference between the savage and the brut is that the savage has no added sugar when the yeast is added back to create the sparkling wine. The brut has the least amount of sugar, followed by several other varieties, including sec, which means dry, but it has more residual sugar than the brut.

In any case, they were both very nice, and we poured glasses for everyone and toasted Lynn's birthday. She was fifty-four, which was my age, so we had a special toast between us. Michael then served the salmon and bratwurst (go figure). We had a wonderful Caesar salad that Nancy had brought, and Michael complemented the fish and meat with grilled green onions and a killer green sauce consisting of olive oil, capers, basil, and chopped hard-boiled eggs. He had also grilled bread with olive oil on the barbecue. It was quite a treat. We drank several times to Lynn's good health, and to the health of us all, and the world, and anything else that came to mind. Dane would just go back over to the filler and fill up another bottle of Merlot.

As we sat and enjoyed the afternoon and the meal, we had several visitors, some for lunch and some just to say hello or to try the wine we were bottling. I heard Dane say more than once, "if you like it, I'm the winemaker. If you don't, it's made from Dave's grapes." He knew that everyone would like it, and they did.

After lunch—or should I say after wine?—we slowly, and I mean slowly, got back to bottling the other half of the Merlot. But soon we hit our stride again and quickly saw the new glass in case boxes go down as our pallet of bottled wine grew. Near the end of the bottling, Dane got a visit from a county inspector who was responsible for groundwater runoff and treatment. Dane excused himself and went outside with the inspector. Fortunately, Lynn's son was learning the corker, and another friend of Dane's named Richard was helping as well. We made quick work of the remaining bottles.

As the flow began to slow, Michael climbed up onto the pallet and looked into the tank, watching it until it was empty. When it was, he asked me to walk the hose up to the filler. This simply means that I held the hose over my head, pushing the remaining wine into the filler, making sure we didn't waste any of the wine. I thought it was appropriate that I had started the morning by draining the barrels, and now I was completing the bottling process by exacting the very last drop of wine from the tank. It was ironic that there was a single bottle left at the end of the process—that and fifty cases of 2006 Page Mill Côté Vineyard Merlot. I thought it was very thoughtful and also fitting when Gary handed me the bottle and said that it was for Denise to try the new wine. I loaded up a case, and the bottle for tasting tonight with Denise.

As we were wrapping up and cleaning up, Dane came back in to tell us that the inspector was giving them a passing grade on everything, so that was great for the winery. After cleanup, Gary and I looked at each other and nearly simultaneously said to Dane that we were done for the day. He laughed and thanked us for our hard work. We thanked Michael for lunch and made plans to carpool tomorrow. We then said our goodbyes and headed out, me with a bottle and a case of our newest wine, the tenth official vintage of the Côté Merlot.

So while today's efforts had nothing to do with the harvest of 2008, it was a deeply personal and quite satisfying experience for me to be such a big part of the blending and bottling of the wine from our vineyard. I shared those thoughts with Denise when I got home that night, and we shared her first glass of the new wine. She enjoyed it just as I had, and just as I hoped she would.

SEPTEMBER 18, 2008

Gary met me at my house at around 8:00 AM. I asked him to take a walk into our vineyard with me to get his opinion of how it looked. We pulled a few grapes, tasting them and checking the seeds. Most of them were turning a nice brown color, a sign that the clusters were ripening. There wasn't much puckering of the grapes, and one of the berries I tasted had seeds that were still green. We agreed that I'd bring samples to the winery on Monday to see where we were. With hot weather, it might be a week until harvest, or maybe three weeks with cooler weather, but we were definitely getting close.

For the first time in over two weeks, the weather was crystal clear, even though it was a chilly sixty degrees when we left Los Altos Hills and when we arrived in Livermore. As a result, it was a beautiful drive, particularly as we dropped into Livermore Valley. The vines were bright green in the morning sun, and the hills were golden brown—classic California wine country.

As we drove in, I described my conversation with Dane about custom crush and the business. Gary agreed that somehow they needed to get away from the small lots, but if they could find a solution to barrel storage, custom crush might be a nice supplement. This fit with my earlier assertion to Dane that if the press was idle, custom processing was a cash generator with almost no downside. The same could be said about excess or reasonably priced barrel capacity, but so far, Page Mill didn't have any excess, as I was about to learn.

When we arrived, we were met with the fact that no one had seen Cindy (Cinderella), the gray kitten and sister to Belle, the black kitten, who was in the barrel room. Gary, who had fed and cared for them as much as anyone, began to look around for Cindy, but he had no luck. Michael had already been looking as well. Unfortunately, this area was out in the country, with hawks and owls, as well as raccoons and coyotes. Cindy was the more adventuresome of the two, and she might have gone out the previous night. We all hoped that somehow she'd just gotten lost and would find her way home. It put a damper on the morning.

The task for the day was to rearrange the barrel storage room and remove about six barrels that were empty among the stacks. Since it was cool, it was a perfect day for it, so we opened up the big doors to the storage room. Dane jumped on the forklift, while Gary and I worked together with the pallet jack to pull out the stacks of barrels so Dane could grab them with the forklift. It was a pretty tight squeeze, and getting leverage with the pallet jack wasn't always easy. Gary said that when you were trying to move a stack of eight fully loaded wine barrels, it was just hard work. In fact, Gary didn't have enough weight to press the hydraulic pump down on the pallet jack at times. I, having a bit more weight, was able to provide the necessary bulk to help get the stack mobile. Most of the time, I just helped Gary to move the stacks, as clearly he had more experience with this than I had.

Dane was a wizard with the forklift, moving the barrels in and out easily, lifting single barrels and the racks of two to four barrels easily. He only really stopped to think about how he wanted to rearrange the stacks, once we got everything out. At one point Gary and I were manipulating a fairly tight space with a stack of nine barrels—two across and four high with full barrels, and an extra empty barrel on top. I was pushing the stack, and Dane asked us to stop and told me to look up. The empty barrel was rocking precariously on the top of the stack ten or fifteen feet above me. He told me to turn my cap around to provide better vision. He also said to be careful, and he reiterated his most important phrase, which was, "I don't want anyone to get hurt. Anything else we can deal with, but no one gets hurt."

Later, as we were again maneuvering a tall stack, Gary told me that often Dane did this all by himself. Not only was it time-consuming getting on and off the forklift and pulling barrels with the pallet jack, but it also took its toll on his back. It was still a challenge with Gary and me working together.

We were about finished when I observed that we didn't seem to have gained any additional space. We had taken at least six barrels out of the stacks, but we seemed to have filled up all available spaces. As we were all puzzling over this, I happened to notice that we had failed to push a stack back against the wall in the first row of barrels. It was hidden by the curtain that separated the barrels from the tasting room, so we hadn't noticed. Once we pushed back the barrels, we gained space for an entire two-barrel stack, so we found our room. Thankfully, we had made the mistake in the first row, which was the best place it could have happened.

Now that we were finished and the barrel room was reorganized, we had gained some space, and while the barrels were out, Gary had a chance to vacuum most of the barrel storage room with the shop vac. All in all, it had been a successful morning, and it was further evidence for earlier conversations about there being no excess barrel space.

It was now about noon, and the other important task for the day was to do a side-by-side tasting of the 2006 Zinfandel and the 2006 Vintner's Select Zinfandel, both of which were being targeted for the next wine club shipment. While I had meetings the next day, Gary had told me on the way in that he and Dane would be preparing those shipments tomorrow. They would then get an email message out to the club members, letting them know that they could pick up their shipments at the winery or have them shipped. The ratio of local to out-of-town members was about ten to one, so there were a number of members who would come out to pick up their wine.

Dane offered to have the winery buy lunch, so Gary and I went off to Zephyr Grill, a great local restaurant that Dane often used for his events. We picked up pasta and pizza, both of which were perfectly paired with Zinfandel.

We returned and set up lunch in the stable. Michael, who had been working on racking the Pinot Gris most of the morning, joined us for the tasting. Gary and I set out two glasses each, and Gary went off in search of the two wines that we would be tasting.

As I tasted each of the wines, first the Zinfandel, and then the Vintner's Select, or VS Zinfandel, I was struck by how good the Zinfandel was *and* how great the VS was. It was quite noticeably a more elegant, bigger wine, with a very smooth finish for so young a wine. As I said, they were both very good, but the VS stood out measurably. We discussed our various impressions, and the others expressed the same view I had. Then we turned to a discussion of pricing. The regular Zinfandel was priced at twenty-four dollars a bottle. In discussing the VS, we considered its stronger attributes, as well as the limited amount of this wine and the need for Dane to begin to create differentiation in his higher-end wines. We all agreed that it definitely should be priced in the thirties but probably not in the forties. As we discussed the pros and cons of different pricing, Gary made the suggestion that we price it at thirty-eight dollars, given its quality and the relatively small number of cases. Gary ran the tasting room and probably had the best and most current view of the Page Mill Winery customer. His idea was reasonable and based on his sense of the clientele. Who were we to argue?

On one of my first days at the winery, Dane had commented to me that it was only in the last couple of years that he had become comfortable with the moneymaking side of winemaking. Not that he didn't want success or to make money, but his passion was winemaking and creating wine that people would want to drink. Charging a premium for premium wines was something that he was only becoming comfortable with—and I still think only to a degree. Dane made great wines and charged a very fair price for them. If they chose the very best of certain varietals or vineyards and created a Vintner's Select, I thought, they should charge a premium for the best of the best. That was also a way to begin to create greater success for Page Mill, and that was what Dane and Gary deserved, given their hard work, the quality of their product, and the enjoyment among those of us who got to partake of their handiwork.

As we continued to eat our lunch, the discussion turned to the stable. Dane commented that with little effort, they could insulate the stable and create more barrel storage. There was even a chiller already set up at one end, so the refrigeration wouldn't be that much, either. In fact, during the winter, the stable was often used for barrel storage. A quick calculation suggested that as many as one hundred barrels could fit in the room. That was the equivalent of twenty-five hundred cases. That kind of capacity could allow for a certain amount of custom crush business that wouldn't necessarily impact the core business of Page Mill and yet could add cash flow to the operation. I'm sure it was something that Dane would think about in the coming months.

After this discussion and cleanup, Dane grabbed a mixed case of wine and headed for Twainharte to celebrate his dad's birthday. Gary and I said our goodbyes as well. Given that I would not be there tomorrow, we discussed sampling several of the peninsula vineyards. Gary would handle what I called the KKK tomorrow morning. This comprised the Kennedy vineyard, which I had checked several weeks back, as well as the Kung vineyard and the Kellenberger vineyard. Steve and Annie Kellenberger were also long-term friends of ours. Steve was one of our daughter Nicole's first softball coaches when our girls were young. Annie and Steve also had a place in Capitola, and Denise and I would see them there on weekends.

On Monday, before I came in, I would get samples from Campi, Arey, and our Merlot vineyard for testing. Early on Monday morning, we would see where we were. Gary and I drove home and said our goodbyes for the weekend.

SEPTEMBER 22, 2008

This would be a very big day for the Côté family. Today Nicole turned twenty-five. We would be celebrating tonight with some of her favorite foods: Caprese salad with fresh tomatoes from the garden, seared ahi, artichokes, and baked potatoes. For dessert, Denise was trying to find "Funfetti" cake and frosting—a throwback to Nicole's childhood, but still a favorite. I was looking forward to our celebration as well, and some of Nicole's favorites were also mine, so dinner would be a treat.

Before heading out to Livermore, I grabbed samples from our own Merlot vineyard, and then I headed over to the Campis' and the Arey vineyard next door to them for samples. The Campi fruit continued to look beautiful, with very little raisining. The Arey vineyard seemed farther along, and many of the clusters were getting a golden color about them.

After I gathered the samples, I met Denise in town for a cup of coffee before heading east. We talked about Nicole's birth, which was at 2:52 AM on the twenty-second those many years ago. We had both wanted a little girl, but we didn't want to know what the ultrasound reading showed. We were blessed with Nicole. And tonight was a celebration for her, and for how far she had come. It also marked her fourth week at Apple, where she was enjoying her new, very busy job. Ironically, it was twenty-five years ago when I had joined Apple myself. Denise had been pregnant with Nicole, and I was a true oddity at Apple—not only married, but we were going to have a baby.

As I drove out to Page Mill, on this first day of fall, the weather was spectacular. Coming up the road toward Pigeon Point, I hit a section of one-lane road under construction and was delayed by twenty minutes or so.

By the time I reached the winery in mid-morning, Lynn was about to leave for the day. She had worked both days of the weekend and had already tested the samples that had been left overnight. When I arrived with my three samples, she simply asked Dane and me to crush them and said she would run the tests on the juice.

As we stood there, crushing the grapes in the sample, I was still thinking about Nicole, and Dane was talking about his girls, when I remembered a story about Nicole.

Denise and I loved to listen to James Taylor. We went to many of his concerts and really enjoyed all of his music. We had numerous tapes we'd play in the car. One of the songs that we all loved was an a capella song called "Traffic Jam." It's a fun song, and the words "Damn this traffic jam" are sung many times throughout the song. When we played it with a very young Nicole in the car, we realized that we didn't want Nicole mimicking the catchy tune, and particularly the chorus. So every time the song was played, Denise and I would sing over James Taylor with the words "Bam This Traffic Jam." It worked, and for years, whenever we heard the song, Nicole would sing it that way, whether we sang along or not. The song probably gave way to later albums and other artists. But one day when Nicole was fourteen or fifteen years old, it came on the radio, and for some reason she heard the lyrics and said to us, "Do you realize what he is saying? All these years I thought it was bam, and it's damn." Both Denise and I broke out laughing, as did Nicole, and it remains one of our favorite stories. Dane, who was a James Taylor fan and the father of two young girls, found the whole thing hilarious.

With our samples crushed, we gave them to Lynn for testing. Dane asked if I'd like to do an ML test; ML stands for malolactic. There is a secondary fermentation process that always occurs with red wines and in some white wines, in which malic acid is converted to lactic acid. Malic acid tends to be tart, and lactic acid tends to be richer, even buttery. This process is what creates the "big, buttery" California Chardonnays that people talk about. Malolactic fermentation is always done in red wines to help smooth out the wine and give it a richer texture on the palate. In general, it is done when primary fermentation is complete and the new wine is dry. The process is caused by bacteria that convert the malic acid into lactic acid. These bacteria are present in most wines, and the process can occur without inoculation of specific bacteria, just as wild yeast starts the primary fermentation process. But in most cases, the winemaker inoculates the wine with the appropriate bacteria to insure that the process occurs and that other bacteria don't create other processes, leading to "off" flavors in the wine.

The ML test is fairly straightforward. It uses paper chromatography to measure the relative amounts of malic and lactic acids in wines, thereby testing for the progress of ML fermentation. The process is fairly simple. Dane marked a piece of paper with the names of the various tanks I'd be testing. I used a capillary tube to draw a small amount of wine out of each tank. I dropped a small sample on the paper, creating about a dime-size stain of wine. (Sometimes I ended up with a quarter-size mark, but the goal was smaller.) I tested samples from the two Zinfandel tanks, all four Petite Sirah tanks, and the Harris Cabernet, the Johnson Malbec/Cab Franc, and the Davigo (standing for two small lots, Davis and Tarigo) Cab/Merlot. Once I had all the samples on my page, Dane had me staple the page together end to end, forming a cylinder. With my samples on the bottom of the cylinder, I lowered it into an airtight chromatography jar containing a developing solvent consisting of butanol, formic acid, water, and dye. The developing solvent travels up the chromatography paper by capillary action, dissolving the sample and separating the acids as it goes. After six to eight hours of development, or before the solvent reaches the top, the paper is removed and hung to dry in a well-ventilated area for several hours or overnight. After the drying period, the paper will appear blue with a series of yellow spots in a vertical ladder-like arrangement. The specific organic acids are seen as yellow spots against the blue background of the chromatography paper, with malic acid below lactic acid on the paper.

Once this was finished, we were ready for the main task of the day: pressing one of the tanks of Petite Sirah, and the Harris Cabernet Sauvignon, both of which were nearly dry. Dane wanted to finish them "off the skins." Dane prepared the crush pad, tanks, and the press, and I moved the two tanks into position. Once I'd done this, I exchanged the fork for the box-dumper, and we were set to go. As I went to grab the Petite Sirah to dump it into the chute, I couldn't get the box-dumper to open up completely so I could grab the tank. It appeared that the hydraulics weren't working. Dane mentioned that there had been a small leak and that maybe we needed to add hydraulic fluid. We both began to look for the hydraulic system under the seat of the forklift. We found the engine, the coolant, the radiator, and what we thought was the hydraulic system, but it wasn't obvious.

Dane decided to check the Web and possibly call someone. He found a forklift-servicing outfit in Livermore and gave them a call. He was hoping that they could simply tell us where the hydraulic fluid went and how much it would cost for one of us to pick it up. Whoever answered told Dane that he'd have the sales manager give Dane a call. I offered to grab sandwiches while Dane figured this one out. When I returned, he had gotten an appointment for them to come out tomorrow and take a look, and to add hydraulic fluid if necessary. We both puzzled about this because the up-and-down hydraulics seemed to work. I decided to look at where I had hooked up the hydraulics when changing from the fork to the box-dumper function. Sure enough, one of the couplers had come undone, so of course there was insufficient fluid getting to the hydraulics.

Dane was ecstatic. I was mortified. He was laughing. I was embarrassed. This was the equivalent of asking, in the tech world that I came from, "Hey, is it plugged in?" when there was a problem—and finding out that was exactly what had happened. For Dane it was a relief that his workhorse forklift didn't have a problem, and that he didn't need to have the service call tomorrow that started at ninety dollars an hour just for showing up. I told him that I guessed it was right that I had bought lunch, as I owed him that for my blunder. He just laughed and said that I only would have owed him lunch if the guy had come out tomorrow, found that we didn't have the hydraulics hooked up, and charged Dane ninety bucks for that bit of news.

With the forklift fixed, I grabbed the Petite Sirah tank and dumped it into the press. Once the cycle started, we sat down to enjoy our sandwiches. Dane was still laughing from dodging the bullet on the forklift. I wasn't sure I'd heard the end of this little episode.

After lunch, we cleaned up the pan, dumped in the Harris Cab, and began to press it. Meanwhile, we began to clean up, and by the time it was finished, we were well on our way to having a clean crush pad again. We cleaned out the press and hosed down the crush pad, and I dumped out the pressed must at the end of the vineyard, using the box-dumper attachment on the forklift that was now working like a charm.

All in all, it was a good day, but I'd learned a valuable lesson about making sure that all the little things were covered—always a good reminder in our busy world, no matter what you do.

SEPTEMBER 24, 2008

I arrived on a near-perfect day in Livermore and walked out onto the crush pad to say hello. Michael walked up to me and said in his most sincere voice, "I understand you fixed the hydraulics on the forklift Monday." He paused for a few seconds to make sure it had sunk in and then broke out laughing. Dane, who was nearby, had a huge smirk on his face, and then he started laughing.

As this was dying down, Lynn came out of the lab, and as if it had been choreographed, she commented, "Hey, Dave, Dane said you fixed the hydraulics on the forklift Monday." With Lynn, there was no pause, just raucous laughter, with Dane and Michael joining in. There was absolutely nothing I could say—nothing!

Before I jumped into the day's tasks, I asked about the ML test I'd done on Monday. Dane pulled out the sheet. Using fumes from a bottle of ammonia, he restored the blue and yellow patches on the sheet. It revealed that the four Petite Sirah tanks had finished ML. This was evident by the fact that the yellow band, where malic acid would have been present on the paper, was now blue for the four Petite Sirah samples. It was also blue for the Johnson Cabernet Sauvignon, but Dane didn't trust that result. He asked me to test again, leaving out the Petite Sirah. So I again gathered samples of the two Zins, the Harris Cab, the two Johnson Vineyard wines (Malbec/Cab Franc and Cab Sauvignon), and the Davigo Cab/Merlot. Once I had the samples on the paper, I stapled it into a cylinder and put it into the solvent.

Today was a day for some general tidying up in preparation for bottling the 2006 estate Petite Sirah tomorrow, as well as the next onslaught of grapes due to begin early next week.

I started first by sulfiting and topping off four barrels of Sauvignon Blanc that represented the excess from the 750-gallon stainless-steel tank, where the rest of the SB was. This meant measuring out fifteen-gram dosages of potassium metabisulfite to be dissolved in the topping wine and added to each of the four barrels. Potassium metabisulfite breaks down to release potassium oxide and sulfur dioxide (SO_2). Sulfur dioxide acts as a preservative in wines. At relatively low levels, it prevents most organisms from growing and acts as a powerful antioxidant, preserving the color and delicate flavors of wine.

The SO_2 levels are checked throughout the barrel-aging process, with a goal at bottling of 35 ppm of SO_2.

After topping of the barrels, I racked the remaining Sauvignon Blanc, from the partial barrel, into steel beer kegs for later use as topping wine. At about this time, Mark LaFleur, the manager of Zephyr Grill, a local Livermore restaurant, arrived to cook lunch for the Wednesday barbecue. Mark and Zephyr were fans of Dane's wines, and Dane was a fan of their food, using them to cater various events at the winery. Mark had been out for a visit a few weeks back on a Wednesday and had offered to cook the team lunch. He was immediately put into the rotation. Upon his arrival, he fired up the grill and brought out several containers of food. Pretty soon, we could all smell the barbecue.

Meanwhile, Michael was "barreling down" the Zinfandel, the Harris Cab, and one of the Petite Sirah tanks. "Barreling down" means just what it sounds like: moving the new wine from the fermentation tanks to new or used oak barrels for aging. I began to help Michael with this process. We also added potassium metabisulfite to the two Petite Sirah barrels. This was the wine from the tank that Dane and I had pressed on Monday, and because it was through the ML process, there was no fermentation to be affected by sulfiting. This was unlike the two Zins, which were still bubbling along, along with several of the smaller lots.

Throughout this process, the promise of lunch was assailing our noses. Out of the corner of my eye, I could see a large pot on the grill, and Mark was also grilling what looked like vegetables and pineapple. When I had first heard about Wednesday barbecue, I had envisioned someone throwing a few burgers and dogs on the grill, but it was much more elaborate. There had been ribs (which I missed), chicken tagine, shish kebab, pasta with red sauce, and grilled salmon. Now what were we having?

Just after noon, Mark declared that lunch was ready, and within minutes everyone had found a way to finish what they were doing, or take an appropriate break. The group descended on the table under the overhang of the barrel storage room, coming from every corner of the winery.

Mark had prepared beer brats with sauerkraut, potato salad, grilled asparagus, and grilled pineapple chunks. There were large hot dog buns for the brats as well. Gary brought out glasses along with a Chardonnay and an Angela's Cuvée, and we all sat down for a wonderful lunch. The food was great, and the group had a lively conversation on politics, the grapes, the state of the economy, Zephyr's business, Page Mill's business, and whatever else came to people's minds. When we were all stuffed, we cleaned up and got back to work. Mark announced that he had put leftovers in the refrigerator. Even though we had devoured the brats, he had made twenty-four, so there were definitely leftovers.

As I went back to the crush pad, Michael had the last bit of his work well in hand. I told him to find me if he needed help, and I went off to assist Gary in the stable. He was working on getting the wine club shipment packed up so he could drop it all off at the UPS store. The shipment included the 2006 Zinfandel and Vintner's Select Zinfandel that we had tasted last week. The club had nearly two hundred members, but only about seventy asked to have their wine shipped to them. The rest came out and picked it up at the winery. Nonetheless, packing up seventy two-bottle shipments was a lengthy task, and it obviously benefited from another set of hands. Gary had built the boxes already, so we set up across the table from each other. I grabbed a box and put the wines in along with the top of the shipper. Gary took it from there, adding the cover letter and tasting notes, sealing the box, and placing the UPS shipment sticker on the front. We moved fairly quickly, but it still took most of the afternoon to get this done. When we had finished, we loaded up Gary's truck, and he took off for the UPS store and then headed for home.

I went around to the crush pad and found Dane preparing the filter for the estate Petite Sirah that we were bottling tomorrow. I asked if he needed any more help today, and when he said no, I said my goodbyes to Dane and Michael for the day.

SEPTEMBER 25, 2008

As I pulled up to the winery and walked onto the crush pad, the place was already humming. As I passed the stable, I saw that we were set up for bottling. Unlike last time, Michael had set up a straight line for production: sparger, filler, corker, spinner, and labeler, all on two tables.

On the crush pad, I quickly jumped in to help move hoses so that Michael could maneuver the forklift. Dane was programming the press, and I took over the pump, which was transferring the free juice from the Petite Sirah tanks to another tank, in preparation for pressing the remaining must. As I was standing there minding the pump, Dick Stark, Dane's father and the founder of Page Mill Winery, came around the corner. We hadn't seen each other in a few years, and after we gave each other a hug, he asked me what the heck I was doing still coming out every day … with a big smile on his face. I asked where he'd been so far this season. He told me that in the last month or so, he had spent most of his time above ten thousand feet, and only yesterday he had been hiking up Mount Dana in Yosemite, but he'd had to stop, as it got too windy and cold.

He had just come down for the day to help with the bottling. It was great fun to see Dick, who had been running the winery when we first planted our vineyard. I remember that throughout the nineties, Dick drove the forklift and ruled the crush pad at the old winery at their home on Page Mill Road.

Dane still deferred to Dick, calling him boss, but it was clear that it was now Dane's winery and Dick was there to help. There was no doubt that Dick was proud of Dane, even though they both loved to give each other shit all day long.

We were ready to bottle, so we got going. Dick worked the sparger and filler, Michael worked the corker, I was back at the newly refurbished spin-ner, and Gary was on the labeler. The first few bottles through the spinner were a bit stiff, but the spinner worked very well. Pretty soon I was doing the "spinner's lunge," as Gary called it, placing the bottle on my leg and using the leg to gently but smoothly push the bottle into the spinner. The result was a very tight capsule. Pretty soon we had picked up speed and were moving the bottles through the line. I could get ahead of Gary because not only was he labeling, but he was also putting the bottles into the case boxes. When he filled a box and sealed it, I moved it over onto the pallet.

Dane came into the stable a couple of times, looking to relieve one of us, but it was going along smoothly. He went back outside and continued to press the 2008 estate Petite Sirah, and we could hear the forklift roaming around the crush pad. As the morning wore on, Gary in particular began to feel it in his back. I had tried to help by moving the full case boxes, but his was probably the most awkward movements on the line, and his back was bothering him.

Dane jumped in at Gary's end, and we continued to fill the pallet. At one point, Michael asked about stopping for lunch, and Dane said it was up to the boss (Dick) to call the lunch break. I'm not sure Dick even heard him, so we continued to plow along. We all agreed that when we had filled a pallet (fifty-six cases), we'd stop for lunch.

We were all a bit tired by now, and so as we got to those last few cases, we were asking often, "Are we almost done?" It reminded me of being a kid and asking my mom when we were going to get there on any car trip we took—and asking that question way too many times for any sane adult to handle.

We all enjoyed the countdown as we filled the last bottle in the last case and Dane put it on the pallet. We filled one more bottle for lunch, and we all went outside under the overhang. I grabbed water for everyone, while Dane and Gary brought out the leftovers from yesterday. We enjoyed Mark's cooking for the second time in as many days, and though the brats were cold, it was again a great meal—only this time, it was accompanied by the newly bottled 2006 estate Petite Sirah.

It smelled fantastic! Before I could take a sip, Dick had taken his first taste. He had a very serene look on his face as he looked up and said to Dane that he had made a wonderful wine. I took my first sip, and he was right. It was a rich, fruity wine with a very long finish and very nice tannins. Gary, who had brought his own sandwich, exclaimed, "This goes perfect with peanut butter!"

To which Michael said, "It is also good with tortillas," which was what he'd brought for lunch.

There was no question that this was a very special wine. I could see the pleasure and admiration in Dick's eyes, and as Dane took a sip, I could tell that he was pleased as well. That had to be the most satisfying part of the job. Dane had worked for two years to process, ferment, barrel, blend, and bottle this wine. It was outstanding at bottling; what about five years from now? And this wasn't even the very best of this vintage, which Dane would bottle as the Vintner's Select. The wine was extraordinary!

We enjoyed lunch and lingered for a while, finishing the Petite Sirah. Finally, it was Dick who said, "Let's get back to work, so I can go home." We decided to change it up for the remaining cases. Dick stayed with the sparger and filler. I moved to the corker, Gary took the spinner, and Michael was on the labeler. We again dove into the task. It was fun to try something different. The corker was an old-style hand corker. It had a pressure plate that I pressed down with the bottle, the bottle being situated underneath the cork. I placed a cork in the rectangular space above the bottle. Then I pulled down on the handle, which compressed the cork evenly, and the final part of the thrust sent a small rod into the now-compressed cork, pushing it into the bottle. Voilà—a perfectly corked bottle. It was actually very easy, and while the corker looked ancient, it worked like a charm … except that Dick observed that the action had been far easier in times past. I chose to use this as an exercise opportunity.

At one point we took a break, and I got some food-grade silicon lubricant and put it on the moving parts of the corker. It definitely made a difference in the ease of operation. Fortunately for all of us, the remaining cases were about half the amount we had done before lunch. Before we knew it, we were finished. We quickly cleaned up, and we were just finishing when Ome, Dick's wife, came by the winery with a close friend. She said hello to everyone. She looked at me and asked, "Why are you doing this?" with a big smile on her face. Dane quickly told her that she couldn't speak to me. I hadn't seen Ome in seven or eight years. She had not changed a bit. She had ruled the place, and that hadn't changed one bit. She had brought along delicious strawberries from a local grower, and she invited all of us to have some, and then some more. They were the freshest, juiciest strawberries I'd had in a very long time, rivaling some that we had picked fresh as a family, when the kids were small.

After a bit, both Dick and Ome said their goodbyes and headed for home. It had been a great day working with Dick, who was full of stories about the old days. Following are two that I remember.

In the late seventies, Dick was up at a Pinot conference in Oregon, long before Pinot was popular in California or Oregon. He mentioned that one of the speakers was Jancis Robinson, a famous wine critic from the UK. She had given Dick (and then Dane) one of the classic lines he used in differentiating between Cabernet Sauvignon and Pinot Noir. She said, "Cabernet knocks your socks off, but Pinot gently, seductively slips them off." Dick said that after he heard that, he used it in every Pinot tasting he ever did. I first heard it from Dane a number of years ago.

The other story provided some insight into Dane's own behavior. Dick told the story of Dane's first sales calls with Dick. Dick quickly interjected that he hated the selling of his wines; Dane agreed. Then he proceeded to tell us how they had done eleven sales calls in one day and gotten eleven orders. Everywhere they went, the proprietors exclaimed, "Dick Stark, where have you been? I've wanted to order your wines." Dick said that almost every one of them would invite Dane and him in for some food and wine.

What's ironic about this story is that Dane had told me a very similar story as to why he had finally gotten a distributor involved. He too was not a fan of sales calls, but he had also experienced getting orders and the happiness of his customers when he would visit. He just didn't feel cut out for that part of the job. I guess now I understand where he got that feeling.

After Dick and Ome left, Gary, Dane, and I loaded up the truck with half-ton bins and FYBs for Leopoldo, who was going to pick several peninsula vineyards over the weekend. It looked like we were beginning to see the next wave of fruit come in. The work over the past few days to free up barrel space and to get fermented new wine out of the tanks and into barrels, or pressed and into tanks, meant that we had space and time to handle this next phase of the harvest.

With the truck loaded, Gary and I left for the afternoon.

SEPTEMBER 26, 2008

Gary and I planned to carpool this morning, and when Gary arrived, he said that he had taken a walk through our vineyard and thought we'd harvest next week. We had been hoping to get an extra week, as several of our family members and friends might not be able to make it next weekend. But the grapes came first. I would pull samples on Monday and bring them in for another set of tests. Based on that, we'd make our determination, but I agreed with Gary. There were already signs of puckering in some clusters, which meant that the sugar was moving up. We'd know more on Monday. For now, we grabbed our coffee and headed for Livermore.

On the drive in, I spoke about seeing Randy and Harry the evening before. They ran Vino Locale, a great wine shop and bar in a restored Victorian house in downtown Palo Alto. The shop specialized in local wines, and they had carried Page Mill wines and, in particular, Côté Merlot for as long as they had been open.

Several years ago, we held an event at our house that benefited Ronald McDonald House at Stanford, a charity that Denise supported. She was on the board of directors and had offered her time in a number of areas for the house. Randy supported this event by pouring wines, and he supported the house in a number of ways over the past few years. The night before, we had seen him at an event at the house. They were again donating their time and the wines for the evening. It was great to see them, and Randy had lamented that he hadn't been able to get the Côté Merlot for a long time, and it was one of his favorites.

As I said, I mentioned it to Gary, who said that there were a number of cases of the 2005 at UDS, which was the local warehouse they used for the tasting room and retail sales. The other warehouse in San Jose held the bulk of Page Mill's inventory and also serviced their distributor, Alexia Moore Wine Marketing. The Côté Merlot was not offered as a general item, as there was only a small amount made. Gary said we could bring some to Randy on our way home that evening, as he had some in the tasting room. We agreed to call Randy later in the day to see how much he wanted.

We arrived at Page Mill to a very quiet crush pad. Dane asked me to take sugars on a number of the wines in fermentation tanks or in barrels. These included a small lot of Cabernet Sauvignon, the Johnson Malbec/Cab Franc, the Lodi Zinfandel, and the Beebe Chardonnay from Livermore.

For all but the Chardonnay, I took samples of juice and used the hydrometer to measure the Brix. The Cabernet, which was the last to be crushed, was still at 6.3 Brix, while the Malbec/Cab France was at 0.8 Brix, and the Zins that were in barrels were at -0.2. For the Chardonnay, which was nearly dry, I used a sugar pill to measure the residual sugar more accurately. It turned out that the Chardonnay still had a little way to go, as it measured about 0.8 percent residual sugar, and for most wines Dane made, he wanted the residual sugar well below 0.5 percent.

The main task for the day was to get the rest of the estate Petite Sirah barreled down. As Dane and Gary rearranged the barrel room, removing empty barrels and washing them for the Petite, I prepared the pump and hoses for the transfer. This meant cleaning everything with peracetic acid and then thoroughly flushing them all with water. My equipment was ready, and Dane had finished moving the barrels and washing eight of them to receive the new Petite Sirah, so we were ready to go.

I began the transfer into the first barrel. As it began to fill, I could see that there was a leak in the barrel. This was fairly common, and I watched as Dane grabbed a cup full of matchsticks, a box cutter, and a hammer. He used the box cutter to whittle the end of a matchstick, and then he hammered it into the leaky spot on the barrel. After hammering it in, he simply broke it off. This did the trick, stopping the leak.

I prepared a fifteen-gram dose of potassium metabisulfite to be added to the first barrel. I mixed it with some of the wine and then added it to the nearly full barrel. As the barrel became full, I turned down the pump to transfer the hose to the next barrel. I spilled some of the Petite on the barrel in my transfer, but I got the next one going. I affixed a card to the barrel stating that it was the 2008 estate Petite Sirah, and I wrote in that I had added the fifteen grams of sulfite. There were also places to mark when topping was done. So this card would mark the progress of this wine from now until it was bottled approximately two years from now.

As I continued the transfer process, I spilled a bit more wine, including spilling some right down into my shoe. Gary got a kick out that. I just said it was going to be my newest creation: "Vin wear." We took a brief break for a quick sandwich, and then I continued the process. I filled eight barrels and emptied two fermentation tanks. There was a bit left in the third tank, but Dane said he would finish it up tomorrow.

By now it was about 2:30 PM, and Dane would be doing a tasting at the Mountain View "Beverages and More" at 4:00 PM with John Ignowski, who was the store's manager and a big fan of Page Mill wines. He had gotten them into a number of Northern California Bevmo stores. In fact, Dane texted him while we were having lunch and found out that there were six cases going to the new Bevmo in Capitola on 41st Avenue—right near our beach house. We had been wanting one nearby, so this was great news!

For our part, Gary and I loaded up his pickup with twenty-two cases of 2006 Côté Merlot, plus a case of '07 Sauvignon Blanc and a case of '07 Chardonnay. Denise and I still had two cases in our allotment, which would probably include the Estate Petite Syrah and the Vintner's Select Zinfandel, among others. Gary was joining us for dinner that night, and we were going to watch the first debate, so he brought a bottle of the Estate Petite from 2005 and the newly bottled 2006 for a "mini vertical," as he called it.

I also called Randy at Vino Locale and asked if he wanted the Côté Merlot, and he said, "Of course," and asked for two cases. So we pulled two cases of the 2005 from the tasting room and added it to our fully loaded truck. At around 3:00 PM, we all departed for the peninsula: Gary and me to Vino Locale and home, and Dane to Bevmo.

We drove first to Palo Alto to see Randy. He was very pleased to get the Merlot, and so quickly. I told him that I had a little pull with the management, so I was happy to get him our wine. He also mentioned that next month, Page Mill would be the featured winery of the month for October. He asked if Dane could come out and do a tasting, and Gary said, "Of course." Randy also asked about having his entire staff come out to the winery on a Monday when they were closed, to see the winery and taste all of the new releases. Again, Gary told him to simply call him to arrange it, saying that he would love to do it. We thanked Randy and said our goodbyes and then headed for home.

On the way home, we stopped off in Los Altos at Draeger's, a local grocery store, to pick up dinner. We were thinking about fish, and when we got to the fish counter, there was fresh, wild-caught opah. The butcher suggested a ginger teriyaki marinade, and we thought that sounded great. Gary had never had opah, and I had only had it in Hawaii. We bought the ingredients for the rest of dinner and headed for home.

When we arrived at my house, we unloaded the wine into the large cellar. We went into the house, and I showed Gary the guest room. After both of us had cleaned up, we opened a bottle of Angela's Cuvée and broke out the cheese and crackers. I also cut up some apples from our tree, and Gary, Denise and I sat down to watch the first presidential debate between Barack Obama and John McCain.

Kent, our vet, called, and Denise found out he was home alone, as Kim, his wife, and their daughter, Brynn, were at a horse show, and their son, Tristan, was out for the evening. We invited Kent to join us, which he did. We watched the end of the debate and then opened the two bottles of Estate Petite and tried them both; Denise preferred the '05, as it was better aged, though she saw the potential of the '06. I actually liked the '06 the best. With some of these two wines remaining, we sat down to dinner. We enjoyed the meal and the remainder of the wines, and then I opened a Windy Oaks Pinot Noir from their vineyard in Corralitos, which is in the southern part of the Santa Cruz Mountains. It was excellent. Dane had told me that he would like to source fruit from this area, so who knows? Maybe we'll have a Page Mill Santa Cruz Mountain's Pinot one day.

After dinner, Kent headed for home to meet up with Tristan, and Gary went to bed. He had to be up and out by seven to get to the winery, to clean up the tasting room and have it opened by noon. Denise and I finished cleaning up and went to bed ourselves. The evening had been a real treat, with great friends, great food, and of course, great wines.

SEPTEMBER 29, 2008

Before leaving for the winery, I pulled samples from our Merlot vineyard, fully expecting the Brix to be up from the 23.2 of last week. This next weekend wasn't the optimal weekend, but as I said, the grapes came first.

After bagging the sample clusters, I drove to the winery. The sky was overcast, with temperatures in the mid-sixties all the way to Livermore. When I arrived, I went into the barrel room, where Dane was working on paperwork. I told him that I'd brought the samples, and he said that Lynn would be back in a bit to run the tests. He asked me to punch down the new vineyards that had come in over the weekend. These included the Merlots from Kennedy and Kellenberger and the Kung Cab/Merlot, all of which came from vineyards in the Los Altos area, near our vineyard. There were also a couple of small custom crush lots of Cabernet and Syrah. For these smaller lots, punchdown really meant trying to smash the grape berries, as there wasn't much in the fermentation tanks or bins.

I also took a Brix reading on the Cabernet from Dublin that was processed midweek last week. The Brix was down from my reading of 6.3 to 3.8.

As I was finishing, Dane came out of the barrel storage room just as Lynn came out of the lab. Lynn was loaded with samples this morning but had plowed through enough to run the test on our Merlot. Surprisingly, the Brix was only at 23.4, which wasn't much of a change from the prior week. The pH was around 3.4, so there was room for that to come down. The TA was 0.68, which was very good. Dane asked me if I wanted to hold off another week before harvesting. I said that it would be better for a number of people, but that the harvest came first. He made the point that he would prefer the

additional hang time of another week, so we agreed that we'd harvest on
Sunday, October 12. This was perfect. It meant that both of my kids could
be there, and we would celebrate Denise's birthday that weekend. Later, I
learned that the weather would cool off later in the week, and there was a
chance of rain, so it made sense to hold off the harvest for another week.
This had already been a very strange year, with vineyards ripening early and
others going very late. It was almost like there were two harvests this year,
one at the end of August and beginning of September, and the other to come
in October.

I called Denise and left her a message about this good news.

Dane asked me if I could handle processing a half-ton bin of Cabernet on
my own. He was working on paperwork and paying bills, and he could use
the time. I was happy to do it. I set up the destemmer with a bin underneath
for the fruit. I pressure-washed a fermentation tank and set it up on pallets,
so the chute would be just above the top of the tank, with the tank and the
destemmer in line on the crush pad. I was ready to crush the Cab.

As I drove the forklift into the stable where the fruit had been left, I
noticed two small baskets of fruit on top of the bin. I went in to ask Dane
what was up. He called Steve, the vineyard manager, who asked that we
process this fruit separately. It was only about sixty pounds of Merlot from a
new vineyard, but Dane agreed to do it. He told me later that he had sent the
vineyard owner his prices for custom crush, and the minimum alone would
make this about six hundred dollars for a case of wine—and that was about
all they'd get. I'll probably never know whether Dane charged him the full
price, but he needed to do it, given the amount of work that would go into
making this small amount of wine.

It started with me hand-destemming the fruit. There was so little of it
that I spent about forty-five minutes stripping the berries off the stems and
filling a five-gallon bucket with the fruit. Dane had gone to the bank and
had stopped off to pick up Chinese food from last night that we would eat
for lunch. When he returned, he laughed to see me still working the fruit
and came over to help me finish it off. We then sat down to a quick lunch.

Earlier that morning, I had heard him comment to someone that he
was having the mid-harvest blues this past weekend, so I asked him what
he meant by that. He said that at this point, he wanted to be finished with
harvest, or so busy that he didn't have time to think about it. This lull that

we were seeing was frustrating because we weren't finished with the harvest, and we weren't able to move it along. The next few weeks would change that, as there were still a number of vineyards to come in: the two Peninsula Chardonnay vineyards, Campi and Arey, the Livermore Cabernet Sauvignon and Syrah, and the Balyeat Zinfandel and Sleepy Holler Syrah, both from the Napa area, and of course the penultimate Merlot vineyard—ours!

After lunch, I got back to processing the Cabernet. I turned on the destemmer and grabbed the bin with the forklift. Since it was only a half ton, I was able to dump it into the chute and then climb up to make sure that the fruit was moving through the destemmer. After making sure it all got destemmed, I washed the bin and stacked it away from the crush pad. I opened up the destemmer and cleaned out the remaining berries that were in the mechanism. I slid the chute over the fermentation tank that I had set up. Once this was done, I used a pallet jack to pull out the bin of destemmed fruit. I grabbed it with the forklift and dumped it into the chute, and on into the tank.

This only took about thirty minutes, and then it was cleanup time. I cleaned the other bin and stacked it with the rest. I took the box of stems and dumped it out at the end of the vineyard. I moved the fermentation tank to a spot on the crush pad near the other tanks and put a plastic skin on it. I then went back to cleaning the destemmer.

As I was finishing with the destemmer, Dane came back out onto the crush pad. He took off his shoes and socks and washed his feet. Then, systematically, he got into each of the tanks and stomped around, as a means of punching down these small batches of fruit. It was much more effective than the big punchdown tool. He asked if I wanted to try it out, but I declined, having done it one other time and not needing to stain my feet deep purple.

When he had finished, he covered the tanks and added nitrogen gas to each tank, just as I was finishing my cleanup of the crush pad.

He looked at me and asked, "Are you getting out of this what you hoped to? Because you are helping me a lot." I told him that yes, I was getting everything I had hoped for and more. I was learning more about winemaking than I had expected, and I was doing most of the various steps in the process. I was also becoming much more self-sufficient, so I truly felt I was helping Dane, freeing him up for other things, or just giving him back some free time during the rush of harvest. My only fear had been that Dane would feel he had to take care of me out here, constantly giving me specific direction—the feeling that he would take as much time explaining something to me as doing it himself. Early on, there had been some of that, but now there were many tasks that I just did, and that was interesting and fun for me, and a real help to Dane—what you call your win-win!

Besides, where else could you sit down every day at lunch, especially on Wednesdays, and enjoy wonderful wines and the conversation of friends? It was quite a lifestyle: lots of hard work, but time to appreciate that work and each other as well. It was very different from the corporate world—a tremendous change of pace, and one that I would cherish forever.

With that, we said our goodbyes. I headed home, and Dane headed out for band practice. I felt particularly good today because not only had I processed the fruit by myself, but I also think I gave Dane enough time in his day to get to band practice—and the Côté harvest was going to happen at a great time for everyone!

SEPTEMBER 30, 2008

This morning, I met a longtime friend for breakfast. We had worked together at Apple twenty-five years ago and had become friends. He has been a serial entrepreneur, and he made the decision some years ago to move to Atlanta with his wife and two boys, both to be closer to family and to afford a nice house—a difficult task in the Bay Area. We had a tradition of meeting for breakfast whenever he is in town. We shared a love of wine, and palates that mostly distinguished what we liked, and that was about all. Matt had joined us for harvest at least once, so we always got to discussions of wine when we met. I was pleased to be able to give him one of the newly bottled Côté 2006 Merlots. He was appreciative as always, though I now had forced him to check his bags for the trip home.

We talked about his new venture, which was a resource site for college-bound high-school students and their parents. He had built an aggregation site for all the information one might need to go through the painful process of college admissions, especially to some of the more elite colleges. He hoped that it would attract enough attention to generate reasonable advertising, and that the community would help to continue to build the site. He was about to launch it publicly. He also hoped to start a site that revolved around wine. We discussed one of his ideas related to wine clubs, which I thought had promise. In fact, Dane and I had talked about this area of his business as well.

We had a great time, as always. He went on to his meetings, and I drove the rest of the way to Livermore.

As I arrived, I noticed that Michael had brought company. He had brought along a friend of his daughter's named Eddy. Eddy made beer and mead and was interested in seeing how wine was made. He was in luck today, as we were going to press a tank of Cabernet Sauvignon, and one of Dane's custom crush clients was bringing in a ton or so of Cabernet to be destemmed. So the crush pad would be busy, even though we still didn't have any new fruit that would become Page Mill wine.

What a difference a few weeks made. I was ready to go. Michael hadn't pressed or destemmed in several weeks, and Eddy was a newbie, like I was a month ago. Michael just needed to get back in shape, as he had been making wine for fifteen years; he was still the expert with equipment, and he began to program the press. But I knew what needed to be done with the bins and the work.

Something was wrong with the press, though, so we needed to wait for Dane to return from an errand.

Meanwhile, the Cabernet fruit arrived in half-ton bins in the backs of two pickups. We had planned to press the Cabernet, so I had the box-dumper on the forklift. In order to get the bins out of the trucks, I needed the conventional fork, so I made the switch. One of the trucks was rather small, so I got the fork under a portion of a bin and dragged it out to the edge of the truck bed. Then I could get the fork all the way under it, and I moved the bin to a shady spot. The next bin came off without a problem.

By the time I got back to the crush pad, Michael and Eddy had cleaned the fermentation tank we'd use. I lifted it with the forklift and placed it on the pallets in line with the destemmer. Then I grabbed another half-ton bin with the forklift, rinsed it off, and shoved it underneath the destemmer to catch the fruit. Now we were ready to go.

Michael's style was different from Gary's. With Gary, whether I was driving the fork or manning the chute, we tended to dump in the fruit and work it from there. Michael's style was to have me dump in the fruit more slowly, even holding off on fully dumping the bin while he pulled fruit out of the bin into the chute and the destemmer. It was just a different style; it had the same result, though, as we crushed the first bin. When Michael was finished, I lowered the bin, sprayed it clean, and moved it out to the front of the winery, where it would be picked up along with the other bin when we were finished. By the time I was back, Michael had used the pallet jack to pull out the bin with the destemmed fruit. I grabbed it with the box-dumper while Michael and Eddy moved the chute over the fermentation tank. Then I dumped the fruit into the tank. We loaded the bin under the destemmer, and I went in search of the other bin.

Within a short time, we had processed the other bin and were on our way to cleaning up the destemmer. I cleaned the bins and moved them off the crush pad. Then I took the bin with stems in it out to an edge of the vineyard where we dumped all the organics. Later these would all get distributed into the Estate Petite Sirah vineyard as soil amendments. Nothing went to waste. When I got back, I moved the tank farther down the crush pad and put a skin on it. Now we were ready to press the Cabernet.

A technician on call discussed the press with Dane and walked through the diagnostics, only to find that two fuses had blown—big fuses. But Dane had spares, and soon we were up and running and ready to press the fruit. Dane had finished programming the press with Michael, and as we prepared to load the press, he went off in search of sandwiches for all of us.

Michael got the press open, and I grabbed the tank with the Cabernet. We dumped it into the press, turned it on, and began to clean up the crush pad. Just as we were finishing up, Dane returned with lunch. I set up the table, and Dane walked up and asked what kind of wine I'd like to drink for lunch. I told him I'd like a red, maybe Zinfandel or Syrah. He said, "How about a Vintner's Select Zinfandel?" That sounded great to me. Lynn had also given us a bottle of her customers' '07 Petite Sirah that she was testing. It turned out to be just okay. I enjoyed the Zinfandel very much; it went perfectly with my sandwich.

After lunch, Michael went back to check the press, with Eddy in tow. Dane grabbed the rest of the bottle and sat down, asking if I'd join him for a few more minutes. He commented that this was the calmest harvest he had spent in his nineteen years of winemaking. When I think back to the old winery and what they went through, I can't imagine how they got the work done. The barrels were spread out in the basement of Dane's family home. I'm not sure how they moved things around, as it would have been impossible to use a forklift in the cramped quarters. In fact, Dane said that once filled, a barrel wasn't moved again until it was empty, making for interesting logistics. A large, one-ton basket press was the Page Mill Winery press for all but the last few years, and it involved grueling physical work to crank down the press over the course of several hours. The current press took as long, but it operated on its own, enabling Dane to take a break for lunch and accomplish other tasks while it was working. And as I said before, it produced about 20 percent more juice, of higher quality, than the basket press. It was a major win for Dane.

But it was still the smoothest, calmest harvest so far. And while I'm sure a part of it was the work that Team Page Mill did in relieving Dane from doing everything, the strange split harvest season had something to do with it as well. My hope was that it also would enable Dane to selectively take on some custom crush work that provided cash flow, and that utilized idle resources like the press, tanks, and people during this lull in the '08 harvest.

I said to Dane that I was looking forward to getting more fruit destined to be Page Mill wine. He agreed and mentioned that Leopoldo would be picking the Arey vineyard Wednesday and bringing it in on Thursday, followed by the Campi vineyard on Friday. So we'd be making the quality backbone of his Chardonnay later this week. That would be good, as I missed Dane's refrain, "Making the wine," which had been absent over the last few days. My guess was that in the next few weeks, we'd see the bulk of the fruit that hadn't yet come in.

As we discussed the Chardonnay vineyards, Dane commented that Leopoldo would be by at around three. He looked at his watch, and it was three o'clock, so we jumped up to get the truck ready. We went out and loaded three half-ton bins on the truck, along with forty or so FYBs for picking. We stacked them up and strapped them down, and it was ready to go. As we walked back onto the crush pad, Michael and Eddy were just finishing cleaning the press. We now had five tanks on the pad, with more coming in. Dane called it a day, so I said my goodbyes. My guess was that he would find more to do later that evening, but we had gotten the major work done for the day.

OCTOBER

OCTOBER 1, 2008

On the way to the winery this morning, I got a phone call from Gary Campi. He and Karen had returned from a trip to France. He said that it was fun and that he looked forward to sharing pictures with Denise and me when we got together. He asked about his vineyard. He mentioned that the Arey vineyard next door was being picked and wondered when his would be harvested. I told him that the Arey vineyard had been a half point or so ahead of his vineyard and that Dane planned to have Leopoldo harvest on Friday. He thanked me for the update and said that he was concerned because there was a chance of rain on Friday night and into Saturday. But hopefully his vineyard would be harvested before any rain.

When I arrived at the winery, Dane and Gary were chatting. As I walked up, Dane asked me if I wanted the good news or the bad news. I told him that I'd like to hear the good news. He laughed and said there wasn't any, but the bad news was that there were twenty barrel spaces in the storage room and about that many barrels and tanks on the crush pad right now. That left no room for the tons (literally over twenty) of fruit still to come in. One answer was to bottle the remaining 2006 reds, which would free up space for fifty barrels. I was sure that Dane would be struggling with this problem as we headed into October and the second phase of harvest.

I went to work testing ML (malolactic fermentation progress) on the eight barrels of Lodi Zinfandel, and on two other tanks with Malbec/Cab Franc and a Cab Sauv/Merlot. I needed to fit ten samples on the chromatography paper. I was in the lab, getting the equipment, when Lynn handed me a small wooden block with what looked like a small version of corrugated metal on it. She said that I should use this to hold the capillary tubes with each sample while I waited for the paper to dry. I asked what she meant, and she told me that in order to concentrate the samples (and fit them on the page), she would touch the bottom of the tube to the paper and let a dime-size circle of wine form on the page. Then she would let the paper dry and come back to that spot again with each sample in succession. That way she could create a small but concentrated sample for the ML test. The block was used to hold the tubes in order while the paper was drying. I used this device and let the paper dry between drops, and I got all of them on the page, with decent spacing and good concentration of the samples. After that, I stapled the paper at the ends and slid the cylinder into the jar of chromatography fluid.

When I finished with this, I began to clean out FYBs that had been used for harvest. I used the pressure-washer to spray them clean and leaned them to drain. Gary came over and began to help me, so within a short period we had cleaned the sixty or so FYBs and had them all stacked on the crush pad, draining.

After we finished, Dane came over and began to program the press. I asked if we had fruit coming in, and he said that the Arey fruit had already arrived and he had gotten the gross weight. Gary and I went out to the truck to unload the fruit. There was some raisining, but in general the fruit looked good, with negligible amounts of mold.

As we were walking out to the truck, I got a text message from George, our friend whose son's christening my wife and I attended two weeks ago. We had talked about my working at the winery, and he had said that he would visit when he was in the area. George was asking if I was working today. I answered yes, and shortly I got a call from him. He was just finishing up a meeting in Dublin, which was fifteen minutes away, and he said he would be out to the winery shortly. I told him it was barbecue Wednesday and that Nancy was making her chicken enchiladas, and he said he remembered that I had told him to come out on Wednesdays for lunch.

Gary and I offloaded the half-ton bins from the truck. It looked like we had over a ton of fruit, maybe a ton and a half. I brought the bins over to the shade of the stable, and we got ready to load the press. Gary worked the chute, and I manned the forklift. Just as I was loading the first bin, George arrived and introduced himself to everyone that was watching. Nancy had arrived and was preparing lunch. Mark from Zephyr arrived, and Lynn came back with cold Coronas. Cruelly, Dane brought over two Coronas with lime, one for Gary and one for himself. He looked at me and said, "No drinking and driving. You'll have to wait until we're finished loading the press." I loved driving the forklift, but I would have traded it for the cold beer right about then.

I loaded three of the bins into the press. Dane said to hold off on the fourth, as he wanted to run a short cycle on the press to make more room. And besides, he said, we needed to break for lunch.

As I washed up and walked over to the table, I was explaining to George what we were doing with the Chardonnay: pressing it right away to get it off the skins for fermentation. I also told him that the tanks of the crush pad contained red wines that went through a slightly different process; i.e., destemming and fermentation on the skins for a week or two, depending on the grapes and the progress of fermentation.

Just as we were sitting down, Richard, who worked for Wente, arrived with a bottle of Chardonnay, so we sat down to beer and wine—not bad. But the real treat was the enchiladas that Nancy had made. She served them up, and we began to eat and chat and enjoy this new tradition of Wednesday lunch at Page Mill Winery. It was a fun group of people that seemed to ebb and flow depending on the Wednesday. Today we had time to enjoy our lunch, as the press was doing its work. I also gave George a mini tour of the barrel room, but he joined right in the conversation around the table too.

As we were wrapping up lunch, Lynn declared that the rotation had started over with her, and that she would be preparing pulled-pork sandwiches next week. Nancy would be in Oregon for the next two Wednesdays, but she promised to be back. Everyone else was planning on enjoying pulled pork next week.

Dane had stepped away to dump the last bin into the press, and Gary went off to load the bins back onto the truck because we needed to get a tare (unloaded weight) at the scales. I stayed at the table for a while longer, and

Dane returned. Soon George said he had to get back, and we all said our goodbyes. Everyone told George to make plans to be back next week, and he said that he was going back to the office right then to arrange his appointments in the area for Wednesday next week.

I walked him out to his car, telling him we would harvest in a week and a half, so he and Natalie should put down the date. He said he would, and I waved goodbye as he left the parking lot. I went over and helped Gary finish loading the bins and securing them on the truck. We then went back onto the crush pad as Dane was starting to clean the press. Gary and I stacked up the FYBs we had cleaned and then loaded and secured them on a pallet.

I asked Dane what else needed doing, and he asked me to go get the tare on the truck and fill it with gas. I headed out for the public scales at Tri-Valley Bekins. I drove the truck onto the scale and went inside. Ruth (I think), who works there, pulled the Page Mill tag and asked me how much I thought we'd gotten. I told her that I thought it was one and a half tons. She gave me the sheet and the net weight, of the Arey fruit was 2,130 pounds, or just over a ton. I thanked her, left, and gassed up the truck before heading back to the winery.

When I arrived, Gary was gone, and Dane was just finishing up cleaning the press. I told him the weight, and he was surprised, as he had gotten what he'd thought was more than that in the pressed juice. Who knows? But that was it for the day.

We were back to "makin' the wine" for Page Mill—it was a glorious day!

OCTOBER 2, 2008

As I arrived at the winery, Gary and Dane were discussing the day's tasks. It sounded like more of a maintenance day.

Our first task was to pull out the pallet and a half of 2008 Estate Petite Sirah, flip over the cases, and load them onto the truck so that Gary could deliver them to UDS, the warehouse in Livermore. When the cases were bottled, they were stored upright to enable the small amount of nitrogen gas to escape the bottle. The nitrogen had been used in sparging and to protect the wine during the bottling process. Within a few days, we needed to turn the cases over to store the bottles upside down, keeping the cork damp and the oxygen out.

While we were turning the cases, Dick Bartlett of Charles R Vineyards pulled up in his truck. He walked up and affably said hello to all of us. He began to tell Dane that Julio was picking his Petite Sirah because the Brix was over 25. He asked Dane whether he was taking any of Julio's fruit. Dane said that he certainly was, and that he was quite surprised that they were picking. Dane quickly called Julio, and they agreed that Dane would be getting about a ton of fruit. Now, whether Julio had forgotten or was simply planning to drop off the fruit, no one knew. Gary told me later that it wasn't uncommon for growers to simply drop off fruit without warning. My own suspicion was that he had forgotten, because he asked Dane to drop off two half-ton bins for the fruit.

Dane said he'd be right over. As Gary and I looked out at the truck, which was loaded and strapped with the bins and FYBs for the Campi harvest tomorrow, and one of the pallets of Petite for delivery, we saw extra work and delay. Dick might have sensed the same thing, as he quickly said that he'd be happy to drop off the bins, pick up the fruit, and bring them back. Dane got a big smile on his face and said he'd be in Dick's debt forever. Dick just laughed as Dane and I quickly loaded two bins on the truck and strapped them down, and then Dick was on his way. I looked at Dane and remarked on what a generous thing Dick had done. Dane said that Dick was a very good friend to him, and to Page Mill.

After we finished loading the other pallet, we strapped them down, and Gary headed out for UDS.

Dane asked me to top off and stir the Beebe Chardonnay. We also needed barrel cards for several of the barrels. A barrel cards is simply a card with all the relevant data about what is in a given barrel. These were the cards I had placed on the Estate Petite Sirah barrels I'd filled a few weeks back. Each card was created from the production database that held all the relevant information about the different Page Mill wines. Dane showed me the database and the barrel card option, which was essentially a template. Dane had historical data on all of the wines he had made over the past ten or so years, so he could go back and see how a given vineyard or varietal had performed in prior years, given the stats on the fruit (Brix, pH, TA, etc.).

With the cards stapled on the remaining unmarked barrels, I set about using the topping can to top off the barrels. The topping can held about a gallon of wine and had a very long neck that came out of the bottom edge of the can, with a curve at the end. The top of the can was half covered so that the wine didn't spill out as you poured it. There was also a small cylinder at the end of the stem. Dane told me that it was used to hold a candle in the dark caves or rooms used for storing barrels, to see how much was being poured in, and that it was in use by some even today.

By the time I finished topping off all of the barrels, it was time for lunch. Gary, Michael, Dane, and I sat down to cold enchiladas from yesterday. They were still great, especially with a bottle of Vintner's Select Zinfandel. We also enjoyed a lively discussion about the upcoming evening's VP candidate debate.

As we were finishing lunch, the Petite Sirah from Julio's vineyard arrived on Dick's truck. I unloaded it, and Gary and I set up the destemmer to crush the fruit. It was almost exactly one ton, and the fruit was beautiful, with the large, very tight dark clusters that are characteristic of Petite Sirah. After destemming, we loaded it into the fermentation tank, skinned it, and put it into the shade.

As usual, the cleanup took as long as the work, which is a testament to both the automation of the destemmer and the importance of keeping the equipment clean.

Gary Campi called me, wondering if his vineyard would be picked this week. I said that the plan was to pick it tomorrow, so he was happy. Later, when Leopoldo came by to pick up the truck and the bins, I confirmed that he'd be out to the Campis' by 6:30 AM.

Gary and I helped Dane rearrange the barrel room, pulling out the empties, bringing in Estate Petite and Chardonnay, and adding the barrel cards to the new barrels in storage. Using a pallet jack, Gary and I moved a stack of barrels—two barrels on racks, side by side, to a height of four barrels—into position so that Dane could get at it with the forklift. He would lift the barrels four at a time and bring them out onto the concrete pad to be rearranged, with empties removed.

In moving one of the stacks, which are very heavy, especially when full of wine, Gary and I bumped a stack of case boxes and knocked two over. Several bottles in each of the cases broke, and the wine drained onto the floor.

Dane came into the storage room and exclaimed angrily, "That has never happened … today!" and then broke into a big smile, giving Gary and me each two demerits. In keeping with Dane's view that as long as no one gets hurt in winemaking, it's all good, we did get demerits for dumb moves— typically two. But we also got our pay doubled for good things we'd done … and if it weren't for the pay being zero, we would be rolling in it.

After we finished with the barrel room, Dane grabbed a rack with two empty barrels on it and headed for the barrel washer. He set them down close to the washer, and we prepared the washer. As Dane picked up the barrels, he had come too close to the barrel washer and began picking it up with the fork, along with the rack of two barrels. As he did so, Michael looked at me with two fingers held up: two demerits for Dane. When I said this to Dane, Michael said it was really the peace sign; he was just too nice to give them to Dane.

We finished washing the empty barrels and called it a day.

As I drove home, I called Gary Campi. I let him know when Leo would come, so he could put their dogs in the garage. I also told him to grab a few clusters of his Merlot and give them to Leo, and I would have them tested by Lynn for Brix and acidity.

OCTOBER 3, 2008

Gary and I drove in together and talked about the Biden/Palin debate, with all of the winks and cute sayings from Sarah Palin. We both felt that while she didn't implode as some had feared, Joe Biden had certainly sounded much more credible.

The skies were threatening as we drove across the bottom of the San Francisco Bay, up into the East Bay hills, and out to Livermore. But the forecast for rain had been downgraded to showers later today and into tomorrow, so I was hopeful that our vineyard would not see too much rain in the next day or so.

This morning, for me, was all about the science. I had to take measurements of Brix and temperature for the ten fermenting tanks we had on the crush pad and under the overhang. These included my hand-destemmed Merlot—all ten or so gallons—the Malbec/Cab Franc, a small lot of Syrah, and the three peninsula red vineyards, Kung, Kennedy, and Kellenberger. There were also three Cabs and the Petite we'd processed yesterday. I completed an ML test on a number of these, plus two Zin barrels and the Harris and Davigo Cabernets. All told, I had ten ML samples to fit on a single page. I used the wooden block that Lynn had showed me and got all ten samples on the page. After that, I stapled the paper by the ends and slid the cylinder into the jar of chromatography fluid.

In the middle of this, Gary came to Lynn and me and declared that he had lost a lot of money in the stock market this week and he'd had no fun at all doing it. So he wanted to take everyone to lunch at the Zephyr Grill, to do something fun while spending his money, and to do his part in stimulating the economy.

Later that morning, Gary came to tell me that the Balyeat Zinfandel from Napa would be harvested in about ten days. The Sleepy Holler Syrah wasn't happening at all. This was a vineyard in northern Napa County. Frost in spring had damaged about half of the fruit, and the heat over the last few weeks did the rest in. This was really too bad, as the Sleepy Holler vineyard had great fruit that made great Syrah.

Gary and I were ready to head out for lunch. Dane needed to run an errand and said he would meet us there. He also said that Angela would be joining us. On the way to lunch, I mentioned to Gary that I had thought about my friend Kent, who had a Syrah vineyard that had developed Syrah disorder, which is a set of symptoms particular to Syrah vineyards. The fruit was fine, but the vines suffered and ultimately died. Kent, knowing he had this problem, had not been as active in his vineyard. With Dane losing the Sleepy Holler fruit, I thought Kent's vineyard could help. I talked about the idea to Gary, and he suggested bringing it up at lunch.

We arrived at Zephyr, and Gary suggested that I give Dane a call to remind him not to forget the wine he was supposed to bring. I got Dane on the mobile, and he said that he had already left, and locked his keys in the tasting room, and forgotten the wine—two demerits!

We had a bottle of Page Mill Sauvignon Blanc, and I enjoyed a mushroom burger and fries. Mark, the restaurant's manager, joined us at the table for a while. I mentioned my idea about Kent's vineyard to Dane, and he was definitely interested, so I told him I'd call Kent and get back to him. We finally decided that we needed to get back to work, so we said goodbye to Angela and Mark and headed back to the winery.

When I got back, I called Kent. He said he would check the vineyard when he got home and call me back.

We spent the early afternoon rearranging some barrels and cleaning up the barrel storage room, turning it back into the tasting room for Gary's work tomorrow and Sunday. As we were finishing up, Leo called to say he'd finished picking the Campi fruit and would leave the truck out front. Dane asked to ride with Gary and me back to the peninsula, where he would pick up the truck and drive it back to Livermore.

On the way over the hill, we talked about parasailing most of the way. Dane and his father were avid parasail pilots, having flown from Mission Peak in Fremont and Mount Diablo locally and done cross-country flights in Mexico. It was fascinating. When we arrived at the Campis', there was no truck in sight. Dane tried to call Leopoldo on his mobile, but he got no answer. On the way to my house, Dane continued to try to reach Leo, calling his mobile again as well as his home number. In the end, with no way to contact Leo, Dane decided to take the ACE train home. This was a train that went from Santa Clara and San Jose out to Tracy, passing through Livermore on its way. Gary was going to take him, but Corky, our friend and Denise's business partner, said she needed to pick up something near where Dane needed to catch the train, so she would be happy to drive him.

While they were talking about this, Kent called and said he had some raisining but the fruit looked pretty good—about one and a half tons. I told Kent I'd give the info to Dane and he'd call back if he was interested. Gary left for home, and Dane and I went in to have a beer while Corky and Denise finished up. I told him what Kent had said, and he took Kent's contact info. As we sat and talked, Leo called, and the truck was in front of Leo's house in Sunnyvale. Dane was relieved and made sure he knew the directions and where Leo had left the keys, and I drove him over. I told him I also wanted to see what the fruit looked like, as Dane would crush it tomorrow. When we arrived at Leo's, there was the truck. The fruit looked good, with a very small amount of raisining. Leopoldo had said he thought it was about 15 percent more than Arey, but we'd see. Dane and I said our goodbyes, and we both headed home respectively.

OCTOBER 7, 2008

Dane was busy on Monday, and when I arrived today, he was away, getting his eyes checked. I ran into Lynn, who was just leaving the lab and heading for home. She told me she'd be smoking fifteen pounds of pork butt today, for pulled-pork sandwiches tomorrow.

I punched down all of the various fermenting tanks, and when Dane arrived, he said he couldn't see because the doctor had given him drops during his eye test. The doctor had said that he could drive, but he wasn't so sure that had been a good idea. We then talked about the day's work ahead, and Dane said we would be pressing a number of the smaller lots today.

With Dane's eyesight blurred for now, Dane asked me to call Kent about the Syrah, as he hadn't gotten a chance to do it over the weekend. I called Kent in his office and left a message. He called me back within half an hour, and I turned the call over to Dane. Dane spoke with him and later told me that he might take his fruit but wanted to check out the vineyard, possibly tomorrow.

We set up the press, cleaned out the hoses, and began with the first small lot. The process was to dump in the lot, pressure-clean the bin that we'd just held it in, press the lot, and pump it into the clean bin. Then we would put a skin on it and gas it, and then we'd take the next lot and dump it into the press and do it all over again. The press held two or three tons, and the seven lots we were processing didn't come close, so we just pressed the juice on top of the skins, which saved cleanup time and got the same result. The very small amount of blending was probably less than a few percent anyway. In the end, we had pressed seven small lots: Kennedy, Kellenberger, Kung, Johnson Cab, a local Syrah, custom crush Cabernet, and my tiny lot of hand-crafted Merlot.

As we loaded one of the larger lots of fruit, Dane said that he would let the press work through a complete cycle on this larger lot, and that it would take about an hour and a half. He suggested a burger at the First Street Ale House in downtown Livermore. The town of Livermore had created a wide sidewalk area downtown, with outside seating at many of the restaurants, including the First Street Ale House. We sat outside, had beer and burgers, and talked about downtown, our families, and birds of prey. I had worked at the Raptor Center while at UC Davis and had the opportunity to work with a number of birds of prey, including hawks, eagles, owls, falcons, and even a turkey vulture.

I told Dane one story about how fast and how protective these birds could be. I took a girl I was dating out to the center one day to show her a pair of breeding red-tailed hawks. The birds were in a large, enclosed aviary and were at the far end of it, sitting in their nest. I told the girl not to get too close to the wire enclosure. She asked why not, and I told her that the birds were very protective and might attack her if she got too close. She looked at me in disbelief, as the birds were a good twenty feet away. She explained to me that there was no possibility of the birds getting to her without her reacting. Of course, within moments, the female launched herself from the perch, and before my friend could move, the bird had reached the wire and raked her with her talons. The hawk drew a thin line of blood on my friend's forehead. It was not serious, but she was so stunned that she was more afraid than anything. I told Dane that while I had felt bad, I'd probably had an "I told you so" look on my face. He just laughed, but he was also amazed by the story and by the speed of the birds.

We got back to the winery and continued pressing the remaining three small lots. In the end, we had them all in bins and all buttoned up and gassed up.

As we were pressing one of the last lots, Randy, the winemaker at Charles R Vineyards, came by. He was ticked off because one of his Zinfandel growers had stiffed him on his fruit. He had requested six to eight tons, and he'd been told that he wasn't going to get any. This was unfortunately becoming a problem of the season. Mostly it was growers saying their yields were down and they could only provide a percentage of what had been requested. Dane was only getting about half of his requested Napa Zinfandel because of low yields, and I've already mentioned that the Napa Syrah was ruined.

When Randy left, Dane and I cleaned up the press, the chute, and the crush pad. As I brought the forklift back from dumping the "cake," Dane was just finishing pressure-washing the crush pad. In the late afternoon fall sunshine, it looked good and clean. Dane said that he hoped to have all of these bins barreled down by the weekend, so that he would be ready for the rest of the harvest, starting with the Côte Merlot next Monday.

OCTOBER 8, 2008

This morning, when I turned on my phone shortly before 8:00 AM, there was a message from Dane asking me to go out to Kent's vineyard, check it out for him, and bring back samples. I called him, and he asked me to be his eyes and his taste buds in the vineyard. I was happy to do it. I called and left a message for Kent, telling him that I would be out in his vineyard, getting samples. I arrived at his house and began to walk the vineyard. The fruit look pruny, meaning there wasn't so much raisining, but the fruit was clearly lacking water and showing some puckering. We had some fruit like this in our vineyard, but Kent's Syrah was 60 percent this way. I took some samples and headed out for Livermore. As I came over the pass, it was another beautiful day in Livermore Valley, with weather in the mid-seventies. Also it was barbecue Wednesday, and Lynn was bringing pulled-pork sandwiches.

When I arrived, everyone except Lynn was there. Michael was figuring numbers of gallons for all of the wines that Dane and I had pressed the day before because we were going to barrel down the wines today. Dane was working on paperwork in the tasting room, but he said hello when I arrived. I gave him the Syrah, and he tasted it and said he thought it made sense to get the fruit. We went into the lab and grabbed the refractometer. The Brix ranged from around 30 in the pruny fruit to 24 in some of the normal clusters. Dane decided to pick the fruit, so he went off to arrange to get it harvested.

Gary had been to UPS with shipments that needed to go out. The weekend had been very good for the tasting room, as several of Page Mill's best customers had come in to buy multiple cases. Also, John Ignowsky, manager of the Mountain View Beverages & More, bought a pallet of '05 California Merlot. (The '05 had a good deal of Côté in it.) He would be selling it at three BevMo stores on the peninsula. So it had been a good week already for sales.

Michael and I began preparing to wash barrels. Several had leaks, so we filled them with water, and Michael fixed the leaks with matchsticks. Some of the leaks were less obvious. For these he used wax that he spread into the spots where the leaks appeared. This usually did the trick, and in many cases as the wine was put into the barrels, the liquid alone helped to swell the oak staves and seal the barrel. I began siphoning out the water in preparation for barreling down.

In the middle of the prep work, Dane came out to say he had a custom press job for John, the winemaker at Big White House Winery. John was bringing in about one and a half tons of Roussanne. Roussanne is a white grape that originated in the northern Rhone appellations, and according to the Web site www.winepros.org, Roussanne probably gets its name from the light-brownish russet cast of its ripe berries. It is a very finicky grape and not very widely planted in the United States.

Michael and I continued our prep work, and when John arrived, I went out with the forklift and grabbed the three half-ton bins of fruit. The fruit looked very good, with the hints of the russet color on the mostly green grapes that were a key characteristic of Roussanne grapes. I switched out the fork for the box-dumper and grabbed the first box. I dumped in two of the three, and we held off while Dane set the press for a light cycle to compress the fruit already in the press, to easily fit the last bin. Once it was in, Michael began pumping the free-flowing juice into John's barrel in the back of his pickup truck.

The press began its work just in time for lunch. Lynn's whole family joined us—Ray, Ben, and Sarah. Also there were Claudia, the wife of Wente's winemaker, Claude; Mark from Zephyr; and Richard from Wente. Along with Dane's A-team—Gary, Michael, and me—and, of course, Dane, we were a big group. Lynn had cooked up some great meat, and along with shredded cabbage, dill pickles, and a variety of rolls, we had the makings of real pulled-pork sandwiches. She had also made a North Carolina vinegar-based barbecue sauce that was very tart, and she had brought an excellent bottled sauce called Sweet Baby Ray's—no relationship to her husband, Ray. Accompanying the sandwiches was a Caesar salad that was a nice comple-ment to the pork.

Gary brought out a magnum of an early eighties Page Mill Cab. So early, in fact, that Dane called his dad to see if he knew when it was bottled. It was capped with a silver foil, and Dane said that his dad had only used those during a few years. Dick couldn't remember, and he suggested to Dane that the bottle was his anyway, and what were we doing drinking it? I'm sure he was smiling to himself as he said this. We also enjoyed two recently released

Zinfandels, including the Vintner's Select, and Richard brought along a very dry Gewürztraminer and a Chardonnay for the table.

Claudia had brought a blueberry cheesecake for dessert, rounding out another wonderful lunch. Dane volunteered for next week, as Lynn was the first one in the second rotation. Dane brought out an old guitar that had been in one of the sheds. It was filthy, but he dusted it off, and then, with help from Ben and his mandolin, he tuned it. We took turns playing music. I played a Lovin' Spoonful song, "Daydream," and everyone joined in, especially at the whistling part. When I was finished, Gary suggested that I look at my fingers; they were filthy from all of the dust on the guitar and its strings. Ben played, Michael played, and Dane played mostly instrumentals, and the guitar seemed to hold its tuning. Before the day was done, Dane hung a hook for the guitar on the toolshed wall. We cleaned up after lunch, and Michael and Dane finished up the pressing for John, and he went on his way.

We then set about the task we'd hoped to do much earlier in the day: barreling down the wines that we had pressed yesterday. By doing this, we cleared most of the bins from the crush pad. The few remaining were placed under the tasting room overhang: two bins of Tazetta Syrah, Julio Petite Sirah, and Cantu Cabernet Sauvignon.

I took off in the late afternoon, as I needed to get home to begin calling people for our harvest on Sunday.

OCTOBER 10, 2008

Today was Denise's birthday. Happy birthday! I gave her a birthday card this morning as a warm-up. It was a cutout of little stuffed bears in ballet outfits, and it said, "Happy birthday tutu you!" It was very cute.

Gary was coming to pick me up, so I made us coffee and brought Denise a birthday cup of coffee.

Gary and I headed out. The plan was for me to bring the truck back tonight for our harvest on Sunday. When we arrived, the truck was not at the winery. We spoke with Dane, who said that Leo had taken it to pick Kent Littlehale's Syrah vineyard and was due back later today, though Dane had called him and had not heard back yet.

In the meantime, I punched down the four remaining fermenting tanks: two Syrah from Tazetta's next door, the Julio Petite Sirah, and the Cantu Cabernet that was a custom crush lot.

Gary was planting a few shrubs around the winery, and I helped him finish it up and pull a few weeds.

Gary had also decided to open up the tasting room today at noon. He had decided to try to open on Fridays as a way to build the business, and as harvest came to a close in the coming weeks, the tasting room could be readied earlier.

Dane had gone to his youngest daughter's doctor's appointment, and when he returned, he asked me to run ML tests on eight lots. I completed the tests and then helped Gary tidy up the tasting room so he could open.

It was a cool, blustery day, with strong gusts of wind and temps in the low sixties. This was the first time that Page Mill had been open for tasting on a Friday in a while, so it was slow. A group of three people came into the tasting room. One of them was on the phone, and the other two stepped up to the tasting bar. Gary asked if they wanted to taste, and the answer was no, they wanted to buy wine. One of them looked at the list of available wines. He noticed the 2005 Merlot, which was "Gary's Pick" and 50 percent off the retail price. "Gary's Pick" was a promotional price that Gary had set up to stimulate sales and move particular lots of wine. The guy said he wanted to buy a bottle of the 2005 Merlot, and Gary helped him with the transaction. Meanwhile, he and the woman with him ate four brownies and filled their water bottle with bottled water. They took their wine and left. Gary smiled and said that at the aggressive price of "Gary's Pick" and with the four brownies and the quart of bottled water they'd consumed, Page Mill might have just broken even on that transaction.

After a little while, we checked again with Dane on the whereabouts of Leo. He still had not heard. We decided to take off mid-afternoon and leave Dane to work the tasting room. We were celebrating Denise's birthday with dinner at St. Michael's Alley that evening, which was our favorite restaurant; Gary was joining us, along with Denise's mother. Just as we were about to leave, Dane heard from Leo, who said he was going over to pick then. Dane asked for a call as soon as he was finished or stopped for the night. He would then let Gary know what was up so he could coordinate picking up the truck and getting it back to the winery tomorrow, so he could bring it for our harvest on Sunday. One way or another, that was going to happen; we just didn't know how, as we left the winery.

On the way out of Livermore, Gary asked if I'd like to stop at Ruby Hill Winery's tasting room. They had only been open a little over six months, and the tasting room manager was also a member of the Page Mill wine club and a friend of Gary's. We stepped into the beautiful new building that housed the tasting room. There was no one there except the staff, but as it was a Friday, this wasn't too surprising. Debbie, the tasting room manager, was there, and she and Gary got into a conversation as we tried several of their reserve wines. They talked about the slowdown in business this year, but they also shared success stories about a limo full of people that had come to Page Mill late in the day on Sunday, and Gary had suggested that they also try Ruby Hill, which was open for longer hours than Page Mill. The passengers had bought sizeable amounts of wine at both wineries, so the two of them congratulated each other on the sales that had helped boost their Sunday numbers, and Debbie thanked Gary for sending them her way. Gary told me later that one of the things he liked about Livermore Valley wineries was the sense of camaraderie that existed among most of the winery people in the valley.

We each bought a few bottles and headed for home.

That night we enjoyed a great meal at St. Mike's and celebrated Denise's birthday. Tomorrow we had a lot to do to get prepared for our harvest on Sunday—the best day of the entire year!

OCTOBER 11, 2008

Today was prep day for the harvest tomorrow. Not only did we need to prepare everything for the harvest, we had to prepare everything for the party afterward. On her birthday yesterday, Denise had done much of the cutting, grating, and measuring for the strata that she was preparing. So today was about assembling the dishes and cooking them most of the way, so that tomorrow we would just need to heat them up. My job on days like this was to be Denise's sous chef and help in any way I could. I picked up a couple of last-minute items and the all-important Peet's morning coffee.

When I got back, Nicole had come over to help for the morning. We spent it putting together seven dishes of the strata, as we were expecting about fifty people tomorrow. This strata was a baked dish made with bread cubes soaked in cream, egg, and cheese, and then layered with herbs (sage and thyme), ham, and artichoke hearts. The dish was then baked for about an hour. We were planning to serve this with a green salad, bread, and fruit, all of which we would get later today or first thing tomorrow morning.

When we finished, Nicole left to take her dog to the beach with friends. Denise went upstairs to shower so we could go out and make our final food purchases for the day. I got out a batch of my red sauce from the freezer. Adam and his girlfriend, and three of his fraternity brothers, were coming home from school for the harvest and would arrive that night for dinner. We'd cook tri-tip, pasta with mushroom sauce and pine nuts, garlic bread, and Caesar salad. These kids were living right—but it was great that Adam would be home for harvest.

Then I went outside to get everything in shape for tomorrow. I brought out tables and chairs, to add to our backyard furniture, giving us seating for forty-five or fifty people. I clipped the rose bushes at the ends of our vineyard rows so that removing the nets tomorrow would be easy. I got out the clippers with the intention of cleaning them, but Denise was ready to go.

We picked up the salad fixings and the fruit, and the rest of the meal for this evening, and headed for home. We got a report from Adam that he was about two hours away. We got everything ready for dinner, and I went to clean the clippers for the harvest tomorrow. There were about thirty-five clippers to clean, and I was just about finished when Adam and his friends arrived. We all gave each other big hugs, and Denise and I met one of his fraternity brothers that we hadn't met before; everyone else, we knew. I finished up the clippers and went to join everyone.

We enjoyed a Bernardus Chardonnay and a Page Mill Chardonnay with some crackers and cheese, and then we drank Côté Merlot 2004 with dinner. After we all cleaned up, Denise and I headed for bed. True to form, the kids didn't go to bed until later. We had a big day ahead of us, and we needed to be up early for Harvest Day 2008!

OCTOBER 12, 2008: HARVEST DAY

Denise and I both got up early and showered. The day was already beautiful, with crystal-clear skies and a very light breeze. While it was a bit chilly at this time of the morning, it was clear that we were in for a glorious day.

The ritual was that I picked up the cake, balloons, fresh bread, and ice—and, of course, coffee. As I was about to leave Peet's Coffee, I got a call from our daughter Nicole. She was coming over to help early and asked if I could pick up a coffee for her. This wasn't just a large coffee like Denise and I drank. No, this was a medium, decaf, nonfat vanilla latte, and when I hung up, I only hoped I could remember it all—oh, and a chocolate croissant.

When I got home, Denise and Nicole were getting the tables ready. It was ten o'clock, and Gary from Page Mill and Shelby, our good friend, were already pulling the nets off. I busied myself getting water, beer, and other drinks into large plastic tubs, setting them out on the driveway, and filling the tubs with ice. Nicole set up a table nearby for snacks and a place for the clippers and the first-aid kit (which we hoped not to use).

Gary went up the street and picked up the truck he had dropped off last night. It had FYBs for picking and half-ton bins for transport. We unloaded the FYBs and set them about the vineyard, and then we got several of the large bins situated on the truck, ready to be filled with grapes.

Adam and his friends were all arriving in the kitchen, where we made some more coffee and had bagels and cream cheese available. (Denise got half of Nicole's chocolate croissant, which was a favorite of hers.) As they were finishing up, friends began to arrive. It was 11:00 AM, and harvest was about to begin.

Within a few minutes, a good group of people had arrived. For some reason, this year we had a number of new people joining us for harvest for the first time ... and we had a new approach this year. So I assembled everyone and went through our instructions. We still used the poster that Denise and I had put together for our first harvest. As we read through it, I emphasized the most important thing: don't cut yourself. Most of our rules revolved around trying to minimize nipping one's fingers while harvesting all of the good fruit. I glossed over the section about disease and rotten fruit, as we rarely had any. I did show people what a truly dried-out, raisiny bunch looked like, but I quickly added that we had very little of it. In general, we wanted all of the fruit, and it looked beautiful, even though there didn't seem to be as much as in years past.

The change from prior years was the use of the half-ton bins. Up until this year, we had filled the truck with FYBs—over two hundred of them every year. This meant that someone had to empty them on the other end to be crushed. By filling half-ton bins, we could use the forklift to dump them into the chute—the thing I had been doing for the last several months.

With the instructions behind us, people went off into the vineyard to socialize and pick grapes. As a few late arrivals came into the yard, we greeted them and gave them instructions as necessary. For the first time in a number of years, I just picked grapes. I had been working the truck with Gary and Adam for the past several years. As picking was a favorite pastime of mine, I was in my glory. I chatted with various friends nearby, and when my bin was full, I took it out to the truck to be dumped into the bins. I took my turn at times dumping the FYBs into the bin. After each full bin, I could go to a different part of the vineyard to mingle with new people each time.

As I went about picking, I noticed that there were just as many clusters as in years past, but there were a number of clusters with tiny green shot among the berries, and others were simply smaller. I did harvest some beautiful clusters, but in years past, these would have dominated the harvest, whereas they were not as common this year. I knew we would be down in tonnage this year, but the fruit still looked beautiful, so I hoped the quality would be there, even if the quantity was down.

It is always a surprise to everyone, even those of us who do it every year, when we are finished. One minute, people are feverishly filling their bins, and the next, they bring it to the truck and realize that there are no more grapes to harvest. It is mildly disappointing to most people, which is the secret, I think, to getting them back year after year. No one has to work that hard or for that long, so it is just fun!

Nicole and I walked through the vineyard, doing the final QC, or quality control. We didn't find too much, which meant people had done a good job of clearing a vine before moving on. We did find a few clusters here and there, but we found more good clusters on the ground than on the vines. Nicole suggested a new rule for next year about making sure that people didn't leave clusters on the ground.

With the QC finished, we brought our last bin to the truck, and Gary and I set about securing the bins. We had only filled four half-ton bins, which meant that we had less than two tons, which was about half of our normal harvest. No matter—harvest was complete, and now it was time to enjoy the afternoon, good food, good friends, and great wine.

As we entered the backyard, people were relaxing everywhere. Denise asked me to get the wine started, so I quickly opened up both red and white (Page Mill, of course), and with the help of friends, I got glasses into people's hands and poured wine. We were serving the Côté 2005, which was drinking very nicely, along with Chardonnay and Sauvignon Blanc.

Then I went inside, opened a bottle of Côté, and filled the huge glass in preparation for the harvest toast. As I walked outside, Denise had gathered the kids, and we went out near the pool to address our friends. We dedicated this harvest to Denise's dad, who had died the previous December. He loved to harvest and to spend the day with family. Last year he had been very sick, but he'd still managed to be at harvest. We had gotten a chair for him, and he'd sat in the vines, picking grapes. It had been hard, but it is an image that I will never forget. He was a great man and a special presence in our lives.

We also thanked everyone for their friendship and their help, for sharing this wonderful day with us. And then we raised the giant glass in toast to the harvest. I carefully took a drink from it and handed it to Denise. Adam told her to chug it. She just looked at him and took a sip. Then Nicole took a sip, and finally Adam. This had become our tradition, and it was so special to have our children here and part of this. Besides Adam's friends, several of Nicole's friends had joined us, so the next generation was beginning to make its mark on harvest.

Just as we were finishing, Gary came into the yard after securing the truck. I called him up and asked that we all honor him as he took a drink from the big glass. He didn't spill a drop!

After the toasts, the food was served, and everyone enjoyed the afternoon. It was a great time to visit and enjoy the food, the wine, and the beauty of the day. Both Denise and I mingled, serving food and wine, and talking with our friends and our children's friends. This truly was a great way to kick off the fall season.

A few people began to say their goodbyes. We gave each of them a bottle of our newly bottled 2006 in thanks for their help. Finally, both of us sat down with something to eat. The food was wonderful, as always, and made all the better because of hard work.

Next came the cake. We always had a big chocolate harvest cake, and this was no exception. The cake was about four inches tall, covered with dark chocolate frosting, and layered with raspberry filling. It was decadent, and it went very well with the 2005 Côté Merlot—I know that for sure.

The afternoon was beautiful, and the remaining guests had clustered in small groups: Nicole and her friends, Adam and his friends talking with Corky and Shelby, and a group of us talking and enjoying the wine.

As I have done on many of these occasions, I went into the cellar and brought out a 2003 to try. Everyone had a taste and declared it to be "bigger" than the 2005, and with its age, it was drinking even better. I kept going. This time I brought out a 1999 and our favorite, the 2001. The 1999 needed more time to breathe but still tasted great. This had been our third harvest, so the vines had still been young, but nine years later, it still had lots of fruit and medium tannins. The 2001 was outstanding. The combination of fruit and tannins was wonderful, and the finish was long, making it a wine that everyone enjoyed. Breaking from the pattern of an odd-year vertical, I brought out a 2002. While not as good as the '01, it was, to me, the next best thing. I was looking forward to next spring, when Denise and I planned to have a ten-year vertical tasting of our Merlot, from the first vintage, 1997, to the most recently bottled vintage, 2006. I was looking forward to drinking the wines, but I was looking forward just as much to the comments and comparisons across the vintages.

This was a great way to end our harvest day. As people left, they all asked to be invited back; we assured them that they would be. Around seven, Adam and his friends left to drive back down to Loyola Marymount, where they were all in college. It had been great to have him home, even for so short a visit. He too felt the importance of being at harvest, as did Nicole.

With everyone gone, Denise and I finished cleaning up and went to bed, satisfied that we had gotten the grapes harvested and enjoyed another beautiful day with friends and family.

OCTOBER 13, 2008

Unlike past years, today I would be part of the next step in the creation of the 2008 Côté Merlot at Page Mill Winery. Every other year, I was back at work the next day, while Dane and Gary crushed the grapes and turned them into wine. But today was my turn to be part of this magic, and it was, of course, the thirteenth.

I went outside and made sure the truck was secure. Unknown to me then, Gary had stopped by earlier that morning to ensure that everything was tightened up and secure for the journey out to the winery. I hopped up into the cab and headed out. I found an empty place to park the big truck to get a coffee for the road, and then I was on my way again. The trip out to Livermore was uneventful. As I drove up Concannon to the intersection of Concannon and South Livermore, one hundred feet from the winery, Lynn was coming up South Livermore and waved. I'm sure she thought it was odd that I headed out past the winery instead of turning in. I had to stop at the public scales on my way into the winery to get a gross weight for the grapes. With that done, I returned to the winery, where I was met by Gary and Dane. Dane asked how the harvest had gone and then asked if we wanted to make some wine! Yes, sir!

Gary unloaded the bins with the forklift as I got two fermentation tanks ready. Gary and Dane had already gotten the destemmer set up. Once we were ready to go, Gary asked if I wanted the honor of loading the first bin. I said yes, hopped on the forklift, and grabbed the first load. I raised it up and dumped it into the waiting destemmer. Gary stood on the chute and made sure the grapes went in. I lowered the bin, cleaned it, and put it back on the truck. When I got back, Gary pulled out the bin of berries from under the destemmer, and I grabbed it while Gary moved the chute over the clean fermentation tank. I dumped the first load of grapes into the tank. We repeated the process with the second bin. I switched places with Gray for the remaining two bins, wanting to participate in all of the processes with my own grapes.

I had now done this many times, but it was very special to be processing the grapes that I had grown and that my family and friends had picked just yesterday. It made this day all the more special for me. When we finished with the last bin, we began to clean the destemmer. I think I did a more thorough job of salvaging all of the fruit that was stuck in the machine this time. I took the stems and dumped them into the vineyard. I brushed down the tanks, to clean any grapes off the walls that might introduce bacteria or bad flavors as fermentation began. Dane and I then put fresh skins on the tanks, and I marked them Côté Tank 1 and Côté Tank 2. When I finished this, Gary was just finishing up with the destemmer. He suggested that I take the truck back to the scales for the tare.

I took off for the scales, and I had to wait a bit when I arrived because the county of Alameda was calibrating the scales. This took about twenty minutes, and then I got my tare, showing that the grapes weighed 3,300 pounds. That was only 1.65 tons, about half of our normal production. I had known that it would be low, but I was surprised by how low it was. When I returned, Dane was surprised as well. He said that he was glad that I had gone to the scales because I probably wouldn't have believed him if he had told me those numbers. There had been reports all over the state of yields being lower, but this was 50 percent of normal. While I was mildly disappointed, I had been expecting a lower yield, and now I was hoping for good numbers that would help create a great wine. But the numbers would come tomorrow, when Lynn was back.

Dane had heard from a local grower who had some Merlot that was not spoken for. Given the yields of ours and the other smaller Merlot vineyards, Dane would go to see it later today and probably take the fruit.

We had sandwiches for lunch, and Scott and Nancy, the couple renting the house at the winery, came by with a bottle of Petite Sirah to share. We tried it and agreed that it needed some time to breathe and open up. As it did, the flavors opened up, and it definitely got better. I still preferred the Page Mill Estate to this wine, though. We had a fun conversation, and with our work done for the day, Gary and I said our goodbyes.

I must have been tired from the busy weekend because I slept all the way home in Gary's pickup. It had been a great few days, and now I was looking forward to these next few weeks with the newly emerging 2008 Côté Merlot.

OCTOBER 14, 2008

Today was a fairly quiet day at the winery. When I arrived, Dane was inside doing paperwork, and Lynn was working in the lab.

Dane looked up and said, "Shall we make some wine today?" We went onto the crush pad, and I punched down the fermenting tanks, starting with the Côté Merlot, which hadn't yet started fermenting and smelled like sweet grape juice. Dane said he liked to let it settle cold for a day or so, and then, given the cooler weather, he would inoculate with yeast tomorrow.

Next I went to punch down Kent's Syrah that Dane had processed on Sunday. It had been inoculated yesterday, so I got to punch it down. Because the grapes had begun to pucker, there wasn't as much liquid as normal. To punch it down, Dane gave me a two-by-six plank that I set across the top of the tank. I stood on the board to get more leverage with the punchdown tool, so I could get the skins and juice mixing. It was a strenuous process, so I completed my morning workout with this tank alone. Then I moved on to a Petite Sirah tank, as well as a Cab and two tanks holding the Syrah from next door, all of which were well on their way to fermenting dry.

While I was doing this, Dane was taking samples for Brix and temperature. He also pulled a larger sample of our must, so Lynn could get the numbers. Dane also pulled samples of the Beebe Chardonnay, which was essentially finished fermenting, and the Campi Chardonnay, which still had 2 percent residual sugar. The Campi tasted like a crisp apple—it was going to be beautiful.

Lynn came back with the numbers for the Côté Merlot. The Brix was 24, the pH was 3.58, the TA was 0.5, and the YAN (yeast assimilable nitrogen) was 146. Dane thought these numbers were very good. We might need to add a little acid, but the Brix was great. I couldn't wait for fermentation to really get going.

With the lower quantity of grapes from our vineyard, Dane was open to sourcing more Merlot. As he was calling around looking for used barrels to buy, one of the calls he made was to a small winery and grower that said he had around two tons of Merlot that he was trying to sell, along with barrels.

Dane asked if I wanted to go on a field trip to check out the Merlot fruit and the used barrels that were available. Of course I did. We drove out Tesla Road and came to the vineyard first. We walked into the vineyard to check the fruit. The far left of the vineyard was Cabernet. This gave way to grafts that had been done that year. Dane thought that at least some of this was Malbec. Farther over, we found what looked to be Merlot grapes that had been grafted two or three years earlier. We both tried the fruit. It didn't seem very ripe, even though the seeds were very brown, a sign that the fruit was fairly ripe. Dane pulled out his refractometer and got readings from 27 to 19. As we walked farther into the vineyard, it became more consistently 21 or 22 Brix, so Dane felt the vineyard was at least a week away. He thought out loud that it probably made sense to take the fruit.

We got back in his SUV and drove the rest of the way to the winery. We walked back into the winery, and Dane commented enviously about some of the equipment that was there. This was another winery started by someone with money, a doctor, who had bought some very nice, brand-new equipment. We met up with Betto, who was the doctor's manager of the vineyard and the winery. He showed Dane the barrels that were for sale. They looked a bit ragged to me, but Dane was very cordial and asked questions about the barrels and how they had been maintained.

He then asked about the vineyard, and we were told that the grafts were indeed Malbec, but also Tempranillo (the famous Spanish grape used to make Rioja) and Cinsault (a red grape from the south of France used mostly for blending). The Merlot was at the far end of the vineyard. We decided to check out that end of the vineyard on our way back.

As we got in the car, Dane echoed what had seemed evident to me: the barrels were too old. Hopefully he would find some newer ones at similar prices, but he could always fall back on these. We stopped at the other end of the vineyard. Here the fruit was not as heavy on the vines, but the Brix was a little higher, around 23 or 24. Dane made a mental note to check the vineyard again at the end of the week, but he said that he would probably take the fruit.

We drove back to the winery, and it was time for me to head back home. Dane was making lunch tomorrow, so he was hoping to finish up early at the winery and go shopping for his second round of Wednesday lunch. I was looking forward to that.

OCTOBER 15, 2008

Today was another beautiful day at the winery. We were experiencing eighty-degree weather, with crystal-clear skies. The first thing I did on arrival was to punch down the tanks we had on the crush pad. We were again getting to the point where there were only a few lots that weren't in barrels: the Syrah from next door, the Julio Petite Sirah, a custom crush Cabernet, Kent's Syrah, and our Merlot.

When this was done, I learned that we would press the Petite and the Cab today. We prepared the crush pad for pressing. I cleaned out a fermentation tank and began pumping off the free juice from the Petite Sirah tank. Once that was done, Michael programmed the press to open, and we situated the chute on top of it. Michael grabbed the now-lighter tank with the forklift and dumped the remaining must into the press. This was a bit trickier, as the tank was four feet by four feet wide and about five feet tall. I stood atop the chute to help guide him in. When he had the tank situated, he began to dump it in. It splashed quite a bit, and I ended up with purple grape spots pretty much head to toe. No one could question what I had done today, that was for sure. Once we got it into the press, we began to pump it into the cleaned out tank with the free-run juice in it.

I also pressure-washed the tank, as we planned to use it for the next wine we'd be pressing, a Cabernet. Just as we were finishing up this first batch, Dane arrived with lunch. He had decided to create a panini bar. He had made homemade pesto and olive tapenade. He bought two kinds of crusty bread, Italian meats, and several kinds of cheeses. He also brought a salad and a very scary-looking pecan dessert—scary good.

I was chosen as the first to grill my panini. The grill was still heating up, so it took a bit of time. I had backed things up with Michael, Gary, Mark from Zephyr and a friend and colleague of his, Diana, and Dane, of course. After a bit, it had heated up, so I removed my now hot and toasty panini, leaving it to the rest to put two in the grill so it moved much faster.

Just as we were sitting down, Richard from Wente joined us with a bottle of Sangiovese from Tamas. We also had a Page Mill '07 Chardonnay and what looked like a shiner. A shiner is an unlabeled bottle that is then sold to a winery for them to put their own label on. I tasted it and knew it was a Côté Merlot. I thought maybe it was an '07 sample, but as Gary correctly pointed out, it had foil on it. It turns out I was close. It was a Côté '05 that for some reason was not labeled. Gary checked the other bottles in the case, finding them all labeled, so this one was destined for our lunch.

The final wine at the table was a bit nondescript, as it was a 2004 Chardonnay and definitely past its prime. But the interesting thing was the label. It was a Mourning Dove Ranch Tesla Vineyard Chardonnay. On the back of the label it said, "Produced and bottled by Red Barn Cellars and estate grown and handpicked for cleanliness by Tesla vineyards." This was most curious, as no one could quite figure out what "handpicked for cleanliness" meant, as most vineyards were still handpicked. The other thing I found curious was the reference to "estate grown." It was not a designation on the front label, but rather a redundant statement in my mind. Every vineyard owner could claim their grapes were estate grown because they grew them. The value of the distinction for most wines was when the winery itself grew the grapes that they then made into their estate wine. Such was the case with the Estate Petite Sirah here at Page Mill.

It served as a lively conversation piece as we enjoyed the lunch that Dane had prepared. Gary was planning to deliver his second round of lunch next week, but Richard offered to make lunch for everyone. Gary gladly relinquished his position for another week. We needed to get back to pressing the Cabernet lot, so lunch broke up, with each of us grabbing a few items to clean up.

Then Michael and I went back to pressing. Because the Petite Sirah had been only a single tank, and the Cab too was just a single tank, we didn't go through the cleaning process between lots. Michael just programmed in a "hard press" during lunch that extracted just about everything from the Petite Sirah. As with the smaller lots that Dane and I had done last week, we simply added the Cabernet to the Petite Sirah cake that was already in the press, programmed the press, and pumped that juice into the free-run juice we had pumped out of the tank already.

As this was finishing up, I got the opportunity to inoculate our Merlot. I measured a half pitcher of 105-degree water and added about twelve ounces of yeast to it. I let it sit for about ten minutes, in which time it began to foam. It smelled just like the pizza dough that Denise and I made. I poured half each into the two tanks of Merlot and then punched it down, along with the remaining tanks on the crush pad. Hopefully by the next day, the tanks would show signs of fermentation starting. I couldn't wait to see the process accelerate with our grapes.

Dane had decided to take the Merlot fruit that we had looked at yesterday, and he mentioned that Cabernet fruit would be coming in tomorrow. We would probably get our last lots of fruit in over the next two weeks, but with the weather, who knew?

With the punchdown complete and the press and crush pad cleaned up, I thanked Dane for lunch and said goodbye to him and Michael. Gary had taken off a bit earlier.

OCTOBER 16, 2008

When I arrived, the first thing I did was to punch down the tanks on the crush pad, starting with the Côté Merlot, of course. As I punched it down, I saw purple foam that showed that fermentation had begun—not in its usual frenzy, but just the beginnings of what would be a furious change of sugar to alcohol over the next few days and weeks.

Dane had me add frozen bacteria called *Oenococcus oeni,* which jumpstarts the malolactic process. This commercial bacteria has only recently been available for use in malolactic fermentation. It is the primary bacteria in the natural process and is now used to inoculate a must in order to get the process moving. Dane also had me add it to the Littlehale Syrah, which was farther along in its fermentation.

The main event for the day was the arrival of two tons of Cabernet fruit from a local Livermore vineyard, the Walker vineyard. It was due to arrive late that morning. In the meantime, Gary and I soaked and pressure-washed eighty to a hundred FYBs that had been used over the last few weeks as picking bins.

When we finished this work, we went into the barrel room to get an update from Dane. He mentioned that in addition to the Cabernet, there was a custom press job coming from Red Feather Winery, and it was due at about the same time as the Cab.

Dane ran a few errands and came back just as he got a call saying that the Cabernet fruit was ready. He jumped into the truck to go pick up the fruit.

As Dane drove off, Gary and I took a break for lunch, and we agreed that both lots would probably arrive at nearly the same time.

In anticipation of this, we set up the crush pad for both destemming and pressing. For the incoming two tons of Cabernet, we cleaned two fermentation tanks and set up one of them in line with the destemmer near the end of the pad, so we could get to it easily. The press was next in line so that we could easily move the chute over any of the three: press, destemmer, or fermentation tank. We also set up the pump and cleaned hoses, putting on two long hoses, one on each side of the pump, so the pump could be located nearer to the truck that held the barrels that we'd fill from the press. We were ready.

Dane pulled in with the truck, and we unloaded the Cab, but it was only two bins—maybe a ton. This was becoming very common, with yields being down in many vineyards, and growers having to short winemakers to try to make everyone happy.

The forklift was outfitted with the box-dumper, and we asked Dane if we needed to switch to the fork to unload the truck. He said no, and then he told us simply to watch him. He was like a surgeon, or so he said, and his forklift was his number 10 scalpel blade. He used the ends of the box-dumper to maneuver the bin into position. Then he grabbed it with the box-dumper and set it down. The other bin was in a similar position on the other side of the truck. He executed the same basic maneuver and was able to extricate the bin from a very tight space on the truck bed. It was fun to watch him use the forklift, as he clearly knew all of the different levers he could pull—literally.

Since Dane was in the forklift, he grabbed the first bin and loaded it into the destemmer. As he did this, I was up top, manning the chute, just as Dan from Red Feather pulled in with his load. He had two bins of Zinfandel must and one of Petite Sirah that he wanted pressed by Dane and then pumped into barrels that were on his truck. The timing was perfect—perfectly bad— and I thought we would have a logistical challenge with the crush pad and the two different processes that needed to happen today.

We finished destemming just as Martin, Dan's winemaker, walked up. I was finishing feeding all of the clusters into the destemmer when he looked up and, with a kid's grin on his face, said, "I love this time of year." Oddly, Dane had told me that it was also his dad's favorite time of year. Most of the grapes were in, the fall weather pattern was emerging, and the reds were fermenting and being pressed on the crush pad. We did have a few more vineyards left to come in, but it was exciting to see much of the harvest in barrels, and the red in tanks, ready to be pressed and barreled down. Besides, it was one of the most spectacularly gorgeous days of the year, 85 degrees and sunny, with the sun lower in the sky, signaling the shortening days and the ultimate coming of winter—but certainly not today, and hopefully not for a few weeks, so we could complete the harvest.

After I climbed down, we moved the chute over the press. Dane loaded in the first bin of Zinfandel while I guided him. He didn't really need the help, but it was safer to have someone up on the chute to make sure everything flowed in correctly. Dane drove off in the forklift to get the next bin and was about to raise it up for dumping when I noticed from my perch that it said Petite Sirah, not Zinfandel. It was a good catch, and the disaster of adding the Petite to the Zin was averted, and Dane got the other bin. He had been told that the two in the back were the Zins—obviously *not!*

With the press loaded and starting to work, we shifted the chute over the waiting fermentation tank. I pulled out the destemmed fruit, and Gary dumped it into the tank. We moved the chute back and got the other load of Cabernet Sauvignon into the destemmer, with Gary working the chute this time. We had to maneuver a bit around the hoses and the press, but all in all, it was very efficient to process both lots of grapes. When we finished, as usual there was plenty of cleanup to do, notably the destemmer and the crush pad.

With this complete, Gary and I put a skin on the Cabernet tank, and I punched down for the second time today; Dane would do it again this evening. The Côté was showing signs of fermentation, and the Littlehale burnt my nose with the CO_2 it was giving off, so it was well on its way. I also punched down the two Syrahs and noticed Dane talking to someone on the crush pad. A few minutes later, Dane came over and told me that he had just agreed to take another five tons of Petite Sirah, and the grower, like me, wanted to take back wine in trade. This would help the Page Mill name for Petite Sirah, which was a great grape in Livermore Valley and one for which Page Mill was already famous.

The press would take a while longer, so Gary and I headed for home. On the way home, I told Gary about the five tons of Petite Sirah, and we agreed that insulating the barn was fast becoming a requirement, not an idea. On the other hand, it meant greater production, which was ultimately Dane and Gary's goal for Page Mill. I have often found that forcing mechanisms, like the additional Petite Sirah, can help to catalyze actions and move the ball forward, when otherwise the idea would stay in the good-idea camp but never get executed.

During the day, I had talked to my friend Gary Campi, and among other things, he had asked about the small amount of grafted Merlot that was still on the vines at his house. I agreed to go out tomorrow morning and bring some samples back in to the lab to see when we would harvest.

OCTOBER 17, 2008

I began my day with a trip to the Campis' to grab a sample of their Merlot. Their two dogs, Lily, the Jack Russell terrier, and Tyson, the Great Dane, were both in their side yard. As soon as I arrived, they began barking. I walked up into the vineyard, where the first row was the grafted Merlot. Since the time they had grafted it ten years ago, they had also remodeled their backyard, and there were only about ten vines left. The fruit looked good, so I took a few clusters from the vines. I also noticed that one of the vines had returned to its table grape roots, literally. I tasted the fruit. It was very sweet and seedless, and not Merlot, of course. When they had remodeled, they had planted another ten to fifteen Merlot vines, but they weren't yet producing much fruit.

I bagged the samples and went down into their yard. Gary had asked me to let the two dogs out of the pen and into the backyard, so I obliged. Tyson and Lily were both barking loudly, but as soon as I let them out, they both came up to me for some affection. I had known both of these dogs since they were pups, so they calmed down immediately. I said my goodbyes to both of them and headed for Peet's in Los Altos for a coffee on the way to the winery.

It was another stunningly gorgeous day as I crested Pigeon Pass and headed into Livermore Valley. When I arrived at the winery, Gary was busy setting up the tasting room. He was going to open again today, as he and Dane had decided to try to open on Friday afternoons whenever they could.

I asked Dane what needed doing this morning, and he told me that a number of his vineyards were due to come in over the next few days. Today we were getting the Merlot that he and I had looked at earlier in the week. He said that the Balyeat Zinfandel from Napa was due in tomorrow. And between Sunday and Monday, all but one of the remaining vineyards would come in. That meant we had Cabernet and Syrah coming in, as well as the five tons of Petite Sirah we'd talked about yesterday.

It was going to be a very busy week next week, but it also meant we'd get everything in during October, with nothing hanging out there into November, when the weather could turn bad and ruin the harvest.

While we were waiting to go and pick up the Merlot, I punched down the remaining tanks, which included the Côté. Our two tanks were definitely beginning to crank. I could smell the CO_2 that was a sure sign that fermentation was under way. As I punched down the Littlehale Syrah, it was definitely in the heat of fermentation and a solid day ahead of our Merlot. Dane also asked me to run an ML test on most of the pressed wines and the two tanks of Tazetta Syrah from next door. I had gotten pretty good at the ML tests and was able to fit nine samples on the test paper easily. Using Lynn's holder for the capillary tubes, I was able to create small, concentrated spots of wine about the size of a dime, fitting all of the necessary samples on a single page. Because I was now mostly drawing samples from pressed wine, I didn't have the problem of getting wine and must on my hands and contaminating the paper, as I had done in my earlier attempts. But in general, as with most things, I was just better for having done this test a number of times now. I stapled the ends of the paper together and put the cylinder of paper into the solution for the test. I'd see on Monday how these wines were doing.

When I finished this task, I went into the barrel room to talk with Gary. He was about to open the tasting room, and I remembered that I needed to get the wine for an event that Denise was holding for her business the next week. She was going to be featuring Page Mill wines at all of her events. I had given the menu to Dane, and he had suggested five wines to complement the meal: the '07 Sauvignon Blanc with the passed appetizers, the '07 California Chardonnay with the salad course, the Côté Merlot with the lamb, the '06 Stuhlmuller Chardonnay with the fish, and the '06 Zinfandel with the duck course. All in all, it was twenty bottles of wine that I needed to pack and bring home with me today. As I was packing it up, Dane came in and said that the Merlot was ready. Did I want to go and pick it up with him? I said of course, finished with the wines for Denise, and then went with Dane to get the Merlot.

We drove out to the doctor's winery again, but this time we weren't just looking; we were picking up the grapes. As we drove up, there were two "porta-tanks" in the parking lot that Dane was envying. In reality, with all of the fruit coming in, Dane had to figure out where to put all of the fermenting fruit and the pressed wine until he got enough barrels for everything. So I think he was beginning to think about ways he could get everything taken care of.

Betto, the vineyard and winery manager, was there and had put the bins of Merlot in the shade of one of the sheds. Dane offered to load the bins, and Betto agreed. Dane jumped on the forklift, while I removed the gates from the truck. We loaded the four bins on the truck and then strapped them down. As I was finishing strapping the bins and Dane was returning the forklift, he came back and told me that I had to see what Betto was doing. I walked back to the crush pad with Dane. There was Betto, having dumped a load of grapes into the destemmer. Rather than berries falling out of the bottom into a bin, and the stems shooting out one side into a box, like our setup, Betto was working a four-inch tube hooked up to the destemmer. Dane told me that it was a must pump. So in this scenario, the destemmed berries were pumped into a waiting tank, rather than falling into a bin to be dumped into a waiting tank. Oh, and this tank was a 600-gallon stainless-steel tank. It was pretty amazing.

As we pulled out of the lot, I noticed that there had to be thirty or forty half-ton bins stacked on the pavement. It was a little scary what a bunch of money could do. It distorted whether this was a true going concern or not. I had no idea how well this winery was doing, but it was clear that it had been funded with a boatload of money. One of my simple observations was that there were two forklifts, one with a conventional fork and one with a box-dumper—no changing attachments for this winery.

One of the things that always impressed me about Dane was that he never commented, let alone complained, about what other wineries had in the way of resources. He would certainly comment about what they had, but it was always by way of comment, nothing more. Whether he was jealous or not, I never knew, and given his willingness to help anyone that came and asked for it, I assumed that he was content with making his own wine—his own way.

We drove back to the winery, and Dane got a phone call telling him that his last vineyard, a Cabernet Franc vineyard, would be picked on Monday and come in on the same day. He laughed and said that was it—all of the vineyards would be in by Monday. He also mentioned that the same vineyard owner had offered him a ton of Grenache, and he was thinking about it for the Angela's Cuvée, his rosé wine, which already had contributions from Syrah, Cabernet, and even the Côté Merlot. I asked him if Grenache, which is a Rhone varietal like Syrah, was used much in rosé. He said that it was, and he cited several rosés from France that had significant contributions from Grenache. I could tell that he was excited by the prospect of it.

When we got back, he unloaded the bins as I set up the destemmer on the crush pad. Gary was busy working the tasting room, so this was the first time in a while that I had worked with Dane. We worked the rest of the afternoon, getting the four bins of Merlot destemmed and put into tanks. At one point, Dane looked at me and said that by Sunday afternoon, he would be out of fermentation tanks. He said that he would use the half-ton bins as fermenters. Given that there were no more vineyards to come in, this was a way to get all of the grapes fermented. It would make for an interesting Monday, with a number of additional vineyards coming in that day.

During the afternoon, Gary had a steady, though small, flow of visitors to the tasting room. He brought several of the groups out onto the crush pad to see the crush in action. I had earlier made the comment to Dane that I called this season "harvest '08," thus *The Harvest Diaries* as a title for my journal. I noticed that Dane called it "the '08 crush." I realized that it was all about perspective. As a grower and therefore a farmer, it was about the harvest for me. As a winemaker, it was about the crush for Dane. I understood the distinction, and I also understood what Dane's father, Dick, had said several weeks ago: that getting the last red-grape vineyards in and crushed was one of the most satisfying parts of the entire year. These last few red vineyards meant that the task of harvest and crush was winding down, and the real effort of creating great wines from these grapes was now in the hands of the winemaker.

I finished cleaning the destemmer and the crush pad and went into the tasting room to say goodbye for the day. Gary had seen several groups, sold a few bottles, and signed up a new club member, which made the afternoon a general success. As I was saying my goodbyes, Dane told me that he had arranged for this rush of grapes here at the end of harvest. He certainly didn't want to leave me with the impression that harvest was a calm affair with lots of wine drinking and lunches, interspersed with grapes coming in. No, he wanted me to experience the literal crush of the last throes of the harvest, so next week would be an exciting week. At the end of next week, we would be hosting a fermentation farm that would cover the crush pad, but we would be finished with the harvest of 2008!

OCTOBER 20, 2008

The days were definitely getting shorter, and there was a crispness to the air that said not only fall, but also the end of harvest, was fast approaching. Also, the crush pad was littered with more fermentation tanks. I saw three stacked up and empty, so that meant that Dane hadn't gotten all of the fruit he'd thought he would over the weekend. Lynn told me that Dane was off running an errand, so I set about to explore the new arrivals and punch down everything. I started with the Côté Merlot. It smelled great and was definitely cranking. The Littlehale Syrah was still throwing off CO2 as well. The Tazetta Syrah seemed to have calmed down quite a bit. There was the Cabernet and Merlot we had crushed late last week, and neither had started to ferment yet. There were several tanks of pressed wine, also from last week, that were settling. They would need to be barreled down soon—and we'd need the tanks.

The new arrivals were two tanks of the Balyeat Zinfandel from Napa, and an unmarked tank that was probably the Nelson Syrah. The newer tanks showed no sign of fermentation, and the tanks were quite full. I had to put a board across the top of these tanks so I could stand on it and get enough leverage to punch down.

While I was punching down the last of the tanks, Dane arrived. He told me that, as usual, things had changed just a bit. The five tons of Petite Sirah that were due on Sunday would come in late today. The Cabernet Franc and the Grenache were being picked as we spoke and would arrive at around 11:00 AM. The Beebe Cabernet would be picked tomorrow, and that was another five tons. Beebe was the same Livermore family from which Dane had sourced Chardonnay earlier in the season—which seemed like a lifetime ago but was only a month and a half.

Planning for the day meant readying both the destemmer for the Cab Franc and the press for the Grenache. He was planning to press the Grenache immediately, leaving no time for the juice to be on the skins. He was hoping to create a very lightly colored rosé, and this technique of treating the red Grenache grapes like a white-wine grape would help to create the light, fresh taste and color that Dane was looking for.

Before I could get the crush pad set, Dane asked me to check the Brix on the Tazetta Syrah, the Littlehale Syrah, and the two tanks of Côté Merlot. The Tazetta was negative 1.2 Brix, prompting Dane to say that we would press the Tazetta before the new fruit arrived. The Littlehale was 4.9, and the two Côté tanks were 5.9 and 7.2 respectively—and all in the midst of ferocious fermentation.

We began to prepare the press and the hoses for the Tazetta. I also got the destemmer and a tank set up for the Cabernet Franc, which was due to arrive shortly. We would need two tanks for the two tons of Cabernet franc, three tanks minimum for the five tons of Petite Sirah, and another three tanks minimum for the five tons of Cabernet Sauvignon coming in tomorrow. So we needed eight tanks. Right now there were five empties on the crush pad. When we finished pressing the Tazetta, we would gain another tank, consolidating the pressed wine from the two tanks into one. That meant that we ultimately needed to get another two tanks. Dane and I discussed barreling down the remaining reds that had been pressed, including a custom crush Cabernet Sauvignon and a Petite Sirah, both of which were in fermentation tanks. If we barreled these wines down, we would have enough tanks to handle all of the grapes that were coming in the next twenty-four hours.

We set up the press and began to pump the free-run juice out of the first tank of Syrah. The main benefit of pumping the free-run juice was to lessen the work in the press and, in some cases, to enable more lots to be pressed in fewer cycles. The other benefit was to lighten the weight in the tanks. We needed to use the box-dumper attachment to dump the must into the press, and that attachment couldn't handle the amount of weight in a fully loaded tank.

After draining the juice, I used a pallet jack to orient the tank so that Dane could grab it with the box-dumper and dump it into the press. We did the same with the other tank, and Dane set the press for its cycle. Just as he finished, the truck pulled up with the Cabernet Franc and the Grenache. It was easy to tell the two apart. The Grenache, which came off the truck first, had large berries in fairly large clusters. The fruit was lighter in color than the other red grapes we'd been working with. Next came the Cab Franc, and it had a similar look to the Cabernet Sauvignon and Merlot to which it was related: smaller berries, good-sized clusters, and dark purple fruit with a blue-gray cast to it.

I had previously set up the destemmer, so I was ready to get going on the Cabernet Franc. Dane helped, in between watching the press and checking the tanks. There were only four bins of fruit, so we made pretty quick work of it. But it did take two of our precious tanks. I asked Dane about the arrival of the Petite Sirah, which was still due today. He thought it would arrive late, so we'd crush it tomorrow. That meant cleanup for the destemmer.

The Syrah was finished, and Dane cleaned out the press while I cleaned the destemmer. When he was finished, we loaded up the Grenache and turned on the press. What came out was a beautiful pink liquid. Dane grabbed some of the juice in a glass, and each of us took a sip. It was stellar—very sweet, with a very round mouthfeel, not too tart, and a gorgeous color. This would be a nice addition to the Angela's Cuvée. I knew that Dane had agonized over whether or not to buy these grapes, but now, seeing and tasting the juice, I knew he felt great about the decision.

With the crush pad clean and no Petite Sirah in sight, I left Dane to complete the pressing. I assumed that the Petite was still coming and that we'd crush it tomorrow morning before the Cabernet arrived. Dane agreed, and we said our goodbyes. He thanked me for all my work today, and for giving him a portion of his evening back tonight.

OCTOBER 21, 2008

Ten bins of Petite Sirah awaited me as I arrived at the winery. I knew what I was doing today. Little did I know that I'd be crushing the five tons solo—just me!

But first, everything needed to be punched down. Lynn stepped out of the lab shortly after I started and asked if today would be a busy day—with a big ol' smirk on her face. I just smiled back, and she said that she too was swamped. There was still an awful lot of activity with new fruit. But we agreed that it was coming to an end; you could feel it. After punchdown, which now included the Cabernet Franc from yesterday, I pressure-washed the remaining tanks, which numbered four. I would need three of them for the Petite Sirah and another three for the Cabernet, so Dane really needed to barrel down some wine.

He was off to pick up some more half-ton bins and take them out to Beebe, where they were picking the Cabernet and were well ahead of schedule. Meanwhile, I finished cleaning the tanks and set up the destemmer *again!*

I also went into the barrel room, cleared out the tasting area, and opened the large door, so we could get empty barrels out of the cellar. While I was crushing the Petite, Dane would be barreling down the two tanks and a few stragglers. I used the forklift to move a pallet of stainless-steel tanks out of the way. They contained the sparkling that Michael and Dane had made the week before I arrived in August, as well as a custom crush Pinot Gris that was tasting quite good.

Dane returned, and we set about removing barrels. They were all at the top of various stacks in the barrel room. Dane climbed around like an acrobat, pulling out the empties. I pulled in the forklift and raised up the fork so that Dane could put a barrel on it. I lowered it, went outside, and removed the barrel. We did this about six times, with Dane at times standing on the fork to maneuver the barrel into position. He looked down at me when he first stepped onto it and said simply, "Don't move!" This task finished, we got several racks, put the barrels on them, and moved them to the end of the crush pad. Dane was now ready to barrel down—but not before he went to pick up the Cabernet, which was now ready.

I turned on the destemmer, jumped on the forklift, and looked at the ten bins ahead of me. I knew it was a matter of taking them one at a time, but I also knew it would take a while.

I got into a rhythm. I loaded a bin into the chute over the destemmer. I left the bin hanging in the dump position over the chute, shut off the fork-lift, and clambered up to make sure I'd dumped all the grapes. While I was up there, I created space for the fruit to fall into the augur that pulled it into the destemmer's mechanics. Once this was flowing, I climbed down from the chute, lowered the bin, and used the pressure-washer to rinse it. I then climbed back up onto the chute and made sure there were grapes flowing. Once set, I again climbed down, pushing the stems into their box whenever I walked by, and put the empty bin out of the way. By the time I got back, there was still fruit to be pushed into the destemmer. Once all the fruit was out of the chute and in the hopper of the destemmer, I climbed down and manually pushed the last of the fruit into the augur.

When the bin was processed, I used the pallet jack to pull the bin of berries out into the open, so I could grab it. I pushed the chute over the tank and got back into the forklift. I grabbed the bin, elevated it, and drove it over to the chute, so I could dump it into the tank. That was the cycle—only nine more to go, and then there was Cabernet coming.

As I finished this first batch, I noticed a small RV pulling up. I went to get the next bin and noticed that Dick and Ome Stark, Dane's parents, were clambering out of the RV. They were on their way to Mendocino to visit friends, and they had stopped to see Dane and to drop off a little something for each of Dane's girls for Halloween. We had a nice chat, and they said they would have a sandwich while they waited for Dane to return. He arrived shortly after that, and we all sat down and had sandwiches together.

Ome kept asking me why I was working here and whether I was crazy. I told her that I was having the time of my life. She looked at me, disbelieving, but went on to say that when Dick had quit his job in high tech, all of his friends would come by because they were jealous. After lunch, Dick and I took a walk outside to see the Petite. He walked right up to a bin and said, "Here's how you taste it," and he took a big bite out of one of the clusters. With his mouthful, he said to just taste the juice, suck it out of the skins, and spit out the skins and seeds. I did as he suggested and got an explosion of ripe fruit in my mouth. It was amazing. He went on to say that he loved Dane's Petite; I agreed. He then asked me how I was enjoying myself. I told him what it meant to me, and the complete change of pace, and he just nodded knowingly.

Soon it was time for them to be on their way. It was always a pleasure to visit with them. They were always so full of life and joy and so proud of their son Dane and what he was accomplishing with what his dad had started.

But soon it was back to the Petite Sirah ...

With the fourth bin processed, I dumped about a third of it into the tank. It was full nearly to the brim, but I needed to get this lot into three bins. I also dumped out the stems at the other end of the vineyard.

As an aside, I had asked Gary why we drove the stems all the way out to the other end of the vineyard. He said "fruit flies." This was also because Dane had stated that only two things really bothered him: the wind and fruit flies, in no order. He just hated, hated, hated them—do I need to be more clear?

Back in the saddle, I continued to crush the fruit. Dane went about barreling down the reds we had discussed. I asked him if we were going to work on the Cabernet today, and he said that it was cool enough for the fruit and we'd have more time to crush it tomorrow. I was actually relieved at this because I had three or four more bins at the time and was beginning to feel pretty tired.

Dane finished barreling down at about the time I finished the five tons of Petite. We worked together to clean up the crush pad, knowing that we had one more big load to process tomorrow. And tomorrow would bring Michael and Gary to help, so it would have to be easier—and of course it was Wednesday lunch day. But more on that tomorrow.

As we were finishing up, Dane asked if he could buy me dinner. I said he didn't have to do that. Then he asked if I'd like to get a glass of wine and an appetizer at Zephyr. I said yes. I think he was surprised but pleased. I knew how appreciative he was of the help I was providing, and I'd enjoy a quick break before the drive home. We agreed that we both looked pretty disgusting, but Dane figured that if we maintained eye contact with the hostess and sat at the bar, maybe we wouldn't look so bad. We arrived, and no one seemed to care what we looked like—and in these economic times, who could blame them?

We sat at the bar and had appetizer pizzas, and Dane ordered a bottle of Steven Kent Chardonnay from Livermore. Steven Kent was part of the Mirassou family, which has been a wine-producing family for six generations, though he was not part of the current Mirassou Winery now owned by Gallo. In fact, he couldn't use the Mirassou name, and so the winery was named for his first and middle names.

We enjoyed our meal, Mark came by to say hello, and the three of us had a great conversation to end a long, hard day. At one point, Dane looked at me and laughed, telling Mark that he had finally gotten me tired—which was absolutely right. But given that the harvest was nearly over, it was good to be tired.

OCTOBER 22, 2008

Today I would have help. I knew there were five tons of Cabernet Sauvignon grapes waiting for me at the winery, but today there would be help. Michael and Gary both would be there, and of course Dane would be there too.

When I arrived, Gary was pulling the bins off the truck that had sat overnight. I walked onto a crowded crush pad and greeted Michael. He was setting up for barreling down the Tazetta that we had pressed Monday. He also said that they were going to press the Littlchale Syrah and maybe the Côté Merlot.

I joined Gary in setting up to destem the Cabernet. I had woken up with a very stiff hand from climbing up and down the chute all day. I mentioned it to Gary, so he took the first shift up on the chute, while I delivered the fruit. It was quite a different day. We helped each other, with Gary making sure that the fruit went smoothly into the destemmer while I cleaned the bin, pushed the stems down into their catch bin, and then helped Gary from the ground by pushing clusters into the augur to move things along. Dane came out onto the pad, and I told him that I'd like to be involved when we pressed the Côté Merlot. He just smiled and said, "You'll do it all."

We had four tanks available today for the Cabernet, so that meant two and a half bins per tank. When I finished with the third bin, we slid the chute over to dump in the fruit, and Gary told me when we had half of the bin dumped. This amount of fruit made it much easier to move the tank with the box-dumper attachment—certainly easier than yesterday, with three and a third bins per tank.

Today was Wednesday lunch, and Richard from Wente had volunteered for this week. Lynn came out and said that he had been called into a lunch meeting at the Wente winery and couldn't make it, but that he would be sending lunch with his girlfriend, who would be joining us.

Gary and I were cranking along in our own little world of Cabernet crushing when Dane came out onto the crush pad and signaled that it was time for lunch. Gary and I agreed to finish the bin we were working, which would put us halfway through the five tons. That seemed like a good stopping point for lunch.

Lunch was served just inside the stable because it was warm but windy—and Dane does not like the wind, remember? By the time Gary and I arrived, the group was seated and about to begin. It was Dane, Lynn, Michael, Gary, and me—the regulars. Today, joining us was Lynn's daughter Sarah, whom I had met two weeks ago, as well as a friend of Dane's. Also joining us and bringing the lunch was Laura, Richard's girlfriend. They had made a tasty cold salad from grains and veggies. The main ingredient was quinoa (pronounced *keen wah*), which tasted to me like a cross between wheat and rice. But it was mixed with carrots, cucumbers, kale, and another form of protein I can't remember. It was in a light vinaigrette-style dressing. We also had chicken that Lynn had brought. All of this was served with a choice of '07 Sauvignon Blanc, Angela's Cuvée, or the '07 Chardonnay. I chose to have a little of each one, and then I went back for more of the rosé.

I was just finishing up when Gary stood up and said he was getting back to work. I was about to reluctantly join him when Michael asked if he could use the box-dumper to load the press with the Littlehale Syrah. I had a reprieve. But it was short-lived, and I knew we needed to finish the crush. This was, after all, the last major vineyard.

I was getting up to join Gary when my phone rang. It was Gary Campi, and he was asking about the small amount of Merlot I had sampled last week. With everything going on this week, we had decided to pick it later in the week. I told Gary that I would be out to pick it personally. When I got off the phone, I told Dane that I'd pick it tomorrow morning before coming in, and that I'd take a few FYBs when I left tonight.

Gary and I went back to work. We processed the fruit throughout the afternoon, while Dane and Michael pressed the Syrah. We all finished late in the afternoon, and Dane, Gary, and I began to clean up the press, the destemmer, the chute, and the crush pad. Michael, meanwhile, set about punching down all the fruit. With a fair amount of new fruit, and some very full bins, Michael, who was not a large man by any measure, found himself on top of the bins to get leverage with the punchdown tool. I knew that workout well, and I would be on it tomorrow morning when I arrived.

With three of us working cleanup, we were finished much more quickly than usual. Michael, too, was finished and was gassing a few of the tanks. Gary said that he'd be happy to meet me out at the Campis' tomorrow morning and help pick the fruit. We laughed when I told him we'd be finished in fifteen minutes instead of the thirty minutes it would take me by myself. I appreciated his company, and I did believe that we would be finished quickly. The other benefit was that Gary had a truck, so we could put the bins in his truck for transport back to Page Mill, rather than putting them in my trunk or on the seat. Gary and I agreed to meet at 8:00 AM tomorrow and said our goodbyes to each other, and to Dane and Michael. On the way home, I called the Campis and spoke with Karen, who was happy we were coming out tomorrow.

Without a lot of fanfare, the major crush was over. In the last week, we had crushed twenty tons of fruit—ten in just the last two days. There might be another small batch here or there, but the major vineyard lots for the Page Mill wines of 2008 were in tanks or barrels, and soon would all be in barrels as the season wound down.

I commented to Dane yesterday that growers, like me, tended to call it "harvest," while winemakers called it "crush." He said he hadn't thought about it, but he agreed that it was the way that people spoke about the season. I guess it just reflected the focus of each vocation, and as a grower, it was and always would be harvest to me.

OCTOBER 23, 2008

Gary Brink met me out at the Campis' house. In fact, as usual he had arrived already and had the bins out, *and* he'd started picking before I arrived at 8:01 AM. Gary Campi was dressed for work and taking out his trashcans when I drove up. He said hi, and that he had to head in to work, but he told me that he and Karen were looking forward to tomorrow.

The Campis, Denise, and I were headed up to the Joseph Phelps Winery Fall Dinner for its wine club members. We had never been to one, but we had heard that it was wonderful. And if it was anything like the Insignia Day, it would be fabulous.

Gary Campi's parting shot was another plea to have Dane treat this as a separate lot, so he could end up with a few bottles from his Merlot vines. I said I'd remind Dane, and I quietly planned to try to watch over the small lot myself.

I went up into the vineyard and said good morning to Gary. I planned to start at the other end of the small row of vines, and we'd meet in the middle. Closer to Gary's end was one vine that had gone back to table grapes. These ten vines had all been table grapes, and Gary, Karen, and their girls never really got around to eating them all, so they had grafted Merlot onto them a number of years ago. I pointed it out to Gary, and he said that Gary Campi had asked us to leave the table grapes on the vines so he could show Eddy and Nancy which one it was. They could then re-graft it or possibly just cut off the competing table-grape wood and let the Merlot take over again.

Because of the steepness of the hill and the fact that the vines hadn't been pruned as well as the Chardonnay vines, it was slow going for both of us. There was some mold, due to the tight clusters, and a few clusters had raisined. But in general, the fruit looked good, and within an hour or so, we had filled about seven FYBs with around two hundred pounds of fruit.

Gary suggested that he pick me up at my house and we could drive to the winery together. I agreed and told him that I needed my morning coffee and would buy him one too for driving; he didn't object.

When we arrived at the winery, we unloaded the "massive" amount of Campi fruit. The question of the day was whether to destem by hand or in the destemmer, and then have to clean it. Due to my previous experience with the sixty or so pounds of Merlot several weeks ago, I opted for the destemmer, even though I'd have to clean it out.

Before we got going, Michael was setting up the press with plans to press the Côté. I told him that I wanted to load the press. He just smiled. First, though, we put the large PVC pipe into the tanks to get the free-run juice pumped into the settling tank we'd be using. Next I jumped onto the fork-lift and grabbed the first tank. Judging where to start pouring was always a challenge. But with Gary's help up on the chute, I successfully poured the two tanks of must into the press, without spilling a drop—a tribute to the

Côté Merlot. Michael programmed the press, and Gary and I went back to crushing the Campi Merlot.

We didn't need the chute, as I just dumped the FYBs directly into the destemmer. As Gary had predicted, each bin took a few seconds to dump, and we were finished in less than a minute. Gary raised his hands and shouted, "A new world record!"

We had crushed the fruit into a large, food-grade plastic bin, and had filled it nearly full. I went over to get a piece of plastic to skin the bin, and as I walked over to it, Michael walked up with a piece of rope and said in his best cowboy accent, "Let me lasso this little dogie." I gave him a big "yee hah," and he cinched the rope. He then handed me a pen to do the honors. I wrote, "Campi Merlot—Yee Hah." Gary then took the pen and wrote, "Bottle Separately," to remind Dane.

When Dane came out to the crush pad a few minutes later, I was cleaning the destemmer, and I told him to look at the bin. He walked over and read the skin, turned with a big smile on his face, and gave me two thumbs up!

The destemmer didn't need much cleaning, as we'd only used it for the seven FYBs. But I took the opportunity to use the pressure-washer to get rid of the tartrate buildup on the stainless steel throughout the inside of the destemmer. Just as the tartrates form on the inside of barrels, they also precipitate out during the crushing process, adhering to the destemmer as a light pink residue. And just as the barrel washer with 180-degree water melts away the tartrates in the barrels, I used the pressure-washer to the same effect. It was very cool to see the tartrates fall away, mostly due to the heat of the water.

Just as I was finishing up, Dane came up to me with a casserole dish in his hand. He said simply, "Lunch." I looked into the dish and saw a beautiful eggplant Parmesan, made with the slim Japanese eggplants that are so tender. I asked him where it came from, and he said that Filippo had dropped it off, probably made by his wife. This was going to be a real treat!

I cleaned up the crush pad around the destemmer and moved it out of the way. Then I went to join Michael, Gary, and Dane for lunch. Dane asked me what I wanted to drink. I said, "Red. Maybe a Zinfandel."

His comeback was, "How about the Côté? That's what we're pressing today, so it's fitting." I certainly couldn't object. The eggplant parmesan was excellent, and for a few minutes, there was simply no talking. After lunch,

Michael brought over what we now called the winery guitar. It was an old Eterna guitar, a brand I've never heard of. It had a small hole in the back, but surprisingly it held its tuning from week to week and sounded pretty good.

Michael began strumming and said he was going to sing a song that his father had sung to him and that he had sung to his own kids. It turned out to be "Oh My Darling, Clementine," so we all joined in, with me singing harmony. Gary, not being the big singer, had gone into the tasting room with clean glasses, but when he heard our rendition of "Clementine," he stuck his head out to listen; I'm not sure if he was enjoying it or just a bit unnerved by us. Michael knew all the verses and led us in the song. The last verse was one I had never heard, but it was very funny … something like, "When I kissed her little sister, I didn't miss my Clementine." We played a few more songs as the press did its work on our Merlot.

Michael and I went out to check the press and found that it had finished. We grabbed two quarter-ton bins and began to clean out the press. What always amazed me was how dry the pressed skins became. Dane had said that this press delivered higher-quality juice, and about 20 percent more than the basket press he and his dad had used, and the dried skins certainly attested to that. Michael and I emptied the press and I took the skins out to the now-large pile at the end of the vineyard. In a month or so, all of this material, along with the stems, would be spread throughout the vineyard as soil amendments.

I walked over to look at the tank of Merlot, which was about two thirds full. Between the free-run juice we had pumped out of the tanks and the juice from pressing, there were about three hundred gallons of 2008 Côté Merlot for Page Mill Winery. That meant nearly five barrels of wine. While that was down from past years, it was still a respectable amount of production from our little vineyard. I was a proud "parent."

As we walked back onto the crush pad, Gary came outside and asked if I could leave now, as he had a pickup and a delivery to do yet today. Michael said he would finish up with the press, so Gary and I said our goodbyes.

OCTOBER 27, 2008

It was cold and overcast today, for the first time in a long time. I was wearing long pants for the first time ever.

The clouds were showing signs of breaking up as I crested the hill and headed into Livermore Valley. I pulled into the parking lot and noticed that Lynn's truck was there but Dane's wasn't. As I walked onto the crush pad, it was full to bursting with fermentation tanks. Every single one of them was being used. Lynn came out of the lab to say hello. I asked her if Dane had been out this morning. She said yes, and that they had watched some video clips from *Saturday Night Live,* but then Dane had taken off; Lynn did not know where.

I figured that the tanks hadn't been punched down, and that would take a while. Sure enough, it was true. I noticed that there were two new tanks without writing, so I couldn't be sure what they were. I pulled off the skins and punched them down. They both looked like Cabernet Sauvignon, and clearly they had just been destemmed, as there was no activity in the tank.

All of the rest of the tanks were in various stages of fermentation. Even the very full Petite Sirah tanks I had processed last week, though they had a thick cap on them, were far enough along that I could get them punched down without climbing up on top of the tanks. It still took me over an hour to punch down the sixteen tanks in various stages of fermentation.

When I was finished, I was sweating and wishing that I had worn shorts. The overcast had cleared, but it was still breezy and only about seventy degrees—but I was hot. I grabbed some water and called Dane. I got his voicemail and left him a message. I figured that I'd record the Brix on all the tanks, and hopefully by then, he would call.

I had just begun the process when he pulled up. His phone wasn't working, and he had been at the phone store, getting a new one, so we laughed when he said that he hoped I hadn't called him. He agreed that I should check Brix on a number of tanks, but not all. He also wanted Brix on our Merlot and the Littlehale Syrah, both of which we had pressed last week. I was also to measure the inches between the top of the tank and the wine to put into his spreadsheet that calculated the number of gallons of wine. The formula was the number of inches times 8.75 subtracted from the total volume of the tank, which was 420 gallons. The Côté had produced 289 gallons, while the Littlehale had produced 210 gallons. Finally, he wanted ML tests on seven of the wines, and I was to use the Côté Merlot to inoculate several other tanks with the ML conversion bacteria that was now going strong in our Merlot.

The Brix on the Côté was -1.9, so it was definitely done. I also looked at the ML I'd done last week and saw that our Merlot was through ML, which was probably why Dane had told me to use it for inoculating the other wines. It looked to me like we needed to barrel it down.

The Littlehale Syrah was at 0.8 Brix, so it had a little way to go, but it too needed to be barreled down. I mentioned that to Dane, and that we needed to do it to get some additional tanks that we could press into, and he said he would be getting some barrels later this week that we could use.

Based on all the Brix, the Aguirre Merlot we had processed ten or twelve days ago was getting ready to press. When I gave Dane the numbers, I could tell he wasn't thrilled about pressing. I asked him what was up, and he said that he had the end-of-harvest blues. When I asked him how his weekend went, he told me that he had made his port, which required adding alcohol at just the right time, which had been 1:00 AM. I told him that he didn't have the end-of-harvest blues; he was just tired. He agreed that was certainly part of it. He was actually hoping to get home early tonight, so we agreed that the pressing could wait until tomorrow.

I finished the ML tests and set the paper in the chromatography solution. I went into the tasting room, where Dane was finishing up some paperwork. He told me that he needed to take a few shipments to UPS, but if I was up for it, we could go for sushi. That sounded great to me, so we took separate cars, as I would leave from the sushi restaurant.

At lunch, the conversation turned to Dane's parents, who had stopped by over the weekend on their way home and had visited with Dane and Angela and the girls. Dane commented on how much he had enjoyed working with his dad. That wasn't surprising, given my other observations when we bottled. Dane genuinely looked up to his dad, enjoyed his dad, and was proud of what his dad had accomplished. It was obvious to me that Dick felt exactly the same way about Dane, with that added touch of fatherly pride in what his son was doing. I asked Dane if he and his brother and sister had helped at harvest time when they were growing up. He said yes, every year. I commented that only he had gotten the bug to make wine. He told me that it had everything to do with the year he spent in France studying. He loved the lifestyle, and the whole philosophy of how the French lived, and how wine wasn't just a business, but rather a part of the fabric of their lives and their families. When he came home, he realized that what his dad was doing was cool, and he wanted to be a part of it.

It was the little insights like this that helped me see what shaped Dane's view of winemaking: that, like for the French, it is more of a lifestyle than a business. While I think Dane understands that it is a business too, and I hope he continues to be more and more successful, I also hope it remains the art and the lifestyle that means so much to him.

After lunch we agreed that tomorrow we needed to press some wine, so I headed for home.

OCTOBER 28, 2008

It was again chilly when I left the house—around fifty-two degrees—but I wasn't going to be fooled again. I was wearing my shorts. By the time I got to the winery, the ground fog was lifting, and the morning was glorious. Most of the vineyards were beginning to turn to fall colors of yellow and orange and red, mixed with the green of leaves that hadn't turned. Other than a few trees that turn beautiful colors in the fall, like the Chinese pistache and the liquid amber tree, California's answer to fall colors is its vineyards, and Livermore Valley was no exception.

At the winery, Dane was out on the crush pad when I arrived. We talked politics for a few minutes and then set about to plan the day. I would punch down all the tanks and then ready both the press and the destemmer, as the last fruit was coming in today. It was all custom crush, and it involved two lots, one of Cabernet Sauvignon and the other Petite Sirah. Dane had no idea when it was coming, just that Steve had taken half-ton bins, so Dane knew that the vineyards were being picked. Our one problem was that now we had truly run out of fermentation tanks. But we would deal with that later. For now, I was all about punchdown, and Dane went into the tasting room to pay his quarterly sales tax—oh boy!

Punchdown was fun today. Even though there were a number of tanks, everything was in the early to later stages of fermentation, so punchdown was much easier, even with caps that were quite thick and tanks that were full. The fullest were the three tanks of Petite Sirah that I had processed last week, representing five tons in three bins. With fermentation, the skins had risen nearly to the top of the tank, so punching down meant pushing through about two feet of cap. The secret was getting that first punchdown through. Once that happened, the rest of the cap would begin to crack and fall apart as I progressed.

Each of the tanks had a slightly different smell, depending on the grapes and the point in fermentation. But nearly all were giving off plenty of CO_2. There were no signs of fruit flies anywhere on the crush pad, and the tanks stung my nose each time I opened one. But they also smelled earthy and yeasty, just like new wine should. Even the Cab fruit that came in over the weekend was starting to ferment, foaming purple as I punched down the cap of skins. The small batch of Campi Merlot was fermenting nicely and smelled wonderful, of fruit and CO_2. Maybe I'm just partial to Merlot!

With fifteen tanks to punch down, it took most of the morning. When I was finished, I decided to check out a fermentation tank that was out in the side yard. My thinking was that if the wooden frame of the tank was intact, even though the plastic liner might have a hole in it, we could use the frame. That's because there was a tank with a fiberglass liner against the fence, whose wooden frame was rotted. If these two could be married to create another tank, we would have a bit more flexibility in what we had to do next. I lifted the tank cover and looked inside. I couldn't see a hole in the liner. Maybe this tank had been put out here in error.

I went into the barrel room to check on Dane. He said he was finished and that we needed to make a plan. I told him about my discovery, and he said he'd take a look. The tasks today were to press the Merlot, barrel down the Côté and the Littlehale, freeing up more tanks, and then, depending on the Cab coming in, destem the fruit. I had set up for everything; that is, the destemmer and the press. Dane said he needed to pick up barrels and we went outside to look at the tank. He couldn't find any holes either, so while he went to get barrels, I set about cleaning up the frame and the liner, both of which had been lying out in the dirt.

First, I cleaned the liner with a hose and filled it with water to ensure that it really didn't have a leak. I couldn't see any holes, and it held water. Next I cleaned up the frame and put the liner inside. Then I used the pressure washer and thoroughly cleaned the liner with 180-degree water. Voilà! We had another tank, so Dane could barrel down while I pressed the Merlot. When he returned, he began to wash the barrels, while I set up to press the Merlot. I cleaned the hoses and the large PVC pipe and hooked everything up to the pump. We had arranged the tanks so that they were close to the press and each other, so Dane could wash the barrels without the pressing getting in his way and vice versa.

I put the PVC into the large tank of Merlot and began to pump the free juice into the tank that I had earlier resurrected. Once this was done, we opened the press and set the chute above it. There was a smaller half-ton bin of fermented Merlot that we had used last week when we were trying to conserve bins. Now it was easy to dump this entire bin into the press, free-run juice and skins together. Then I dumped the larger fermentation tank into the press. It had been lightened by pumping the free-run juice into the settling tank. With that, Dane programmed the press, and I cleaned out the bin and the tank, so we still had a tank for the fruit that was due in later today for destemming.

Dane continued to wash barrels until late in the afternoon, when the fruit arrived. It was about a ton of Cabernet Sauvignon fruit and a ton of Petite Sirah fruit. Dane unloaded the Petite, and Steve went back to get a weight on the truck, representing the tare for the Petite, as he had weighed it before coming out to Page Mill. He then returned, and Dane offloaded the Cabernet fruit, and he went back to get a tare for the Cabernet (the Petite tare represented the heavy for the Cabernet).

By now it was nearly 5:00 PM, and Dane wanted the fruit to cool down through the evening, so he decided not to destem. The press needed another hour or so to finish, and I needed to be home a bit earlier tonight, as it was "proposition night." Nicole, our daughter, had asked that we talk about the twelve propositions on the California ballot. Both Denise and I agreed that we could use the discussion as well, so we were having dinner together to discuss them.

Dane said he'd finish up, which probably meant that he'd stay until late and barrel down the wines we'd discussed. I reminded him that tomorrow, Gary and I would be at the warehouse, going through the pallets of library wines to take inventory for a sale of library wines in the new year. I was looking forward to it. He laughed and asked what he would do without us. I told him that Michael would be there to help, so he shouldn't be lonely.

The subject of end-of-harvest blues never came up, and I suspected it wouldn't. I think Dane was sore and tired from a long weekend, and he'd already told me that Mondays were tough. He was back with the usual gleam in his eye, and more than once today he said, "Makin' the wine," so I knew he was happy. I headed for home.

OCTOBER 29, 2008

Today was a real change of pace. I met Gary at CWT, the warehouse that held the bulk of Page Mill's wines, and all of the library wines. CWT stood for California Wine Transport, and it was a large warehouse that serviced many wineries. I met Gary out front at around 8:30. Our goal today was to go through a number of the library pallets to catalog what was there. Gary and Dane wanted to serve some library wines at their upcoming harvest party and hold a library wine sale after the first of the year. The "Holy Grail" for this exercise would be to find twenty-five cases of a library wine that could be offered as a special treat to wine club members, but that would be quite a bit of wine.

As we walked to the section of the huge warehouse where Page Mill wines were stored, I commented to Gary that the size and number of pallets suggested that CWT was like the warehouse at the end of the first *Raiders of the Lost Ark*. Gary laughed and said that sometimes it felt that way. As we walked into the depths of the building, I was amazed at the height of the pallets and the diversity of wines and spirits. There were many of the smaller names in California wine, and a number of French and Italian wines that were probably stored at CWT by U.S. distributors for these international wineries.

We arrived in the section where Page Mill was stored, and the crew at CWT had already pulled out a number of pallets of older wines. We began to work on the first pallet, and quickly we divided the wines into their various varietals. At least half of the boxes either had fewer than twelve bottles (a case) or they were mixed vintages, and even mixed varietals sometimes.

The first pallet seemed to be Zinfandels of various ages, so we began to build a pallet of these wines. Gary catalogued what we stacked onto each of the layers of the pallet. At one point, I found a case of 1977 Zinfandel. This was only the second vintage that Dick Stark, Dane's dad, had made. I read the back label that described the fruit from San Miguel on the central coast of California. The last sentence made me laugh. It referred to this being a younger wine that would be enjoyed best by drinking it in the next two to three years, and it said that it wouldn't hold up to long-term aging. Here we were with a case of it, thirty-one years later. It would be interesting to try. As we went along, there were numerous vintages of Zinfandel from the eighties, nineties, and 2000s. Gary thought he had the makings of some interesting vertical tastings, with the number and variety of Zinfandels.

We kept working, and we began to find Pinot Noir and Merlot, which we set aside for their own pallet. When we had finished with several pallets and what seemed to be most of the Zinfandels, Gary had the warehouseman bring out what looked like a pallet of Cabernet Sauvignon. As we began to work through it, there were indeed a number of Cabernets from different years, though like the previous pallet that was mostly Zinfandel, there were several cases of other varietals, mostly reds. Soon we had another pallet that was catalogued and was composed of Cabernet only.

Next up was the Merlot pallet. We already had a number of cases from the prior work, and we found several partial pallets that had Merlot cases. One had twelve cases of Côté 2000 Merlot, which I knew was great. In fact, I only had three bottles of the 2000 left, and I was sure it was drinking very well. There were also a number of cases of the 1999 Côté.

The next two pallets were mixtures of primarily Dane's and his father's private collections—some Page Mill, but many from other wineries. We went through these pallets to pull out the Page Mill library wines that Dane might like to sell. Mixed in these and other pallets were cases of older whites, primarily Chardonnay, that were probably well past their prime, but we just put them together and catalogued them so Dane and Gary could discuss it later. In all, we ended up with similar-sized pallets of what we simply marked "Personal." One case had a few bottles of a wine called Ome's Sweet Revenge. It was a 1992 wine, and from the label, it was impossible to tell what varietal or blend it was, except that it was a red wine. The label was filled with poetic descriptions of life and the joy of drinking wine, so I was sure it was one of Dane's first attempts at a label. Dick's labels tended to be more descriptive of the wine, not the experience.

There were two pallets with a number of cases that had unlabeled wines in them: twelve cases of one that looked like a Pinot, and five cases of another that Gary thought was a Charlot (a blend of Chardonnay and Merlot). The Charlot, if that's what it was, was a 1999 vintage and made like a white wine, so it wasn't clear how it would age. Gary took samples of both of these unlabeled wines for "analysis" at lunch tomorrow. In all, he ended up with a case of wines that needed to be tried.

We went through several other pallets and were able to build catalogued pallets of Cabernet, Merlot, Zinfandel, and Pinot Noir, in addition to the pallet of Dane's personal collection. There were still a number of pallets that needed going through, but Gary called it a day, rather than pulling out more of these pallets. Also, the warehouse tended to quiet down in the early afternoon, having started early in the morning. We were not able to find the twenty-five cases of great library wine for the wine club, but then there were a number of additional pallets we could check on our next trip.

It had been an interesting break from the winery, but I looked forward to getting back out there tomorrow.

OCTOBER 30, 2008

This was the first day that I went out to the winery and the weather really looked threatening. It had been overcast a few times, but it always burned off. There was a chance of rain today, and the weather looked like we'd get that chance.

When I arrived, the place was already hopping. Thursday was a day when all of the regulars were there—Dane, of course, Michael, Gary, and Lynn. I also noticed Dick Stark in Dane's SUV, reading the paper. I remembered that he said they might come back on Thursday for the lunch that Michael's wife, Leighann, was preparing—paella on the grill. Leighann was not available on Wednesdays, so we easily accommodated her request for Thursday to get the benefit of her cooking.

I had finally remembered to bring the orders for Côté Merlot that Denise and Corky had gotten at their event last week. I gave them to Gary for follow-up. I also made sure that Dane had Denise's order for her opening event this weekend, which included four cases of wine: Chardonnay, Sauvignon Blanc,

Zinfandel, and Côté Merlot. Gary said he'd pick up the Côté from CWT, and the rest from UDS tomorrow morning. Dane also created an account for Denise and her caterer so he could send them invoices electronically.

I stepped onto the crush pad and found Michael starting to barrel down the Côté Merlot and the Littlehale Syrah from the settling tanks that we had pressed into a few days ago. I began to help him with this, first cleaning a few breathable bungs for the barrels. The wines were still fermenting a bit, so the breathable bungs would allow the CO_2 to escape.

He asked me to take over while he went and prepared the grill for Leighann, who would soon arrive with the paella. Preparing the grill meant taking the top off the barbecue to fit the large paella pan and setting up the briquettes so he could start the fire later this morning. While I was filling the barrels, Dane and Dick came onto the pad, and we got talking about the wines that Gary and I had "found" yesterday. I mentioned Ome's Sweet Revenge. Dick asked me if I knew the whole story on that wine. I told him I had only read the label.

Dick said that sometime in the early nineties, they had a couple of barrels of red wine that weren't very good. Dick had suggested just dumping it, but Dane thought they should bottle it and sell it cheap. Shortly after this discussion, Dane went on vacation, and Dick bottled the "cheap" wine and labeled it "Dane's Red." Dick said it was truly bad wine, but it sold for two dollars a bottle—an early version of two-buck Chuck, I guess.

At this point, Dane took over and said that the next year, they again had a couple of barrels that weren't too good. This time Dick was on vacation, so Dane bottled and labeled the wine "Dick's Blend" to get even.

Dick cut in, saying that his blend was actually pretty good, and reluctantly Dane nodded.

A year or so later, they made a Zinfandel that they just couldn't ferment dry. It had a few percentage points of residual sugar, which I knew Dane hated. He was about to get rid of this wine when Ome, his mom, tried it and liked it. She got a bit energized around the fact that she too was an owner of this winery, and she never got a wine with her name on the label. This wine was one she liked, and she said she would sell it herself. In honor of her desire, and in keeping with this tradition of labeling, they called this wine "Ome's Sweet Revenge." To Dick and Dane's chagrin and surprise, Ome sold it to her friends, with some coming back several times to buy multiple cases at a time.

I remember in the early 2000s when Dane also had a Zinfandel he couldn't ferment dry. He bottled it, and it became one of his best sellers that year. He chalked it up to America's love affair with sugar. What a great story!

While we were talking about these older wines, Dick mentioned that he and Gary and Dane had discussed sales of the older wines and had set a few dates. On the second weekend in December, they would hold a tasting and sale of older Pinot Noir, and the third weekend in December would be the same for older Cabernet Sauvignon.

I went back to my barreling down. While we were working, Lynn came out of her lab, looking bleak. She said to Michael and me that she was sorry, but she would miss lunch because she wasn't feeling well and needed to go home. We wished her well and hoped she felt better. Michael said he hoped there would be a good number of people, as Leighann had made a wonderful meal for twelve. I used it as a reason to give George a call. He had joined us once for lunch, so I thought if he was in the area, he'd enjoy it again. I left him a message and went back to finishing the Côté Merlot.

With the barreling done, I cleaned out the tanks, and we had spares now for further pressing. We were going to press the Walker Cabernet Sauvignon, so I got the pump and the hoses ready and cleaned the large PVC pipe so we could pump the free-run juice first. We got the clean tank ready and began to pump the juice. Meanwhile, Michael readied the press for the remainder of the must. Our goal was to get the press loaded in time for lunch, as Leighann had arrived and was preparing the paella on the grill in a huge, flat-bottomed pan.

When the free run was finished, Michael got the forklift and grabbed the tank. Gary and I were watching, and just before he was about to dump it in, he asked us to check for skins. Gary and I looked at each other and then at Michael, not understanding. "Skins. You know, skins," Michael said. Finally we got it.

A week ago, Michael had double pressed a wine, meaning he had dumped a wine that was settling back into the press. It simply drained through the press, and we pumped it back into the tank. But we laughed about new marketing language we could use on the bottle that would describe this wine as double pressed. You would be amazed at the kind of stuff people will add to labels to create some sort of differentiation—like "handpicked for cleanliness."

Of course Michael had the Walker Cabernet must in the tank, and he dumped it into the press. I pressure-washed the tank while Michael set the press cycle. We cleaned up and walked over to the overhang where the table was set up. Gary walked over to us with a glass of what was clearly older wine. He said it was a 1997 Pinot Noir. He handed Dick the first glass, and Dick got this serene look on his face as he began to smell the wine. He said that he loved the smell of old wines, and this was a classic, in his mind. When he took a sip, he savored it, smiled, and said, "This is red velvet."

I got my glass and swirled it around. It smelled a little musty to me, but good. Then I took a sip. It was spectacular, with plenty of fruit, but a smoothness characteristic of a well-aged wine. It had a long, smooth finish that stayed with you. At about this time, George arrived and he too enjoyed his first sip. I let the wine breathe and drank it very slowly as it was changing right before our eyes, and getting better and better. Ome had not arrived, and we had finished the bottle that Gary had brought back from the warehouse. I noticed that Dick had saved a little in his glass, and when Ome arrived a few minutes later, he brought it over for her to try. It was such a simple yet thoughtful thing, and she enjoyed her taste of this extraordinary wine that her husband and son had made.

Michael quietly began nudging us to start eating. Gary and I needed little prodding as we filled our plates with Leighann's wonderful cooking. I could smell the saffron, seafood, and spices. There were scallops, fish, shrimp, chicken, and sausage, along with the rice and other veggies. She had also made a light green salad with a vinaigrette dressing and roasted pumpkin seeds. I think we had hit the ultimate in our Wednesday (Thursday) lunch; no one was going to top this meal.

But the wines were up to the challenge. After that Pinot, Gary brought out a 2000 Sangiovese that was very good, but for some reason, Dane didn't like it. The rest of us did.

He also brought out an unlabeled Pinot that we had decided was probably a 1999 Nonpareil, which was the designation they used for the "N" block of Bien Nacido vineyard in Santa Maria Valley. Page Mill received grapes from both the N block and the Q block. Each was made separately, and in certain years, if the wines were particularly good, they created a Nonpareil, or a

Quintessence, which came from the Q block. I had never had a Nonpareil Pinot Noir, so this was a real treat. It had more fruit than the 1997, but it was still silky smooth in texture with a long, rich finish.

Then Gary opened a 1995 Napa Cabernet that was still full of fruit, but with silky tannins in balance with the fruit. I knew there were five cases of this wine, which should sell for a high price.

We drank these wines and again congratulated Dick and Dane on creating such a tasty wine. Dick asked me if I'd ever heard how he priced his 1985 Cabernet Sauvignon. He credited that vintage with changing the fortune of Page Mill. He said it was an ageless vintage, one of the best of the century for California Cabernet Sauvignon. He had created his Cabernet from Napa fruit and believed he had made a great wine. As background, Dick said that he sold his first Napa Cabs for $4.75 a bottle in the mid-seventies, which shocked me. He said that by the mid-eighties, he had upped the price to $12.50. Even for the mid-eighties, I thought that was a very inexpensive Cabernet.

Dick believed he had something special in his 1985 Cab, so after he had bottled it and was ready to release it in 1987, he took it down to a newly opened wine store in Palo Alto called Vin, Vino. The proprietor, Victor, did a blind tasting of seven high-priced Napa Cabernets and Dick's wine. Dick said he spent an hour just smelling the wines, and then another hour tasting the wines. He then ordered them by rank and gave the list to Victor to see how his Page Mill Cabernet Sauvignon had fared among the Napa Cabs. To his delight, Dick had picked his own wine second. He was thrilled, and he decided to raise his prices. I asked him how much he'd sold his '85 Cab for, and he said twenty dollars a bottle, which was a very good price in the late eighties. I asked him if it sold out, and he laughed, saying, "Immediately, so I should have priced it even higher."

Everyone was enjoying the wines and the meal, but the conversation and the presence of Dane's parents made this a very special lunch. Dane told me later that it would be difficult to surpass this meal, and he was right, because of the food and wine, but also because of the company of these wonderful, special people that I had had the pleasure of working with for the harvest.

The rest of the day seemed anticlimactic. We finished pressing the Walker Cabernet, and I punched down the fifteen tanks still on the pad, just as it began to rain. Dane got on the forklift and began moving tanks under the overhang while I finished punching them down.

When I finished, Dane asked me if I'd mind dropping off some wine to a customer in Palo Alto. It was three cases, including the same wines that Denise had ordered for her event on Saturday. I headed out to deliver the wine, with a light rain still falling.

OCTOBER 31, 2008: HALLOWEEN

When I arrived at the winery, the weather was again threatening, but there was no rain. Gary had picked up the case of Côté at the warehouse in San Jose and was going out to UDS to pick up the other wines, along with his needs for the tasting room that weekend.

Dane and I went out to all the tanks. I punched down while he took sugars. I buttoned them up and gassed them all.

Gary arrived back, and we unloaded the truck, putting most of the wine in the tasting room and taking the four cases for Denise out to my car. Gary was opening the tasting room for the afternoon, and after checking with Dane that there wasn't anything that needed to be done, I said I would take off.

I asked Dane about what needed doing next week. He said that we would press most of these wines during the course of next week, but the big chore for the week was readying the winery for the holiday party next Saturday. I said goodbye and walked out to my car. The combination of the weather and the lack of activity on the crush pad left me feeling that harvest and crush were really over. We still had fifteen tanks and a number of wines to press and get into barrels, but the rush was over. Even the weather seemed to be saying it was time to let the wines mature and mellow in the barrels, to become the whites of next year and the reds of two years from now.

NOVEMBER

NOVEMBER 4, 2008

It was Election Day, and while it wasn't raining, it was crisp and cold, with clouds blowing across the sky. When I arrived at the winery, I followed a gravel truck into the winery. Dane was coming out to meet the truck driver as I pulled up. He said hello and followed the truck driver out to the front of the winery, where the truck dumped its load of gravel. I'm sure it was meant to fill holes and add stability to the dirt road leading to the winery, which was showing signs of becoming a muddy mess.

When Dane came back, I asked what needed doing. He said we needed to punch down and take numbers, so I began to punch down the tanks as he measured Brix and took samples for an ML test. It was windy but dry, and soon we had completed our task. It was clear that fermentation had slowed down with the cold, but the wines were nonetheless nearing completion. It was much easier to punch down even the fullest of the tanks. When Dane was finished with the numbers, he said that he wasn't planning to press any wines today.

Instead we got ready to top off the wines in the barrel room. We cleaned the topping can and a length of hose, which we hooked up to the topping barrel with a topping gun: a trigger with a long nose for adding wine to barrels up in the stacks. Dane used nitrogen gas to drive the topping wine. While he topped the barrels, we began to redo "Dane's Brain," which was the whiteboard containing all positions of the wines in barrels. It reminded me of the work I did over three months ago before harvest began. With all the movement during the course of harvest, very few of the barrels were in their positions from that inventory in July.

Along with topping the barrels and verifying barrels for "the Brain," I also measured potassium metabisulfite for addition to a number of the barrels. As Dane pointed out to me, two people made this job tolerable. Dane could stay up in the stacks of barrels, giving me the wines and their positions and then using the topping gun to fill the barrels, augmenting some with sulfites I had measured and added to the topping can. We finished two stacks of barrels and decided to break for lunch.

Dane took me into Livermore to a Vietnamese restaurant, where he had pho (Vietnamese soup) and I had pad Thai, which is a Thai noodle dish. On a cold, blustery day, the food warmed us.

We headed back to the winery and punched down all the tanks again. We then went back into the barrel storage room and finished topping another stack of barrels. By this time, it was after 3:00 PM, and Dane had to be in Los Gatos for a tasting at 5:30 PM. We cleaned up the tasting room and both headed out for the day. I suspected that with Michael and Gary on hand tomorrow, we'd probably be pressing some wines, but I'd have to wait and see what tomorrow brought.

I drove home that afternoon listening to a talk-show host going on about the election. When I arrived home, I spent the evening watching the returns. At 8:00 PM Pacific Time, when the polls closed in California, the various networks declared that California, Washington, and Oregon had all gone for Barack Obama, and that he would be the forty-fourth president of the United States. Denise and I listened first to John McCain's well-done concession speech and then Barack Obama's victory speech. Several of the newscasters commented correctly that Obama's speech was less about victory and more about the job ahead. He also said less about himself and more about the people that had gotten him there, and about all of us, whom he needed in order to get work done. He challenged everyone to change and to believe "Yes, we can!"

I heard from both of my children in the next few minutes. Both of them had voted, and both of them saw this as a historic time. Among many of the things that the Obama campaign had done was to energize youth to get out and vote. Denise commented that hopefully this was the beginning of enfranchising the younger generation. We all hoped that change would come, and change for the better for all of us.

NOVEMBER 5, 2008

On this day, I arrived at the winery feeling that we were starting a new day. Whether that was simply because the campaign was over, or if in fact Barack Obama would bring the change he spoke of, it did feel like a new time.

But for the work at Page Mill, we were still winding down, and so the crush pad was somewhat inactive when I walked onto it. Michael was just starting to punch down and take numbers for the remaining tanks. I joined him, punching down while he took Brix measurements. When he finished a tank, I also buttoned it up.

Today, the plan was to press the Nelson Syrah from Livermore Valley, which was in a single tank, and the Balyeat Zinfandel, which was the Napa Zin that Dane and his father, Dick, had been sourcing from the north end of Napa County for over twenty years. With the arrival of cooler weather, fermentation had slowed down for all of the wines. As an example, the Zinfandel had been fermenting for about three weeks. Earlier in the harvest, reds were fermenting to dry in less than two weeks.

Michael and I cleaned the hoses, and I set the four-inch PVC pipe into the Syrah tank to begin pumping the free-run juice. When we finished this, I removed the hose from the tank and connected it to the pan below the press. Then I used the forklift to dump the remaining must and juice from the tank into the press, and Michael turned on the press. As the press began to work, I arranged the Zinfandel tanks in preparation for pressing the Zin after lunch.

After the wonderful lunch we had had last week, Dane and I had talked yesterday about getting pizza for lunch today. But Gary had come prepared with an excellent meal that he was making for us. As Michael and I finished up, a small group began to assemble around a table that Gary had set up. Dane went into the tasting room and brought out several bottles of wine. The regulars were there—Dane, Michael, Lynn, Gary, and I—but we were also joined by Nancy, Lynn's friend who had returned from Oregon. Scott and Nancy, friends who rented the house at the front of the winery, joined us with their friend Jim, and like a few weeks back, Laura, Richard's girlfriend, joined us, while Richard was at a seminar. Rounding out the group was Steve, who managed several vineyards and brought custom crush fruit to Dane. The table was set up in the stable, but the weather was so nice that we added another table for the larger group and set up mostly outside in the sun.

Gary had created a Greek lunch for us that included stuffed grape leaves and spanakopita, and as if that weren't enough, he brought out a pastitsio, which is Greek lasagna. He had heated it up in Scott and Nancy's oven. The three dishes were very tasty, all with subtly different flavors that meshed well with each other and the wines. I started with a glass of the '07 Chardonnay, the gold medal winner, but quickly moved to the '06 Estate Petite Sirah, which went very well with the food that Gary had prepared. Everyone seemed to think so, as we quickly finished the bottle, and Dane went inside for another. With the harvest winding down, the group seemed to linger at lunch, enjoying the beautiful fall afternoon and the wonderful food and wine.

I thought about next week and realized that it would not be sufficient to just buy pizza. I would need to come up with something to fit the season, and while I couldn't compete with paella or Gary's Greek feast, I could at least make a valid showing. I was already thinking about a great chili recipe or a French beef stew, both of which Denise and I had made for harvest parties. I would be okay.

Eventually, Michael and I had to get back to pressing. The Syrah was finished, and we moved the PVC pipe and hoses to the Zinfandel tanks to pump over the free run. One of the Zinfandel tanks had been treated with the same enzyme that he had used on the Lodi Zin earlier in the season, so we needed to keep the two separate. After we pumped the juice out of the first bin, which had the enzyme, we loaded it into the press. Michael set the press for a couple of short, hard presses over about ten minutes. This would get 90 percent of the juice out of these skins. Combined with the free run, we had most of the enzyme-treated juice in one tank. We then switched to the second tank and pumped the free-run juice first, and then we added the remaining must to the press and went through a full cycle with all of the skins in the press. This would take about two hours to complete, and I had a dinner that evening, so Michael stayed on to finish and clean the press. I cleaned up the crush pad and said I'd see him next week, and that I would be making lunch. He smiled and asked if he was ever going to meet Denise, or did she really exist? I told him that I'd talk to her about coming out next week, and we said our goodbyes and gave each other a hug. Michael was a genuinely sweet guy that I had come to really enjoy. I valued the friendship we had built in this short time.

NOVEMBER 6, 2008

I was treated to another spectacular fall day in Livermore Valley. At Page Mill, that day would be all about getting ready for the holiday party that was to occur this Saturday. I would not be at the winery tomorrow (Friday), so I was anxious to help in any way I could. Little did I know that this was to be a forklift extravaganza day!

First, though, I punched down the remaining tanks, buttoned them up tight, and gassed them all. I would be moving them into a tight cluster on the edge of the crush pad because with the holiday party and a busy weekend for Dane and Gary, there would be no pressing of wines until next week. The reason to get the tanks all together was that Dane wanted to get a tarp on them, as there was rain forecasted over the weekend.

Before I could begin moving tanks, I needed to clean up the crush pad and clear it so that the forklift could maneuver easily.

When this was done, I began moving the remaining seventeen tanks just out beyond the crush pad on the gravel, into tight clusters of six tanks, which could be tarped easily. I also moved five pallets of empty bottles out of the stable and onto the same graveled area. Dane and Gary would use the stable for several of their food and wine stations during the party on Saturday. Gary was working on the wine for the party, figuring out what was on hand and what was needed from the warehouse. They had also decided to use some of the wines that he and I had catalogued in the warehouse. He chose several old Cabernets and old Zinfandels, as well as a couple of older Côté Merlot, all of which he would need to pick up at the warehouse tomorrow.

After a quick lunch, during which we discussed the setup for the event, we moved the tents and formed a cohesive covered space. Then I began precision forklift work for the rest of the day. Dane wanted to use barrels to frame the space for his party and add to the winery atmosphere. He had me set stacks of barrels in a row, two barrels wide by three high, to create a virtual wall between the tents and the crush pad, which improved the ambiance of the tented area immeasurably. I moved stacks of two by two and then added a third set of two barrels to make the stack three high. It was made more challenging by the fact that I was setting these up on uneven gravel, rather than the smooth cement of the crush pad. When I finished this most difficult type of forklift work for me—these barrels were full of wine, and the ground wasn't level—Dane said that I was now an excellent forklift driver. I asked if I had passed the Stark Course in Forklift Driving, and Dane said yes enthusiastically.

Gary took off for the day as I finished up cleaning the crush pad. I went into the tasting room to wish Dane a great event. I was sorry not to be there, but we had a long-planned weekend away with friends. Dane and I discussed the plan for next week: to press everything and barrel down as much as possible. If we cleared the crush pad and got everything into barrels, next week would clearly mark the end of harvest.

NOVEMBER 9, 2008

While this was a Sunday, and the day had nothing to do with making wine, it was a day about Page Mill.

Denise and I and our friends Jim and Marcie stopped at Page Mill for tasting on our way back from Arnold, where we had spent the weekend. Arnold was a small town just up in the forests of the Sierras, about 4,500 feet high. We had also visited Murphy's, a small Gold Country town that was now a tourist destination, with boutiques and tasting rooms for the local wineries. It seemed that every county in California was creating a wine industry, and Calaveras County was no exception. They were mostly known for their reds, with Syrah and Zinfandel leading the way. We tasted a few and found a couple of Syrahs and Petite Sirahs that we really liked.

The tasting room was busy when we arrived, and Gary had had a good day of sales, with both investors and others buying a good amount of Page Mill wines. Since I knew my way around, I asked Gary if I could barrel-sample the '07 Côté Merlot for Jim and Marcie. Of course he said, "Sure!" I got the wine thief and filled a glass.

The color was beautiful, darker and richer than I had ever seen our Merlot. The bouquet was excellent, with a hint of oak and a strong aroma of fruit. I tasted it, and the richness was immediately evident. This wine would age for another nine to twelve months, but it was already a bigger Merlot than we had ever made, with deep fruit flavors, good tannins, and a long finish. Jim and Marcie tried it and looked genuinely astonished at how good it was. Jim asked me about futures—and he was probably serious. Denise tried it, looked at me, and just smiled. We had talked about how good I thought the '07 was, and she was very pleased, as I was too. Gary tried it and also just smiled with pleasure.

It was about 4:30, and Denise suggested that we go for an early dinner at the Zephyr Grill in town. We had been talking about eating there, and here was a perfect opportunity. We had a great meal, and Mark stopped by to say hello just before his charity event started. Dane was pouring his wine for the event, and when he arrived, he also stopped by for a visit. He looked more relaxed than he had all last week, so I knew the investor presentation must have gone well. Now was not the time to ask, and I knew I'd see him tomorrow.

NOVEMBER 10, 2008

Today was a beautiful fall day, sunny with small, wispy clouds. The leaves were changing everywhere and certainly throughout the vineyards of Livermore Valley. I arrived at the winery and found Dane getting ready to press a couple of small custom lots that he had received late last week. We finished pulling off the free run, and he loaded up the press. While we were pressing, I cleaned up the crush pad and also cleaned a longer length of hose that we would use to barrel down some of the Page Mill tanks.

Dane said that this would be a short day, as he had been busy over the weekend with their holiday party on Saturday night and his investor meeting the next day, which he said went well. He said the investors had asked a number of questions, but in general they thought he was doing pretty well, given the difficulties of the year. Nonetheless, there is a certain amount of stress associated with all presentations.

While the press continued to do its work, I set up the hoses to barrel down a Cabernet and a Merlot that had been settling for a couple of days. Dane had acquired a number of used barrels from a nearby winery. They were only a few years old and in very good shape. Dane loaded a pair onto the barrel washer and got them ready for the wines. Once he was finished, I muscled the empty barrels onto a rack and began filling the barrels with the Cabernet. Dane cleaned two more pairs of barrels, and we arranged them on the crush pad so that I could easily move the hoses from barrel to barrel. When I finished with the Cabernet, I moved on to the Merlot. Meanwhile, Dane had gotten us sandwiches, which we ate as I finished barreling down the Merlot.

When we were finished, we pumped the remaining pressed wine from the pan into the tank for settling. Dane called the winery and told them they could come and barrel their wines tomorrow after they settled for a day. By now it was 1:00 PM, and Dane said we wouldn't get to any of the Page Mill pressing today, but we'd get it all done in the coming few days. We cleaned the press and the crush pad and called it a day—Dane going to a massage and band practice, and I, unknowingly, to a broken water main.

November 11, 2008

As I said above, I found out on my way home yesterday that we had a broken water main. I needed to be there with the plumber, and so I had sent email to Dane, telling him I wouldn't make it today. But the other task for the day was preparing tomorrow's lunch. I made a smoky chipotle and dark beer chili. While this wasn't as elegant as several of the meals I was following, this was a great chili and a perfect meal for a fall day, so I was feeling good about lunch tomorrow. And to top it off, Denise would be joining us for the last lunch of the 2008 harvest/crush.

NOVEMBER 12, 2008

This morning, I got up and turned on the water main so that Denise and I could shower and then turned it off before I left. The break was fixed, but we needed to let the new joint set for twenty-four hours. I gathered up all the food for lunch: chili, sour cream, cheddar cheese, green onions, and corn bread, as well as the utensils, plates, and napkins that Denise had put together for me. Once I got to the winery, my plan was to slowly heat the chili through the morning.

It was another stunning fall day—sunny and in the mid-seventies. Dane had pressed the five tons of Cabernet Sauvignon yesterday and was just starting the Petite Sirah when I arrived. I got out the winery hot plate, turned it on low, and set the chili pot on the burner. Then I went out to the crush pad to help Dane. I made sure that the hoses were cleaned and set the large PVC pipe into the first tank to draw off the free-run juice. I did this to several tanks, and then we dumped the remaining must from these tanks into the press. We were hoping to get all five tons of the Petite pressed today. After putting several tanks of must into the press, Dane ran it through a shortened cycle to get the bulk of the juice off the skins and create room for the remaining tanks of Petite.

With the press working, I went into the stable to help Gary with the wine club shipment, all the while checking my chili frequently. The shipment was to include a bottle of the newly released 2006 Estate Petite Sirah that we had bottled in September, as well as a bottle of the 2006 Stuhlmuller Vineyard Chardonnay, an excellent Alexander Valley Chardonnay that Dane had been making for a number of years. While I was filling the packing boxes for the wine club shipments, Lynn arrived and said that her husband, Ray, and maybe her daughter Sara would join us for lunch. I told her that Denise was coming, and Lynn was looking forward to meeting Denise. My only disappointment for the day was that Michael was not going to be there. He had said the previous week that he would try to come out, but I knew he was busy with projects at home. I had hoped that he and Denise could meet because Michael, along with Dane, Gary, and Lynn, had been such a big part of my harvest experience.

Dane and I pumped the free-run juice from the remaining Petite Sirah tanks into a new tank, just in time for lunch. It was noon, and my strategy of slowly heating the chili had worked. It was boiling, and nothing was sticking to the bottom of the pan. Mark arrived, as he'd said he would when we saw him at Zephyr Grill on Sunday night. He was followed shortly by Richard and a friend. Now all we needed was Denise. I called her, and she said that she was just turning on to Vallecitos Road from Pigeon Pass, so I told her that she would be at the winery in ten minutes. Ray arrived, and Sara was able to come as well, so we had a great group and a beautiful afternoon.

Everyone was enjoying a first glass of wine when Denise arrived. I began to dish up the chili, but Mark came over, handed me a bowl, took the ladle, and said that everyone could serve themselves. Denise had brought a dessert she'd made that required a bit of assembly, which she did before settling down with a bowl of chili. As usual, we had lively conversations and great stories. Dane brought out a magnum of 1994 Napa Zinfandel, which was very nice, particularly as it opened up with a bit of time and air.

After a long, leisurely lunch, people began to leave. Denise and I packed up the remnants of lunch and put it into her car, and she said her goodbyes to Dane and Gary and Mark. Shortly after that, Mark left, and Gary went back to packing up the wine club shipments. I went back onto the crush pad to help Dane finish pressing the Petite. We were able to get it all into the press, and then Dane put it through a full cycle. Dane said it was the most he had ever gotten into the press; juice just rushed out as the press was closed and began to rotate. I pressure-washed the empty tanks and cleaned up the crush pad. When I was finished, Dane said that the press had another hour to go. Since it was after 4:00, he suggested that I call it a day. We said our goodbyes, and he thanked me for the chili, which he thought might last him through the night. I agreed and headed for home.

NOVEMBER 13, 2008

When I arrived this morning, Dick Stark was there. He shared with us that he was using the winery as a "pee break" on his way to catch a BART train in Walnut Creek. He was headed to the city to be with a friend who was fighting ALS. I told him that we hoped to finish pressing today, and that tomorrow would be my last day of the season. He looked a little sad, as did

I. Gary quickly suggested that I'd be back for bottling, to which I agreed happily.

After Dick had gone, Dane and I set out to finish pressing everything today. The quantity wasn't that large; it was the number of lots still left to do. Dane figured we could get it all into the press. I cleaned the hoses with sodium percarbonate and then citric acid. I set up the pump and pressure-washed a tank for the juice. Then I stuck the PVC into the first tank to pump the free run. We started with the Cabernet Franc and then moved through three more lots, including two Cabernet Sauvignon and a Petite Sirah. All of the fruit was local from Livermore Valley. Dane had sourced 60 percent of his fruit from Livermore Valley this year. He had again increased his year-on-year production, but he'd spent less on grapes and less on the travel necessary to get the grapes from all over the state, as he had done in past years.

While the press was doing its job, Dane and I filled the stable with the barrels that had been stored outside from last week's barreling down. Dane had created a space for a row of two barrels, two high, on one side of the stable. There was still room on the other side for a long table to accommodate the blending party that Dane was holding this weekend. He had donated the party to a local charity auction. We were able to get forty-four barrels in the stable without much effort. If he insulated this center section of the stable and used it all for barrel storage, he could fit over a hundred barrels in the space, which would be a huge benefit for his custom crush business, as well as his own production for Page Mill Winery.

I could tell that the weight of harvest was beginning to lift from Dane. He had been in a good mood all week. I'm sure the added stress of his investor meeting had made the prior week even tougher. But here we were finishing the pressing for the season. The process with these smaller lots was to set the press at very high pressure for a shorter cycle time. While this did not squeeze every last drop out of each lot we put in, between the free run and this process, Dane figured he got 95 percent or more of the juice from each of the tanks. After the Cab Franc and the two Cabernet Sauvignon lots, Dane cycled the press for a while longer, and he and I headed into town, where we had a beer and split a hamburger.

We sat outside in downtown Livermore with the weather in the upper seventies. It was spectacular. Knowing tomorrow was my last day, Dane asked if I had gotten what I'd hoped for from harvest. I told him that it had surpassed my expectations, based on what I had learned and the fun I'd had. I thanked him for his knowledge and his willingness to share it. I also told him what a pleasure it had been to work with him, and everyone associated with Page Mill.

After lunch, we went back and pressed the rest of the Petite Sirah. The last lot of pressing we did was the small amount of Campi Merlot. It had fermented in a food-grade plastic bin because it wasn't even large enough for a half-ton bin. I put it on a pallet, and Dane used the forklift to raise the pallet, with me and the Merlot, up over the chute, so I could pour the must into the press. It was somewhat funny that the last bit we pressed was this small lot of fruit that Gary and I had picked several weeks back. After I dumped it in and Dane lowered the forklift, we high-fived—the last of the wines was being pressed.

It was after 5:00, and Dane knew that he had an hour or so before the press was finished, so he suggested that I leave for the day instead of waiting around. I guess it was one of the benefits of being a volunteer laborer; Dane would stay on, finish up with the press, and clean it before he was done for the day, and I could just go home. I knew that tomorrow would be my last day, and I had mixed emotions, knowing that it needed to end at some point, and yet not wanting to give up the work I had been doing. But for now, I just left for home.

NOVEMBER 14, 2008: THE END OF HARVEST

Here it was the middle of November, and it felt like the middle of summer. The whole week had been unseasonably warm, but today was warmer still. As I headed out for my last day at Page Mill Winery, I decided to wear shorts. It was seventy degrees out when I got in my car and headed out from the house at 8:15 AM. That was as warm as most mornings in August and September.

It was a beautiful day, and as warm as it was, there was still the feeling of fall in the air. As I drove through Fremont, there was still some lingering fog, but as soon as I crested the Sunol Grade, it was clear. By the time I reached Page Mill, it was seventy-five degrees. When I arrived, the winery was fairly quiet. Dane's truck was there, but not Gary's. When I walked into the tasting room, Dane was at the computer, and there were balloons tied up on the chair which signaled that Gary had been there and that he was going to open the tasting room at noon today, which he had done for several weeks now. I asked Dane where Gary was, and he said that he had gone to UDS to pick up cases for the weekend and would be back soon.

I asked Dane if we were barreling down today. I guess I knew the answer, as there wasn't anything else left to be done. He said yes and told me that I should get the hoses ready, and he would start to wash barrels. Gary returned, and I helped him bring the case boxes into the tasting room. He mentioned that there was a bus of twelve to twenty people arriving at 2:00 today, so he would have at least one large group this afternoon.

After the hoses were ready and Dane had washed the first two barrels, we got into a rhythm. He washed a pair of barrels, and I filled the two he'd just washed. When they were filled, he moved them out with the forklift and replaced them with two more, so I always had a pair of barrels to work with. We began to move through the remaining tanks of wine that had been settling over the past few days since our pressing. I started with the Napa Zinfandel. As I filled the barrels, I would write the year, the varietal, and the vineyard with a Sharpie on the barrel ring. Later, Dane would create barrel cards for them, but for now it kept things straight.

At one point, when Dane was putting one of the empty fermentation tanks away, I asked him if he was feeling good about harvest coming to a close. He asked me if I hadn't seen the permanent smile on his face—and yes, he was happy to see it come to an end because he would see more of his family and enjoy some free time. But it also meant he had completed the harvest/crush, and his wine was all in barrels, which has to be a huge relief to any winemaker. So it wasn't any wonder that he went about his work today, and had all week, with a much happier and satisfied demeanor.

We continued to barrel down the remaining tanks, moving from Zinfandel to Syrah to Merlot to Cabernet Franc and on to Cabernet Sauvignon. I barreled down over twenty barrels by the time 2:00 PM came around. I needed to leave today at 2:00 because I had an interview at 4:00 PM back in Los Altos. It was a clear reminder that the harvest was over and I had no excuse now but to begin my job search. I wasn't quite finished with all the tanks, but Dane would get that done either later today or tomorrow. In any case, within a day, there would be nothing but empty tanks on the crush pad, and all of the wine would be in barrels. It was a fitting end to the season and a clear demarcation point for the completion of crush, or harvest, as I liked to call it. Make no mistake—there was plenty of work to do in turning these young wines into the mature, quality wines that we could all enjoy. But for now, there was time for rest and a slower pace.

I finished up a barrel of Cabernet Sauvignon and told Dane that it was time for me to go. We gave each other a big hug, and I genuinely thanked him for the experience. He just looked at me and said how thankful he was for all my help. He told me that harvest had been just a little easier and a bit more fun for my having been there. I thanked him for that and said goodbye—not for long, I hoped. But it was the end of the season and the end of an experience I never thought I would have, and I never could have imagined how satisfying it would be.

I drove away from Page Mill Winery on a beautiful fall day, ending my harvest diary.

EPILOGUE

DECEMBER 13, OF COURSE

Last night Michael and Leighann hosted an end-of-harvest dinner for all of us. Dane and Angela, Gary, Lynn and Ray, Nancy and her husband, Richard and Laura, and, of course, Denise and I were all in attendance. The evening was filled with good food, good wine, and all of our stories from the 2008 harvest. I was pleased that Denise had a chance to meet Michael and Leighann because Michael had been such a big part of my harvest experience.

Today we were out at Page Mill for the library Pinot Noir tasting. Denise's brother Emory and his fiancée, Annette, joined us for the afternoon and dinner at Zephyr Grill. Unfortunately Dane wasn't there, but Gary was holding court with Jan, one of the longtime volunteers in the Page Mill tasting room. And the added treat, especially for Denise, was that Dick Stark was pouring the library Pinot Noir for the afternoon. Many of these wines were the ones that Gary and I had "discovered" at CWT, the San Jose warehouse. It was fun to visit with Dick, as always, and Denise hadn't seen him in a number of years. The whole day made for a fitting close to this journal.

In the month since I left the winery, I have reflected on my time there. It was everything I had imagined and so much more. I had talked about doing it for so long, and it truly felt like I had been given a gift.

The work itself was invigorating. Spending these past months outside has been a blessing. Unlike so much of what I have done throughout my career, this was work in which you saw the result every single day: the grapes were crushed, or pressed, or in barrels. It was fun work as well, something different every day, and while it was hard work at times, it was satisfying. The work itself was not so different from what I expected.

What was different were the other experiences and, of course, the people. Dane is the heart and soul of Page Mill, and I enjoyed the opportunity to make wine with him. But what surprised me were the other times. On Mondays and Tuesdays, Dane and I worked alone. Lynn, of course, was in and out for her lab work, but these were days when Dane shared his knowledge and love of wine and winemaking with me. For my part, I shared with him my thoughts on business, both his and that of the world of technology. They were interesting conversations for me and for Dane.

Dane is a caring and passionate man. He loves his family, and he loves making wine. He probably knows more about making wine, and the art of it, than most winemakers. This was apparent by the number of other winemakers in the valley who just stopped by to talk with Dane. And I enjoyed the same benefits. I asked all of my questions, and I feel that I understand the process of making wine much better—but the art is still very evident and a bit elusive for me, I think. But hey, I can always drink and appreciate good wine as long as there are people like Dane to make it.

Working with Dane and the rest of the team—Gary, Michael, and Lynn—was one of the great joys of my time at Page Mill. There were no real egos; everyone just got the work done. Everyone was quick to pitch in and help each other, and laugh when any of us screwed up—I think I led the league in this category. Maybe that's the benefit of volunteer laborers. Dane knows he can't really boss us around, and we're there to make wine, so it works perfectly. But it was one of those times in my life when everything came together to create a unique and magical experience that I will never forget, and it will never happen again.

Everything I did contributed to the production of the 2008 wines at Page Mill Winery—absolutely everything. And everything I did and experienced contributed to one of the greatest life experiences anyone could have. I am blessed to have been given the opportunity, and while I wasn't paid a nickel, I am a much richer man for having done it!

RESOURCES

WINERY WEB SITES

Note that many sites now require you to confirm that you are over twenty-one to enter—no idea why!

www.pagemillwinery.com/
www.charleskrug.com/
www.jpvwines.com/
www.robertmondaviwinery.com/flash/index.html
www.rubiconestate.com/site.php
www.bvwines.com/
www.louismartini.com/
www.franciscan.com/flash/index.cfm
www.beringer.com/beringer/index.jsp
www.sterlingvineyards.com/en-row/home/
www.buenavistacarneros.com/
www.sebastiani.com/home.asp
www.edmeades.com/
www.navarrowine.com/main.php
www.ridgewine.com/#home
www.cask23.com/index-flash.htm
www.williamsselyem.com/

www.dunnvineyards.com/

www.caymus.com/

www.pineridgewinery.com/

www.chandon.com/web/index.cfm

www.closduval.com/

www.opusonewinery.com/

www.vsattui.com/

www.stfranciswinery.com/?gclid=CLWRv_ijoJUCFQ8QagodQincjw

www.chateaustjean.com/stjean/index.jsp

www.matanzascreek.com/

www.schugwinery.com/schugwinery/index.jsp

garyfarrellwines.com/

www.rochioliwinery.com/

www.robertstemmlerwinery.com/

www.simiwinery.com/

www.souverain.com/

www.rodneystrong.com/rodneystrong/index.jsp

www.arafanelliwinery.com/

www.trefethenfamilyvineyards.com/

www.zdwines.com/

www.duckhorn.com/home.php

www.cakebread.com/

www.whitehalllane.com/

www.pezziking.com/

www.savannahchanelle.com/

www.testarossa.com/

www.davidbrucewinery.com/

www.byington.com/index.php

www.fernwoodcellars.com/winemaker.html

www.bargetto.com/

www.hunterhillwines.com/

www.soquelvineyards.com/aboutus/index.asp

www.troutgulchvineyards.com/

www.silvermtn.com/index.shtml

www.windyoaksestate.com/

www.buonwine.com/

www.peterfranus.com/
www.grothwines.com/
www.darioush.com/
www.robertsinskey.com/
www.domainccarncros.com//indcx.cfm
www.etudewines.com/etude/index.jsp
www.medlockames.com/medlock/index.jsp
www.josephfamilyvineyards.com/
www.ferrari-carano.com/
www.zichichifamilyvineyard.com/
www.wilsonwinery.com/
www.stuhlmullervineyards.com/index.php

ITALIAN SITES

Castelletto di Montebenichi – where we stayed
www.castelletto.it/en/index.htm
Cinque Terre tourism site
www.cinqueterre.it/en/index.asp

LIVERMORE WINERIES

www.pagemillwinery.com/
www.charlesrvineyards.com/
www.wentevineyards.com/default2.asp
www.concannonvineyard.com/
www.johnchristophercellars.com/
www.fenestrawinery.com/
www.stevenkent.com/
www.bigwhitehouse.com/
www.redfeatherwinery.com/Welcome.html
www.pg100.com/bodegasaguirre/
thomascoynewinery.com/

www.cedarmountainwinery.com/
www.garrewinery.com/index.html

OTHER WEB SITES AND BOOKS

About Brookside Winery in the fifties
www.oldandsold.com/articles02/losangeles3.shtml

About Secondi Guasti and the Italian Vineyard Company
www.csupomona.edu/~library/specialcollections/guasti/index.html

Info about the industry
www.winebusiness.com/

Winemaking products
www.grapestompers.com/index.asp

Just what it says—definitions of wine terms
www.winedefinitions.com/index.htm

Santa Cruz Mountains Winegrowers Association
www.scmwa.com/

Livermore Valley Winegrowers Association
www.lvwine.org/

General info site with blogs on a variety of topics
www.wineintro.com/

Community for wine enthusiasts and winemakers
www.crushnet.com/cms/

Site for the Complete Winemaker, a Web store and retail store in Napa
www.tcw-web.com/

A wine site hosted by a famous British wine critic
www.jancisrobinson.com/